THE MISFORTUNES OF ALONSO RAMÍREZ

JOE R. AND TERESA LOZANO LONG SERIES
IN LATIN AMERICAN AND LATINO ART AND CULTURE

The Misfortunes of Alonso Ramírez

THE TRUE ADVENTURES OF A SPANISH AMERICAN WITH 17TH-CENTURY PIRATES

By Fabio López Lázaro

UNIVERSITY OF TEXAS PRESS, AUSTIN

Requests for permission to reproduce material
from this work should be sent to:
Permissions
University of Texas Press
P.O. Box 7819
Austin, TX 78713-7819
www.utexas.edu/utpress/about/bpermission.html

♾ The paper used in this book meets the minimum requirements
of ANSI/NISO Z39.48-1992 (R1997) (Permanence of Paper).

Library of Congress Cataloging-in-Publication Data

López Lázaro, Fabio T.
The misfortunes of Alonso Ramírez : the true adventures of a Spanish American
with seventeenth-century pirates / by Fabio López Lázaro. — 1st ed.
p.   cm. — (Joe R. and Teresa Lozano Long series in Latin American
and Latino art and culture)
Includes bibliographical references and index.
ISBN 978-0-292-74389-2
1. Ramírez, Alonso, 17th cent. 2. Pirates—History—17th century. 3. Dampier, William,
1652–1715. 4. Puerto Ricans—Biography. 5. Captivity narratives—History—
17th century. 6. Voyages and travels—History—17th century. 7. Seafaring life—
History—17th century. 8. Sigüenza y Góngora, Carlos de, 1645–1700.
Infortunios de Alonso Ramírez. 9. Spain—Foreign relations—1516–1700.
10. Latin America—History—To 1830. I. Title.
G535.L63 2011
910.4'5—dc22

2011005074

ISBN 978-0-292-72997-1 (E-book)

First paperback printing, 2012

To Gwenyth

Contents

Acknowledgments

LIKE ALL BOOKS, this one owes a great debt to many people: numerous archivists and librarians in Europe and the Americas, generous colleagues who listened to talks about the project and commented on drafts, my editors at the University of Texas Press, and patient family and friends who lived with Alonso Ramírez as another interesting but somewhat challenging part of our lives. Over the years I incurred a significant debt to my colleagues in the History Department at Santa Clara University as well as to those beyond my campus who at one point or another provided support, encouragement, and critiques. The College of Arts and Sciences and the university provided much-needed financial subventions which enabled significant research trips to archives in remote places. Among the many people to whom I am particularly grateful, several stand out for making this project possible: Tom Turley, Barbara Molony, Gerald McKevitt, S.J., David Ringrose, Asunción Lavrin, Isabel Aguirre, Carla Rahn Phillips, Helen Nader, Frank Dutra, Felipe Fernández-Armesto, Rachel Fuchs, Lewis Fisher, and David Starkey. Without the pioneering efforts of James Cummins, Alan Soons, Estelle Irizarry, and Antonio Lorente Medina, who searched through some of the published sources, I would not have begun archival research into Alonso Ramírez's historicity. At an early stage, Fr. José Antonio Oquendo Pabón of Puerto Rico responded graciously when asked about Ramírez's traces in "Borinkén." At a much more advanced stage, Consuelo Varela of

Seville's Escuela de Estudios Hispano-Americanos was instrumental in keeping me motivated. I deeply appreciate the help of Don Enrique Terrones González, chief archaeologist at the Instituto Nacional de Antropología e Historia (INAH) Center in Quintana Roo, Yucatan, Mexico, who provided me with advice and photocopies of the extensive work that he and others have done on the Maya coastal ruins of that state. This made it possible for me to posit an identification for the ruins described by Ramírez in 1690. The errors in this book, of course, are mine.

Above all, my greatest pleasure is to acknowledge the support of my wife, Gwenyth Claughton. Throughout a voyage which took twice as long as the original Ramírez voyage to complete, she helped me bail water when research times were tough, kept my hand steady on the writing tiller, and helped me navigate difficult historical issues with her insight. There can be no better companion on such a voyage.

Abbreviations

AE	*Armada española desde la unión de los reinos de Castilla y de Aragón* (Fernández Duro)
AGI	Archivo General de las Indias (Seville)
AGN	Archivo General de la Nación (Mexico City)
AGS	Archivo General de Simancas (Spain)
AHM	Arquivo Histórico de Macau (Macao)
AHN	Archivo Histórico Nacional (Madrid)
AHNSN	Archivo Histórico Nacional, Sección Nobleza (Toledo)
AHPM	Archivo Histórico de Protocolos de Madrid
AM	*Arquivos de Macau*
AN	Archives Nationales (Paris)
ANAM	Archives Nationales, Archives de la Marine (Paris)
APCE	*Acts of the Privy Council of England, Colonial Series* (ed. Grant and Fitzroy)
BL	British Library (London)

BL IOR British Library, India Office Records (London)

BN Biblioteca Nacional (Madrid)

CDMFN *Colección de documentos y manuscritos compilados por Fernández de Navarrete* (Fernández de Navarrete)

CSP *Calendar of State Papers, Colonial Series: America and West Indies* (ed. Fortescue)

DIPCA *Documentos inéditos referentes a las postrimerías de la Casa de Austria en España* (Baviera and Maura Gamazo)

DNV MS draft of *New Voyage* (Dampier) entitled "William Dampier's Second Voyage in the South Seas"

ICS *Los infortunios de Alonso Ramírez* (ed. Cummins and Soons)

IO 5582–5583 British Library, India Office Records, E/3/47, 5582 and 5583

KA VOC Koloniaal Archief, Verenigde Oostindische Compagnie (The Hague)

NA National Archive (the old Public Records Office) (London)

NV *A New Voyage round the World* (Dampier, 1927/1968 Dover edition)

Ou-Mun *Ou-Mun Kei-Lèok* (Tcheong-ü-Lâm and Ian-Kuong-Iâm)

RAH Real Academia de la Historia (Madrid)

RRSFC *Records of the Relations between Siam and Foreign Countries in the Seventeenth Century*

A Note on the Translation

I HAVE USED ESTELLE IRIZARRY'S 1990 facsimile of the original 1690 book as the base for this translation. The English version re-creates as much as possible the style of the original seventeenth-century Spanish text, without unduly moderniz-ing it. My aim has been to strike a balance between this desire to convey its original Baroque qualities and the need to maintain readability. The spelling of names (including the lack of accents) has not been modernized; nor have names been systematically corrected. Thus "Joseph" appears instead of "José" and the governor of the Philippine Islands as "Cuzalaegui" not "Curu-zeláegui." The correct or modernized form for these names can be found in the notes. The paragraph structure follows the original.

THE MISFORTUNES OF ALONSO RAMÍREZ

Introductory Study

Introduction

> Truth is stranger than Fiction, but that is because Fiction is
> obliged to stick to possibilities; Truth isn't.
> MARK TWAIN, *FOLLOWING THE EQUATOR* (1897)

N 1690, DURING THE HEYDAY OF PIRACY, when attacks terrorized the Spanish empire from the Caribbean to the Philippine Islands, a little book entitled *The Misfortunes of Alonso Ramírez* was published in Mexico City. The book described how the second most powerful imperial official, the viceroy of New Spain, met a man by the name of Ramírez in Mexico City in the spring of that year. Ramírez, a poor Spanish American carpenter from Puerto Rico, created a dramatic impression: his face, chest, and hand had been severely scarred by a gunpowder explosion, and he had lost all his hair. But the story that Ramírez told his sophisticated audience was even more remarkable. After being taken captive by English pirates near the Philippine Islands three years earlier, Ramírez and his twenty-five Asian and American companions had been forced to work as slaves aboard the pirate ship.[1] Having witnessed how the buccaneers repeatedly pillaged southeast Asian ships and cities without mercy, the nine men ended up circumnavigating the world in the pirates' company until they were freed off the coast of Brazil. Ramírez said that he had managed to steer a frigate which the pirates had given them across the Caribbean to Mexico but was shipwrecked on the dangerous reefs lining the eastern coastline of Yucatan. He now appeared on April 4, 1690, before Viceroy Gaspar de la Cerda Sandoval Silva y Mendoza in Mexico City, the Count of Galve and New Spain's highest judge, because local Yucatan officials suspected he was a smuggler or, even worse, a pirate.

Not surprisingly, given Ramírez's improbable story, most scholars have maintained that *Misfortunes* must be a piece of fictional writing. They have overwhelmingly attributed the extravagant depiction of events to the literary skills, scientific knowledge, and political agenda of Don Carlos de Sigüenza y Góngora, the king's cosmographer in Mexico City. According to the book itself, he was commissioned by the viceroy to write it. Sigüenza is one of the greatest cultural talents of the Spanish-speaking Americas in the early modern period (along with the protofeminist poet Sor Juana Inés de la Cruz). The importance of *Misfortunes* as one of colonial Latin America's great literary achievements has earned it the status of the first Latin American novel.[2]

Nevertheless, some scholars have not agreed with this assessment, positing that many of the events and people described in the book must be historic. Ramírez's real-life existence, though unproven, has been maintained by literary scholars like Marcelino Menéndez y Pelayo, Cayetano Coll y Toste, Concha Meléndez, Josefina Rivera de Alvarez, and Manuel Alvarez Nazario. Others, like Willebaldo Bazarte Cerdán and David Lagmanovich, have believed that the lack of historical evidence tilts the balance in favor of Sigüenza's creative imagination. Many readers, like Raúl Castagnino and Enrique Anderson Imbert, have preferred to sit on the fence, arguing to various degrees that *Misfortunes* contains a mix of fictional and historic elements attributable to Sigüenza's pen. Lucrecio Pérez Blanco, for example, theorizes that Sigüenza, as an *arbitrista* (protonationalist lobbyist), wrote the book as a critique of the imperial government's lack of attention to America's woes and a defense of Latin American identity and needs against Old World arrogance and ineptitude. At the other end of the interpretive spectrum, Francisco Vidargas points out that Sigüenza always preferred historical or "objective" accounts to fiction. Most recently, Estelle Irizarry has cast doubt on Sigüenza's input by proving statistically that the language used in *Misfortunes* does not match that of any other works by Sigüenza.[3] But only a few investigators, like James Cummins, Alan Soons, and Antonio Lorente Medina, have gone to the effort of substantiating that many of the people mentioned in *Misfortunes* did in fact exist.[4]

Based on European, Asian, and American archival documents, the present study proves incontrovertibly that Ramírez existed and that his narrative is not a novel but a historical account, though full of distortions and lies.[5] We can now state that Ramírez was a real person and that his story in *Misfortunes* is corroborated by solid evidence. For example, the dramatic meeting between the Count of Galve, still fresh from Spain on his new appointment, and the wounded pirate captive did in fact take place in the spring of 1690, although this was not the first news of Ramírez's shipwreck that the viceroy received.[6]

On January 27, 1690, Galve reported the important news in a letter to his brother in Madrid, the Duke of Infantado, the right-hand man of King Carlos II (r. 1665–1700):

> My dear brother, friend, and lord: attached to this letter you will find a copy of the one I have just written to His Majesty, giving him an account of the [latest] voyage of the Windward Fleet . . . with notice of the news of the pirate Lorencillo's armaments and supplies . . . , to which I add another re- markable and strange piece of news, consisting of the loss of a Manila vessel on the shores of the Province of Campeche,[7] toward its southern reaches. It carried three Chinese, a Spaniard, who is a native of Puerto Rico island and acted as captain, another Spaniard born in Puebla de los Angeles, and a black boy [*negrillo*].

Galve's letter then related the essential narrative that was repeated in the Sigüenza text, published five months later (in June), with certain important details:

> The declaration which this captain has made relates that, as captain of a royal ship in Manila with a crew of twenty-five men, he was taken prize on those coasts by two English vessels. After leaving most of his captured crew on the coast, these pirates took the rest of his men with them, eight in all.

Galve's letter told how the "pirates continued their corsairing [*corso*] among those islands, taking many prizes from the Portuguese, setting course for the coasts of Bengal [Indian Ocean], until they arrived on the Island of San Lorenzo [Madagascar]." The English pirates then took the eight Spaniards with them around the Cape of Good Hope, crossing the Atlantic to the coast of Brazil, "where they set free the aforementioned vessel, giving them an English wag- goner [sea chart] to steer by so that they might from there sail for Puerto Rico, toward which they [the Spaniards] set off" across the Caribbean.

Galve's confidential letter suggests that at that point he did not suspect Ramírez was lying: "Finding pirate ships in all these locations, they were forced to head out to deeper waters; fleeing from land but finding themselves short of supplies, they resolved" to head for whatever inhabited island they might be able to reach. "When they had adopted this plan, a sudden storm arose which threw them on the coasts of Campeche, where the vessel was lost." Forty days of wandering on the beaches left the castaways ill; two died. By good fortune a beachcomber found the despondent and lost sailors and notified the local Spanish officials, who ordered that they be brought to the town of "Tixhobuc [Tijosuco?]." "Divine Providence saved these lives," Galve rhapsodized, "releasing them from such a long and unprecedented voyage and from so many successive dangers; I have consequently ordered that the Captain be brought to this court to inform me in greater detail of his ship's course."[8]

The basic January narrative of the shipwrecked captain's experiences matches the plot of Sigüenza's text of *Misfortunes*, printed in June, but Alonso Ramírez was not mentioned by name in any archival document until the viceroy sent a second letter to his brother about the shipwrecked Puerto Rican on July 1, 1690. In it Galve announced that he had commissioned the publication of Ramírez's narrative in the following terms:

> My dear brother, friend, and lord: attached to this letter you will find twenty [printed] relations of the voyage which Alonso Ramírez, a native of Puerto Rico, made from the Philippine Islands to the Province of Campeche, where he lost his way. Having ordered that he be brought to this Court [Mexico City], I then commanded that a declaration relating his course and the misfortunes he suffered in such an unheard of and unprecedented navigation be taken down in writing; the strangeness and incredible nature of his story prompts me to send it to Your Excellency. I have had it published so that many copies can be forwarded to You in the eventuality that You should desire to distribute it amongst our friends, for I have only remitted it to the Marquis of Vélez. All of which I now submit for Your information, whose Excellent person I hope God will preserve for many years, as I truly wish He will; Mexico, July 1, 1690. I place myself, Your brother and greatest friend, at Your Excellent Lordship's feet.[9]

It is thus clear that the viceroy commissioned Sigüenza to write down Ramírez's account. Chapter 2 explains why the viceroy felt that it was a useful piece of propaganda in the concerted campaign against pirates and the enemies of the monarchy of Spain which the Marquis of Vélez, Spain's chief minister in charge of American and naval affairs, was organizing in 1690. He chose to ignore the many improbabilities in Ramírez's account, such as the oddity that Ramírez had never tried to land in Puerto Rico even though his course through the Caribbean took him quite close to the island, because the story could be useful.

The archival evidence also demonstrates that the famous English pirate and naturalist William Dampier was in fact the man who took Ramírez captive near the Philippine Islands in 1687. This is not incidental to understanding Galve's patronage of Ramírez. The English identity of Ramírez's captors interested Galve because it confirmed what he and his brother, the king of Spain's close advisor, feared most during the opening years of the global war (1688–1697) against King Louis XIV of France. They were afraid that Spain's new ally, England, was not to be trusted, that English greed would lead English politicians, like pirates, to seize American islands from the French but refuse to give them back to their rightful owner, Spain.

My analysis also strongly suggests something which neither Sigüenza nor the viceroy apparently realized or expressed: at some point in his supposedly forced cruise with the British pirates through Asian, Indian, and African waters, Ramírez joined them, probably early on. Chapters 2 and 3 present new evidence that proves Ramírez consorted with two separate pirate crews. Chapter 3 examines the evidence concerning the odd frigate which, unbelievably, Ramírez said the pirates gave him and which, more unbelievably, the Count of Galve accepted as Ramírez's by law. The fast frigate might be salvageable; moreover, it was full of valuable Asian (most notably, Siamese) treasure, some of it quite useful for Galve's military projects against buccaneers and the French. An analysis of Galve's letters and Spanish law governing the distribution of shipwrecks points to the cargo in Ramírez's fast frigate as the ultimate reason for Galve's patronage. Piracy attracted commoners like the carpenter Ramírez into its ranks; but in the right context the proceeds of piracy could also attract the highest officials, dedicated administrators like Galve who were willing to turn a blind eye when valuable cargo could be used to defend empire. The legal implications of Galve's patronage reveal the very sinews of power.

Misfortunes thus acquires tremendous historical importance in addition to its proven significance as one of colonial Latin America's unique cultural texts. It provides deep insights into the cultural, legal, and maritime history of the most important early modern empire, linking the working-class world of Ramírez to the high diplomatic circles in which Galve and his colleagues schemed. The historicity of the book increases its value as a source for the study of colonial Latin America within world history. Read in the context of Spanish America's struggle against French, English, and Dutch pirates, interlopers, and invaders,

Misfortunes constitutes the only extensive eyewitness account of maritime predation written by a member of the society most victimized by pirates between 1630 and 1730: the subjects of the king of Spain around the world. In a similar vein, the book also deserves to be read beyond the Hispanic world for its intertextual insights into the workings of legal and illegal maritime trade networks. Because Ramírez voyaged with Dampier, one of the most famous English pirates of all time, their accounts can no longer be read separately. Ramírez's book offers important new insights into pirate history as well as regional histories. English scholars, for example, will find that their views of Dampier's activities need to be revised. Ramírez's account corroborates Dampier's description of one of the first European recorded visits to Australia in *A New Voyage round the World*.

Political historians will realize that *Misfortunes* also contributes to our understanding of the evolution of international law. Its publication fits Ethan Nadelmann's contention that the criminalization of piracy by the concerted efforts of Spain, England, and Holland in the late 1600s was the first major step forward in the establishment of "global prohibition regimes." This slow process accelerated in the 1680s as former colonial rivals began to collaborate (after the modern international diplomatic system really got underway with the Peace of Westphalia in 1648) to prosecute economically deleterious and morally repugnant activities like maritime predation. The repeated horrors perpetrated by English pirates, as narrated by Ramírez, are material evidence of the growing consensus of moral activism, based on "religious faith . . . humanitarianism, universalism," and "compassion," which ultimately led to Western European colonial prohibition regimes.[10] The Anglophobia of *Misfortunes*, on the other hand, also demonstrates how tortured was the path to this diplomatic consensus.

Thus this study attempts to avoid isolating Latin American colonial history by placing it firmly within Pacific, Asian, and European networks of contact and exchange and transoceanic communities of solidarity and power. Kenneth Banks has argued rightly that, contrary to popular images, capitalist enterprises and missionaries' efforts did not function "as a finely tuned machine whose parts always worked together smoothly and efficiently in response to the dictates of the chief engineer." Early modern "absolute" states as complex as the monarchy of Spain possessed an equally "fragmented voice."[11] The machinations of politicians and businessmen, like those of Dauril Alden's preachers, were foiled by "time and distance."[12] But we would be well advised to read Ramírez's adventures in their historic context, not just to hear the voices of such imperializing disjunctures but also to capture the voices of solidarity within the fragmented world of the Spanish monarchy.

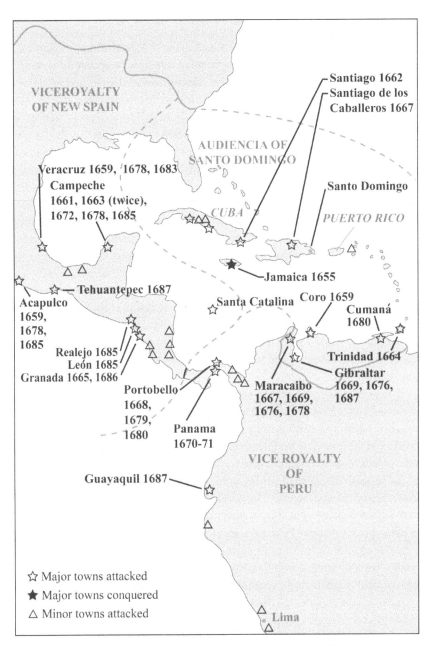

MAP I.I. Major pirate attacks in the Caribbean, 1650–1690. Some of these attacks, most notably in 1659, 1678, and 1683, were carried out by Caribbean-based buccaneers serving Spain's enemies during war as adjunct troops. Based on Galvin, *Patterns of Pillage*; Gerhard, *Pirates of New Spain*; Haring, *The Buccaneers in the West Indies*; Juárez Moreno, *Piratas y corsarios*; Kemp and Lloyd, *Brethren of the Coast*; Lane, *Pillaging the Empire*; Lucena Salmoral, *Piratas, bucaneros, filibusteros y corsarios*; and Sáiz Cidoncha, *Historia de la piratería*. Cartography by Elwood Mills.

The empire was as ethnically diverse as Ramírez's African, Filipino, Chinese, and American crew. What kept this network of territories together for so long? What bridged the oceans separating the galaxy of colonial cities and provinces which a seventeenth-century Spanish political philosopher called the world's first example of a "portable Europe"?[13] A fully historical contextualization of *Misfortunes* will clarify the processes which bound the empire together in the late seventeenth century, at a time when historians have traditionally maintained that the empire was in decline and the bonds were the weakest. These territories were linked by elite structures of linguistic, economic, legal, and religious administration. For a brief moment the public acceptance of Ramírez's account as truthful constituted a denunciation of pirates, foreigners, and non-Catholics for endangering and terrorizing the multiethnic solidarity which characterized the early modern entity that we call the Spanish empire, more a federation of states loyal to one king than a monolithic nation. The common purpose of Ramírez's companions, however fragmented and self-interested their interests may have been in reality, served the romanticized vision of their sufferings as described emblematically in *Misfortunes*. The civilian fear of pirate attacks on their Catholic world was shared by all levels of a highly hierarchical society, as varied as Ramírez's crew, and reinforced the elite superstructures of worldwide monarchy.

The second half of the seventeenth century perhaps witnessed the apogee of these unifying processes, notwithstanding colonial consciousness of European negative racial and cultural stereotypes about non-Europeans.[14] Christopher Storrs has recently critiqued the thesis that Spain's empire was in decline in the second half of the seventeenth century, arguing convincingly for the "Resilience of the Spanish Monarchy," demographically, economically, and even militarily. The story of the interaction of Ramírez and Galve in 1690 supports his theory that skillful management and an expanding imperial enfranchisement of local peoples, not English or Dutch help, sustained this "resilience" between 1665 and 1700. "Spain saw off most of its enemies, above all in the Caribbean and north Africa, without outside help," as Storrs believes, precisely because of Madrid's administrative flexibility in perennially negotiating with elites and commoners around the world. Although Spain's fortunes seemed to be at a particularly low ebb in military matters, recent research has provided a more balanced, archivally based understanding of a relatively efficient and successful Spanish navy. For example, it may have lagged behind other navies in artillery carriage design and usage in the early 1600s, but Spanish ships held their own in firepower despite reverses.[15] The successes of fleets flying Spanish flags during the reign of Carlos II have been seriously underappreciated. Ramírez's habitat was amphibious: the world's first truly global—and largest—territorial-cum-maritime composite monarchy.[16]

The full story of Ramírez's *Misfortunes* should include an examination of how it catered to locals' sense of self and place. Beleaguered by pirate attacks but increasingly involved in administration, local elites were at the zenith of their power. From the perspective of the periphery, Madrid's evident inability to exert authority over its colonial subjects in this period, which led Mark Burkholder to pick 1687 as the low point of the Spanish colonial process, can be seen as these elites' greatest moment of investment in the machinery of empire. Financial reforms in the 1680s broke all precedents by creating public budgets: Galve himself, as we shall see, championed accountability and transparency. As Madrid's constant supervision seemed to diminish, local elites in America "came into their own," writes John Lynch, reaping the rewards of shouldering empire. Between 1674 and 1700 four supreme court judges, eighteen provincial governors,

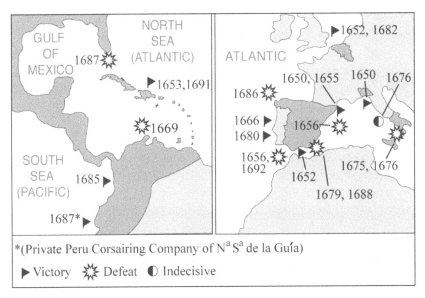

MAP I.2. Major Spanish naval victories and defeats, 1650–1700. Based on Fernández Duro, *Armada española*. In selecting the combats that merited mapping as "major," allowance has been made for the relative size of American versus European engagements. Cartography by Elwood Mills.

twenty-six important city mayors, and fifty-six royal inspectors (*corregidores*) in America were "creoles" (Europeans born outside of Europe), Alfred Crosby's famous "Neo-europeans"—an unprecedented number.[17] Moreover, Bartolomé Yun Casalilla's analysis of finances has revealed the degree to which this new-found American aristocratic confidence in a remarkably Euro-American empire connotes "a much less subordinate relation between the colonial elites" and the metropolis. Americans had a mature society by 1690, legitimately proud of their nineteen universities, sophisticated urban life, profitable economics, and estab-lished Catholic religious and social traditions. Their currency was the *world's* currency. They lived in states whose ancient Pre-Columbian roots were increas-ingly praised by their intellectuals; and these states were kingdoms, not planta-tions. As John Elliott has recently pointed out, it was the English, French, and Dutch settlers in outlying posts like New England and the lesser Antilles who were the poor cousins in comparison to Spanish Americans.[18]

The research of Julián Ruiz Rivera and Manuela Cristina García Bernal alerts us to the way Spanish subjects' transoceanic networks were working toward economic revival and institutionalized solidarity. In the 1660s registered Span-ish merchants dominating Spanish commercial networks connecting Europe, America, and Asia began to pay fixed annual amounts, calculated regionally, as a subvention for the naval protection which the crown provided to their fleets (budgeted for the crown's contribution at 150,000 ducats): Andalusian mer-chants paid 170,000 ducats, Peruvian ones 90,000, New Spaniards 30,000, and New Granadans 30,000.[19] The growing participation in empire by regional mer-cantile elites belies premature theories of economic or manufacturing decline. Between 1650 and 1700 most legally registered merchantmen on the Europe–New World routes had been built in Spanish yards, 37.2 percent in Spain and 27 percent in Spanish America (versus 35.4 percent in foreign shipyards). By the late 1600s established shipping families with both commercial and aristocratic credentials had one foot in Europe and one in America. Their interests culmi-nated in the creation of a Commerce Committee (Junta de Comercio) in 1679 which aimed to slow down the deindustrialization of their local economies, as a service-oriented monarchy with a problem of bullion-draining consumerism became excessively dependent on offshoring manufacturing and production.[20] It was only natural, then, that successful inhabitants of Mexico and Peru saw recent non-Spanish arrivals in the New World as dangerous, heretical foreigners wanting in on a good thing. Galve's strategic use of the carpenter's story in 1690 appealed precisely to that mind-set.

At lower social levels Galve could rely on what we must, for lack of a better phrase, term Hispanic solidarity, based on the increasing sense among the population at large that all the king's subjects suffered from pirates and enemies. European-born soldiers stood together with American militias made up of whites, mestizos, blacks, and mulattos in defending Veracruz (in 1683) as well as the towns and villages of Yucatan. The sense of urgency was shared across oceanic boundaries as well. The humble priest Cristóbal de Muros, who met Ramírez in Yucatan in 1690, had made a donation the previous year expressly for the global fight against pirates from the Pacific to the Mediterranean. In 1691 Cubans loaned the cash-strapped governor money to finish building forts. Commoners were encouraged by elites in this patriotism: the president of the Santo Domingo Supreme Court, a man with painful experience of buccaneer attacks, praised sailors and soldiers serving the monarchy with the Roman poet Horace's oft-used phrase "Dulce et decorum est pro patria mori" (It is sweet and right to die for one's homeland).[21] The English were astonished at this level of interracial and interethnic collaboration. One English governor in the Leeward Islands east of Puerto Rico ranted in 1689 against the incomprehensible Spaniards, "a dastardly and mongrel herd of mulattos, mustees and other spurious mixtures, [who] are now certainly become the very scum of mankind."[22]

We should not exaggerate or romanticize this multicultural collaboration or believe that commoners' loyalty to the empire was anywhere near universal. Galve himself was disgusted with the pervasive corruption of colonial administrators, churchmen, and businessmen. Additionally he was frustrated by popular uncooperativeness and aware of the seriousness of Spain's military challenges.[23] Two years later, on June 8, 1692, the viceroy would face an ethnically charged riot in Mexico City caused by escalating food prices which destroyed part of his palace and the city archives. Sigüenza, who saved the archive, acrimoniously blamed the "plebes": "Indians, blacks," the racially mixed "creoles," and low-class Spaniards.[24] Equally prejudiced posters appeared on the palace walls shortly thereafter, lambasting Galve and his ministers for hiding in the Franciscan convent while the citizenry ran amuck: "Apartments to rent for native Cocks and Castilian Chickens."[25]

The point is to consider how Galve saw in Ramírez's *Misfortunes* a catalyst for widespread governmental as well as popular support of the monarchy among creoles and Americans in general who shared a keenly developed sense of identity within a world of rival dynastic states. Like Sigüenza and Galve, Ramírez claimed to be a great Spanish patriot in the sense of a broad, transoceanic, early modern Hispanic patriotism. The historical significance of this phenomenon is becoming clear through the research of Alejandro Cañeque, Tamar Herzog, and Jorge Cañizares-Esguerra.[26] It was not a limited "European" identity, or even a Euro-American one, but rather a global identity co-terminal with the boundaries of the monarchy. Pirates and heretics were its antithetical "Other." *Misfortunes* appealed to this identity and made a modest but not unnoteworthy contribution to its construction.

CHAPTER 2

The Viceroy, the Carpenter, and the Pirate

Let God destroy France, and Religion will take care of itself.

DON PEDRO DE RONQUILLO,
THE SPANISH AMBASSADOR TO ENGLAND (1689)

OW WAS THE ACCOUNT of a Spanish carpenter taken captive by pirates in the Philippines useful to the viceroy of New Spain in 1690? To answer this question we must understand Galve's concerted struggle against Spain's enemies and his equally firm distrust of its allies. We must appreciate the state of the monarchy's global politics in the late 1600s. As complex new alliances reversed traditional religious enmities, Spanish Catholics and English and Dutch Protestants found that they had to stand together against perceived common enemies. To save themselves from Louis XIV's expansionist France, as ambassador Ronquillo put it, they would have to jettison religious prejudice. But old arguments about pirates—and fears of rivals stealing colonies—endangered this newfound diplomatic pragmatism. Furthermore, the new politics of these transoceanic dynastic states blurred ethnic boundaries confusingly: in 1690 an English-speaking Irish subject of Spain was being named admiral of a mixed Hispano-Anglo-Dutch fleet to be sent against France and its buccaneer allies, while a Dutch- and French-speaking, Flemish-born former Spanish naval officer was rapidly becoming the most feared pirate captain ever to be active in the Caribbean.[1]

PIRATES AND THE SPANISH EMPIRE FROM THE MEDITERRANEAN AND ATLANTIC TO THE PACIFIC

Don Gaspar de la Cerda Sandoval Silva y Mendoza (1653–1697), Count of Galve, served as viceroy of New Spain from November 20, 1688, until February 27, 1696. He died on March 12, 1697, shortly after landing in the port of Santa María, Spain, probably stricken by an epidemic ravaging the country.[2] We already know from the archival documents that Ramírez's story so impressed the viceroy in the spring of 1690, only a year after he arrived in Mexico City, that he immediately wrote letters to his elder brother in Madrid, Gregorio María de Silva y Mendoza (1649–1693), the Duke of Infantado. This brought Ramírez's story directly to the ears of the king himself. As Spain's wealthiest aristocrat, *camarero mayor del rey* (Head Gentleman of the Bedchamber), *sumiller de corps* (Groom of the Stool), and a member of the Council of War and Council of State, Infantado was Carlos II's closest personal advisor.[3] On July 1 Galve told Infantado that he had commissioned Sigüenza, Mexico's premier intellectual, to create the book in order to distribute it among the brothers' political friends at court, including the powerful Don Fernando Joaquín Fajardo de Toledo (d. 1693), Marquis of Los Vélez, former viceroy of Naples and now chief naval minister.

These three men formed a concerted political triangle from the late 1680s until 1693, with the aim of preserving the monarchy from its internal and external threats. Galve was viceroy of New Spain, the king's most profitable overseas possession; Vélez was head of the Council of the Indies and Spain's chief naval minister; and Infantado was the personal advisor of Carlos II. It was Infantado and Vélez who convinced the king that Galve should be appointed viceroy.[4] Vélez signed off on the 1688 notice of appointment along with Don José de Veitia Linaje, a key councilor who was spearheading a revolutionary financial reform. Some historians credit Spain's turnaround in the late 1600s to this reform, but at least one contemporary in Mexico City saw it as "the king diving into everybody's money." Certainly Veitia's reputation for implementing policies aimed at curtailing fraud in the Indies trade was justified.[5]

Galve's correspondence clearly demonstrates that in 1690 he was motivated by his dutiful concern for the king's subjects. In a highly revealing personal letter to his brother written shortly after taking up his post in Mexico, Galve described a nightmare he had after an evening of too much eating followed by reading Francisco de Quevedo's satire *El alguacil alguacilado* (The Police Officer Policed) and thinking about his brother's news that a Commission for the Reform of the Royal Treasury (Junta de Hacienda) had been created.

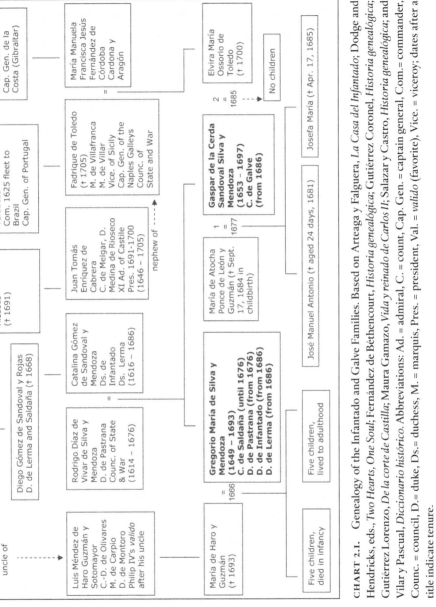

CHART 2.1. Genealogy of the Infantado and Galve Families. Based on Arteaga y Falguera, *La Casa del Infantado*; Dodge and Hendricks, eds., *Two Hearts, One Soul*; Fernández de Béthencourt, *Historia genealógica*; Gutiérrez Coronel, *Historia genealógica*; Gutiérrez Lorenzo, *De la corte de Castilla*; Maura Gamazo, *Vida y reinado de Carlos II*; Salazar y Castro, *Historia genealógica*; and Vilar y Pascual, *Diccionario histórico*. Abbreviations: Ad. = admiral, C. = count, Cap. Gen. = captain general, Com.= commander, Counc. = council, D.= duke, Ds.= duchess, M. = marquis, Pres. = president, Val. = *valido* (favorite), Vice. = viceroy; dates after a title indicate tenure.

Galve dreamed that he had been elected to serve on the commission despite his inexperience and impracticality ("lo pobre Adbitrista") and was forced to present his solutions to the monarchy's worldwide problems before anyone else at the opening meeting. In a premonition of his later interest in Ramírez's story, Galve's characteristic first response to the committee's queries was to stress military preparedness, especially preventative measures which paid particular attention to coasts, "the bridges connecting His Majesty's disparate dominions." For this global imperial policy, an overall realistic budget was essential. It should prioritize financing the immediate needs of "Our Monarch's possessions": "tumbling ruins" for whose "illness" Galve diagnosed the following cures. The king should set an example for his vassals by economizing in his own household. Pensioners who did not really need government support were to be cut off. Only experienced men would be appointed in future to political and military posts, based on their merit. "Powerful men" who had diverted government funds or failed to pay their taxes were to be ruthlessly prosecuted, while the common workers' petty evasions should be ignored, to build morale and popular support. Agents of "integrity and intelligence" were to scrutinize financial records for instances of graft and unnecessary taxes, from the king's accounts down to the lowest municipal account books, in order to alleviate the hardships in the day-to-day life of commoners. These people, whatever their intelligence, would as a result "recognize the king's goodwill." Tax farmers were to be eliminated, "for it is illogical and scandalous in any republic to allow such exploitative [atrevido] men to become wealthy at the expense of common taxpayers." Church fraud should be publicly exposed. Finally, equal government work was to receive equal pay.

In his dream—or in his reformulation of it in the letter for Infantado's benefit—Galve anticipated that self-interested critics would denounce his policies as too radical or unrealistic, but he maintained dramatically that laws should apply to all "regardless of status." There was no better rule "to measure merits" and destroy "such contagious corruptions [corruptelas]" than "the proper distribution of the king's favors." Galve's vision of a meritocracy would have been surprising or shocking to many of his contemporaries. It is equally surprising and ironic—given the brothers' concerted fight against France—that Galve's key example of the successful application of these measures was Louis XIV. Since the signing of the Peace of the Pyrenees on November 7, 1659, stated Galve, Louis had raised his nation from a similarly "attenuated state." To compete with France in the world Spain had to become more like it, a remarkable forecasting of what in fact occurred when the Bourbon dynasty took over in 1700.[6]

In the New World Galve was particularly concerned for the welfare of the coastal inhabitants of his jurisdiction, New Spain, who had suffered repeatedly at the hands of brutal pirates for two generations. The modus operandi of these pirates was well established by 1690. Contrary to popular myth, ship-to-ship combat was rare, and the king's convoys were almost never serious targets. It was the medium-sized to small local communities of the Gulf of Mexico and the Caribbean who suffered the most, very much like the victims of corsairs in the Mediterranean. Unlike them, however, New World victims of pirates were rarely kidnapped to be sold into the slave trade or individually ransomed. Instead, the entire town's inhabitants were rounded up, jailed in churches, tortured to extract any personal wealth, and then collectively ransomed to government officials, who were usually too weak militarily to respond effectively. On his maiden voyage to Mexico from Spain, Galve himself had a chance encounter with English pirates. While sailing on the night of September 12, 1688, near the dangerous coral reef of El Sisal, thirteen miles off the northwest tip of Yucatan, the fleet on which Galve was traveling to New Spain clashed with two pirate vessels. After a fierce battle, they took one of them and captured its crew. This personal experience brought home to the new viceroy, even before he officially took up office, how exposed the king's subjects were to maritime predation.[7] This conviction was reinforced upon his arrival in Veracruz in 1688, when locals told him of the destruction of the city five years earlier by the worst buccaneer of the 1680s, "Lorencillo" (Laurent de Graff). In the company of the "Chevalier de Grammont" (François Granmont de La Mothe), this ex–Spanish officer from Spain's Low Countries had led 1,200 men aboard eleven ships in a terrifying fifteen-day sack of New Spain's principal port city.[8]

Lorencillo extorted the last drop of wealth from the already decimated and tortured inhabitants by placing two thousand of them in one of the city's main churches. The pirates surrounded the church with kegs of gunpowder, holding them prisoner for days and threatening to burn them alive. Five hundred civilians died in the attack. Six thousand traumatized survivors told their bone-chilling stories to officials from the capital who visited the city to investigate shortly after the attack. Eyewitnesses said that the buccaneers had demanded two million pieces of eight from the incarcerated inhabitants, but only half had been collected. One man who experienced the horrors of the church incarceration simply confessed that he was speechless: "Where do I find the tears to describe it?"[9] Now, during the winter of 1689–1690, Galve learned that Lorencillo was planning another attack, either on Veracruz again or on Merida, the capital of

Yucatan Province.[10] What shocked Spanish contemporaries was that such unprovoked attacks on civilian populations in the Americas during times of peace were frequently countenanced by cynical officials in England and France. When Galve took office, he found reports that pirates had cost the king 60,000 crowns between 1660 and 1685, with 350 ships taken and at least a hundred villages, towns, and cities sacked.[11] Buccaneering was coastal terrorism, not high-seas adventure. When Ramírez told his story of suffering at the hands of English pirates at court in Mexico and in his autobiographical book, he was preaching to the choir.

Galve and his brother were committed to a policy of defending Spanish America, Spanish Europe, and Spanish Asia at all cost. For them, Spain had legally kept sovereignty over territories discovered in the Indies until it ceded them to other states. Because of this diplomatic principle, Caribbean islands not ceded (for example, to France) which nevertheless contained non-Spanish settlers remained "lands which that nation occupies *against* our nation," Galve noted in a letter to his brother in January 1690 (just one day before writing about Ramírez). Their inhabitants had to be considered illegal immigrants into the Spanish monarchy's jurisdictions.[12]

The brothers did not trust Louis XIV's promises not to back further piratical endeavors. The French king replaced Tortuga governor Jacques de Pouançay with Pierre-Paul Tarin de Cussy after the 1683 Veracruz attack, giving him an "explicit order to suppress the buccaneers." But men like Galve believed that Louis tacitly continued to accept Caribbean pirates as a necessary evil of his imperial ambitions, much as Jamaica's Assembly did by ensuring that prosecutions for piracy against non-English shipping miscarried.[13] And indeed the French *guerre de course* (privateering war) did not end in 1684.[14] Galve's knowledge of the deleterious effects of piracy hit home early in 1689 as he took up the reins of power in Mexico City. When Galve and his wife, Elvira, arrived in Mexico City on Sunday, May 8, they heard the gruesome news that Fr. Diego de Aguilar, a Mercedarian based in Acaponeta (near Mazatlan), had just been kidnapped for ransom by English pirates. To prove that they were serious, the pirates had sent Fr. Diego's ears and nose to members of the government.[15] Local news was made worse by reports from across the Pacific. The viceroy's commitment to protecting the king's subjects was galvanized by confirmation that the foreign predation on the king of Spain's subjects was now accelerating worldwide.

For most of the seventeenth century Spain's Asian possessions had been spared European piratical depredations, although Philippine governor Gabriel de Curuzeláegui had exaggerated in a 1685 report to his immediate superior, the viceroy in Mexico City, when he described the islands' recent "tranquillity and peace." Serious maritime threats had come from Chinese forces, particularly the Taiwan-based "pirate" (or hero) Koxinga (Coxinga, Kuo-hsing-yeh, or Cheng Sen), whose death in 1662 cut short an imminent invasion of the Philippines. In the 1670s the Philippine government feared that Sipuan, another Chinese "pirate," was seeking an anti-Spanish alliance with the English and withdrew from the southern island of Mindanao to bolster its garrisons. Pressure continued to come from the south as well. Although Spain was kicked out of Mindanao and Muslim raids persisted, diplomacy was prevailing over war by the 1680s (a factor which explains part of Ramírez's story in the next chapter).[16] Chinese (*sangley*) immigrant rebellions in 1639, 1662, and 1686 had been severely punished; repressive measures had been put in place, including the order for the expulsion of all non-Christians from the islands in November of that year (another fact connected to Ramírez's story). Some gossiped, moreover, that Galve's officials in Manila were letting almost all of the revenue from the Chinese-Philippine trade and the Philippine-Mexican-Peruvian trade, "the globe's most powerful commerce," slip through the king's fingers into a massive black market.[17] Galve himself confessed secretly that the office of viceroy of New Spain "has been denuded of authority and respect" through recurrent maladministration.[18]

Curuzeláegui's 1685 report thus underestimated external and internal difficulties. Two years later the governor's gloomier reports to the viceroy in New Spain stressed problems, especially that "enemies" were now "infesting our coasts." What was worse, bad luck and typhoons had prevented regular communication across the Pacific between the Philippines and New Spain, the Manila government's key revenue source. One Jesuit summarized "the present state of affairs: no soldiers, no ships, and no militiamen at our disposal; God grant us delivery from all of our current fears."[19] Where had these enemies come from?

The new European and Euro-American pirates of the Pacific had entered the South Sea, as it was then known, in dozens of ships. Beginning in 1680, several companies of thousands of men came across Panama or around Cape Horn, territories within the jurisdiction of the viceroy of Peru. "It is noteworthy," wrote the viceroy in 1689, "that they entered by the Straits of Magellan around the months of May and June, during the time of year in this hemisphere when we feel winter's greatest rigors, it having been thought impossible prior to this event for anyone to dare navigate the straits at that time of year at a latitude of 53°." No one he consulted could remember any other ship having succeeded in doing so before. "This knowledge," he commented, "undermines even further any confidence we had in our safety from their attacks."[20]

The invaders were buccaneers and entrepreneurs from the Caribbean, New England, Britain, France, and Holland. Several factors motivated this invasion, including Captain Henry Morgan's highly profitable sack of Panama City in 1670–1671, which demonstrated that concerted pirate operations could attack even the biggest Spanish targets. An important 1670 Anglo-Spanish treaty led some northern European merchant investors to believe (erroneously) that they could now trade legally with Spanish markets on the Pacific coasts of the Americas. A big boost to pirate operations came when non-Spanish captains discovered that they could get copies of a complete set of Spanish navigational charts for the Atlantic and Pacific. The charts were originally taken from the *Santa Rosario* by Bartholomew Sharp's buccaneers on July 10, 1680, off the Peruvian coast. Copies were sold piecemeal by William Hacke in London (tradition maintains that he sold only limited charts for exorbitant rates from his usual seat in a corner of the Prospect of Whitby, a pub in Wapping, in London's East End). The subsequent capture of Spanish pilots and more charts in the South Seas by other pirates, like Basil Ringrose and John Cook, made sustained Pacific piracy possible.[21]

Governors from California to Chile and across to the Philippines began to fear that their jurisdictions might suffer a slow erosion of Spanish control, as had happened on the smaller Caribbean islands between the Franco-English settlement of San Cristóbal (St. Kitts) in 1624 and French entrenchment in Antigua and Monserrat in 1660. Viceroys and merchants particularly feared the loss of the galleons which connected the Philippine Islands with the Americas (though none was ever taken in the 1600s).[22] The founding of Manila in 1571, linking America with Asia, marked the year "when all important populated continents began to exchange products continuously," as Dennis O. Flynn and Arturo Giráldez have remarked. The year 1680 may be taken as the time when the Spanish administration truly began to worry that its control over the critical Manila-Acapulco link in global commerce was seriously challenged, by pirates, not by the navy of a declared enemy.[23]

Galve's response to these threats significantly accelerated the slow implementation of the previous viceroy's policies, initiated after the brutal sacking of Veracruz in 1683, which had proved that even heavily garrisoned cities were woefully unprepared for such predators. Galve increased coastguard patrols (especially the fast, shallow-bottomed galleys and large oceangoing canoes [*piraguas* or pirogues] which could penetrate mangrove coastlines), diverted funds to strengthen the Armada de Barlovento (Windward Fleet) cruising the

Caribbean, encouraged an effective reform of local militias, and allotted impressive resources to fortifying the main ports (Veracruz's "Fortress" was a fortress in name only). Unofficially, Spanish pirate attacks on French, English, and Dutch shipping and settlements on the Lesser Antilles were encouraged. We have no evidence, however, that Mexican merchants organized antipirate fleets like the Armada de Nuestra Señora de la Guía then operating quite successfully out of Lima, Peru.[24] As a Chinese official of the time pointed out, catching pirates and smugglers was like standing at the water's edge trying to catch passing "fish and birds."[25]

Nevertheless, Galve was not just thinking defensively. When he met Ramírez in 1690, Galve was planning an amphibious attack on French and buccaneer bases on Hispaniola and Tortuga islands. Perhaps his bold thinking was encouraged by his family connections in the navy. His father-in-law was Don Fadrique de Toledo, the commander of the Sicily and Naples galleys, a highly respected officer. Don Fadrique's own father, as captain general of the Atlantic fleets, had ousted the Dutch from Brazil in 1624–1625 and 1635.[26] The seventh Duke of Sessa, the maternal grandfather of Galve's wife, was the chief naval commander in charge of the sensitive area around the Straits of Gibraltar.[27] Galve's 1690 campaign against Tortuga ultimately succeeded in 1691. Sigüenza celebrated this victory in print, remembering the Tortuga-based buccaneers' destruction of Veracruz in 1683 as "Spanish justice" punishing "French treason."[28] Galve's measures garnered him the king's approval in 1692 for the way he had "undertaken measures . . . for the safety of those provinces . . . so that the inhabitants may experience freedom from pirate invasions."[29]

WHY THE VICEROY COMMISSIONED *THE MISFORTUNES* IN 1690

This is the larger political context for Galve's public acceptance of Ramírez's story. *Misfortunes* was intended to form part of a larger initiative, a complicated global naval alliance against the expansionist French king Louis XIV. Beginning in 1688, this collaboration forced Catholic Spaniards into mistrustful cooperation with the Protestant English and Dutch. The viceroy commissioned *Misfortunes*, a story of how Spaniards had been enslaved by English pirates off the Philippines, because he belonged to the aristocratic court party which was then cautiously steering Spain's cooperation with England and Holland against France. Simply put, Galve, Infantado, and Vélez mistrusted their newfound allies and believed that London and Amsterdam, like the predatory Tortuga buccaneers, aimed to deprive France of its New World possessions at Spain's expense. This court party suspected that the English and Dutch wanted to expand their occupation of the Americas, which Madrid considered legally Spanish until proven otherwise.

In a joint memorandum in 1689, the members of the Council of the Indies and State Council reminded King Carlos II of the grounds for his legal dominion in the Americas. It was based in part on the 1494 Tordesillas Concord and Alexander VI's papal bull, which others might dispute, but more importantly on rights of discovery, centuries of conversion, and sustained occupation and settlement. These factors vitiated *res nullius* arguments that unexploited pockets of territory were free for the taking. This sound combination of diplomatic agreements and practical realities, in their minds, was built on underlying legal principles of possession which were generally accepted by rivals even if their application was not. Subsequent northern European imitation throughout the world was the best form of flattery. This "exclusive [*privativo*]" jurisdiction did not require recognition by another state. Thus "English, Dutch, or French territorial claims were only legitimate if and when Spain formally recognized them."[30]

The greatest governmental fear in Spanish circles around the globe—which Galve, Infantado, and Vélez shared—was jurisdictional erosion. Whether northern European rivals wanted to call them planters or interlopers, migrants to the Americas without Spanish documentation were considered illegal immigrants—or even criminals. In December 1688 the Jamaica governor ordered that English navy ships as well as privateers should attack the newly arrived Basque privateers whom Spain had commissioned to fight both evils, piracy and smuggling. This led to a state of *de facto* American war while England and Spain were not only at peace *de lege* but negotiating an alliance against France.[31] The alliance with the maritime powers of England and Holland against France, concluded in 1689, heightened these legitimate concerns. On March 7, 1689, Vélez warned the king of the danger that allied Dutch and English naval forces might refuse to return French territories which they might occupy, thus threatening Spanish sovereignty in the Americas. Vélez suggested measures to counter the eventuality that one of Carlos II's allies might deny *de facto* the Spanish king's *de lege* title of "sovereign of the Indies." Specifically, he recommended commissioning ships to accompany allied maneuvers in order to reestablish Spanish sovereignty wherever required. The government immediately issued secret instructions to Spanish colonial officials to prevent allied English or Dutch forces from occupying French American possessions by any means necessary. A project to commission

English and Dutch ships as Spanish vessels, under the command of an Irish-Spanish admiral by the name of Arturo O'Bruin, was put into motion to ensure that the monarchy's flag was present at any allied Caribbean engagement.[32]

In commissioning *Misfortunes* Galve's publicity campaign against pirates and dodgy allies was twofold. First, Ramírez's story was constructed as a public event to arouse Hispanic indignation against buccaneers and other predatory foreigners, and Ramírez undoubtedly acquired regional celebrity status for a time. Second, once the book itself arrived in Madrid in late 1690, it encouraged Spanish councilors there to adopt a policy of keeping Spain's dangerously powerful Grand Alliance partners against France at arm's length, particularly in terms of American campaigns. This popular and high-level campaign argued that England and Holland were allies under duress, which explains why *Misfortunes* catered to a relatively old-fashioned but enduring stereotype—England was perfidious (*la pérfide Albion*), a place which bred heretics and pirates who preyed primarily on their archenemies: Spanish subjects.[33]

Misfortunes portrayed Ramírez as a long-suffering victim of violent English criminals, enemies of humanity (*hostis humani generis*), whose criminal actions were born out of deeply engrained English jealousy of the Spaniards' empire. Galve intended to pluck Hispanic heartstrings through Sigüenza's masterful presentation of Ramírez's tribulations. The book sounded a rallying call against what one Spanish senior judge in Peru called "the projects of emulation, envy, hatred, and ambition harbored by foreign nations, particularly the English." Anti-English sentiment among Spanish observers was heightened by the continued publication of inflammatory English pamphlets. These tracts justified pirates' pillaging of the Spanish Empire through stereotypes of Spaniards as latter-day conquistadors following in the footsteps of Hernán Cortés and Francisco Pizarro, who "rifle, plunder and bring home undisturbed all the wealth of that golden world," despoiling the "poor, naked and innocent people" of the Americas with "unprecedented cruelties, exorbitances and barbarities."[34]

Thus Ramírez's account of captivity at the hands of Englishmen served a cautious, even cynical, policy vis-à-vis Spain's allies put forth by Galve, Infantado, and Vélez in 1690. The pathos of Ramírez's story in *Misfortunes* appealed to a broad Hispanic audience, from Yucatan villagers who suffered directly at the hands of buccaneers to European politicians who were negotiating scabrous military collaborations. It exposed pirates for what they were, criminals "who recognize neither government, nor homeland, nor loyalty to anything [*señor, patria, ni obediencia*] other than the sea and applying themselves to stealing anything they can get their hands on, today here, and tomorrow elsewhere."[35] Implicitly, *Misfortunes'* English pirates provided useful analogies to faithless allies. They were intended to function at the highest political level as emblematic reminders to officials in Madrid: if the English or Dutch allies refused to hand back Caribbean islands now occupied by the French at the end of the war, they would essentially be refusing to play by the rules of multilateral wartime collaboration. They too would be pirates "who recognize neither government, nor homeland, nor loyalty to anything." The political utility of Ramírez's account of English perfidy relied on accepting it as true, but did he tell Galve and Sigüenza the truth and nothing but the truth? Did Ramírez invent his story?

THE HISTORICITY OF RAMÍREZ'S NARRATIVE

Substantial Spanish and English archival evidence as well as other eyewitness accounts can be used to gauge how much of Ramírez's story about pirate captivity was true. We have no evidence about Ramírez's life before his capture by pirates, so we can tentatively accept that he was a Spanish carpenter from Puerto Rico. Ramírez's version of the important events in his story focused on how he was attacked by two ships on March 4, 1687, while returning to Manila from the northern provinces. Governor Curuzeláegui had placed Ramírez in command of a poorly armed single-deck frigate and instructed him to bring back "supplies" urgently needed by the presidio in Cavite from "the northern province of Ilocos":

> Upon the fifth day of our return passage, beating upwind to gain entrance to the Marivelez channel and reach port, around four in the afternoon we spied two vessels on the landward side. I, assuming along with my crew that they were the ships given to Captains Juan Bautista and Juan de Caravallo to go to Pangazinan and Panay to seek rice and other necessaries for the presidio in Cavite and the surrounding area, continued tacking even though they stood to windward of me, under no apprehensions whatsoever, for there was no reason for any.
>
> My state of mind could not but be changed as soon as I beheld, within a short compass of time, two pirogues paddling at full speed toward us, and it gave me an extreme shock to recognize them, upon their close approach, as enemies . . . they did not immediately board us, and we answered their shots with our muskets from time to time, one man aiming while the other fired;

in the meantime some of us were engaged in cutting our bullets in half with a knife so that, by doubling our munitions, we might prolong our ridiculous resistance. Almost without delay, the two larger vessels which we had seen before and from which the pirogues had been sent came upon us, and we struck our topsail flags and main, requesting to be given quarter just as the fifty Englishmen boarded my frigate with cutlasses drawn; it was all over in a trice . . . It was six in the afternoon on the fourth of March in the year 1687.

A Jesuit report in Madrid's Royal Academy of History (manuscript RAH 9/2668) corroborates that pirates did indeed take Spanish ships off the entrance to Manila Bay on March 4, 1687.[36] RAH 9/2668 forms part of the Jesuits' annual reports summarizing events in Manila between June 11, 1686, and June 24, 1687. It mainly focused on the escalation in the vitriolic disputes involving the Dominican bishop and his successor, the Jesuits, the Philippines Supreme Court, and Governor Curuzeláegui.

As part of these attempts to undermine each other's spiritual and political authority on the islands, posters appeared in Manila in the 1680s which lambasted the Jesuits for their commercial materialism (one stated: "If anyone wishes to buy CROCKS, POTS, or DISHES, he can get them at the Jesuits'"). The Jesuits fought back. One accused the governor's principal allies, the Dominicans, of giving him 50,000 pesos to run a smear campaign against the Jesuits on the islands, "whose population, led by the Jesuits, cries out for liberty; we are living under the fist of Pharaoh himself." Ultimately the bishop suspected the Jesuits of a criminal escalation in the mutual smear campaign. One morning a poster was found plastered on Manila walls which implicated the governor and his *valido* (favorite), the bishop, in the destruction of the monarchy itself. The conspirators were depicted exulting over the beheaded body of the king, whose arms and legs were tied "by their intrigues"; a little rhyme at the bottom of the picture "exhorted the people and soldiers of Manila to come to the King's assistance." After years of verbal sparring, violence erupted.[37]

In late February 1687 two hundred troops stormed the Jesuit residence, took everyone inside captive for nine days, and searched for incriminating evidence. Several brothers were ultimately arrested. The entry in RAH 9/2668 for March 4, 1687, recording this shocking news reveals key evidence both corroborating Ramírez's account and making it problematic:

On March 4 (the day on which the first violent search of [the college of] the Society took place) the English pirate captured a royal sloop [*balandra*], which was coming from Pangasinan laden with three thousand *caváns* of cleaned rice.[38] *Item*, he also captured a *champán* [sampan] belonging to the alcalde of Pangasinan, which came laden with rice and other products.[39]

A comparison of the RAH 9/2668 report with Ramírez's version of events seems to corroborate that pirates did take Spanish vessels on the date that Ramírez mentioned, a sloop and a sampan. But the report apparently does not mention Ramírez's frigate. Clearly, the Jesuit report and Ramírez's story do not mesh. Archival documents can help us determine whether the events referred to in these two accounts can be reconciled.

Ramírez related in Chapter 2 of *Misfortunes* that he had allowed the pirates to come too close to his ships because he mistook them for two vessels commanded by Captains Juan Bautista Gambaldo and Juan de Caravallo, which were to return to the Manila presidio with rice and other supplies from the provinces of Pangasinan and Panay. RAH 9/2668 generally corroborates this account; other evidence provides additional information about these two individuals.

Juan Caravallo was indeed salaried in the Philippine Islands at the time as a "seaman on the Manila *nao* [Manilla-Acapulco galleon]." He probably belonged to a family with established roots on the southern island of Cebu and was certainly the Caravallo named as the principal suspect in a 1670s case involving 12,000 pesos' worth of goods smuggled into Mexico from Asia. By 1695, however, he had risen to the rank of sergeant and was serving as the *despensero* (purser or steward) aboard the *Santa Rosa* on its regular runs between Manila and Acapulco. Hence it is likely that Caravallo had already attained that rank if he was given command of a Pangasinan or Panay supply ship in 1687, as Ramírez stated. Likewise, Juan Bautista Gambaldo was the *guardián del galeón* (boatswain or assistant to the quartermaster) on the Manila *nao*, a petty officer whose job was to maintain the ship's seaworthiness by inspecting and repairing "sails and rigging at sea," careening it, and loading and unloading cargoes.[40] The duties of Caravallo and Gambaldo thus fit the roles which Ramírez ascribed to them, but we are left wondering which man commanded which ship, the larger royal sloop or the smaller sampan owned by the alcalde.

But why did Ramírez say that one of these two ships was returning from Panay (an island beyond Mindoro Island to the south of Luzon) when the careful annotation of the Jesuit report tells us that only two ships were taken and both were from Pangasinan? Were three ships really sent out by the governor on exactly the same mission, commanded by Ramírez, Caravallo, and Gambaldo? We should note at this juncture that Pangasinan and Ilocos are essentially the same region of Luzon Island. Colonial Pangasinan was the capital city of the southernmost part of the northwestern region of Luzon, and Ilocos was the northern part.[41] Ramírez himself told Sigüenza (see Chapter 4 of the translation) that one of the Philippine Islanders who reached Yucatan with him, Juan Pinto, was from Pangasinan. Could Pinto have been the representative of the Pangasinan alcalde who owned the smaller sampan? Was Ramírez being intentionally obscure? RAH 9/2668's report that two ships were taken by pirates on their return leg from Pangasinan, not from Pangasinan and Panay as Ramírez stated, is confirmed by an unexpected published source: the pirates themselves.

In the winter of 1687 the precise movements of the English pirate company cruising those waters were carefully logged by a man aboard their ship who would become famous, William Dampier (1651–1715). Biographers have called Dampier both "a pirate of exquisite mind" and "the devil's mariner." He had a checkered career as a pirate, incipient naturalist, and Royal Navy officer during the last two decades of the seventeenth century.[42] In his *New Voyage round the World*, published ten years after 1687, Dampier described his voyage aboard the *Cygnet* with the piratical crew of Captain Charles Swan, a man who claimed to have been forced into piracy by his men.[43] After several unsuccessful attempts to pick off galleons along the coast of South America or Mexico and a lackluster set of land raids, the *Cygnet* broke off from its companion pirate ships, which were carrying several thousand buccaneers, and made an excruciatingly long voyage across the Pacific to the Philippine Islands in 1686. There the crew demoted Swan for his lukewarm performance as a pirate leader on January 14, 1687, on Mindanao, the only substantial Philippine island not controlled by Spanish authorities. In his stead they elected a man by the name of John Read as their captain.[44] The *Cygnet* left Mindanao with Dampier aboard, but without its "tender" (companion ship: a smaller bark stolen from Spanish Peruvians almost two years earlier), because its hull had been so eaten by sea worms that it looked "like Honeycombs."[45] Dampier tells us that the pirates captured two small prizes as they cruised along the west side of the Philippine Islands in February, seeking to intercept either the Manila *nao* or a rich merchantman. Two versions of his account survive, each of which elucidates our investigation of Ramírez's capture. The first narrative is a handwritten and annotated draft version of the second, a much more elaborate text published as a book entitled *A New Voyage round the World* several years afterward. At the time of the voyage Dampier seems to have been the navigator aboard the *Cygnet*, but on occasion he temporarily commanded subordinate vessels taken by the pirates. In any case, no other log of the *Cygnet*'s movements survives. For clarity, Dampier's annotations to the draft account appear in the following transcript in parentheses and mine in brackets:

> The 23rd day in the morning we took a small vessel that came from Manila bound for a town called Pangosanam [Pangasinan] on the north side of the island of Luconia [Luzon] (Pangosanam is the name of a town about the northeast end of Lutonia) and in the evening took another three mast ship about 100 tons loaded with rice and had 190 pieces of dungaree for making sails. She had twenty-five men aboard and came from Pangosanam, the same town whither the other was bound. The commander of her was boatswain of the Acapulco ship which we heard of at Guam [the events at Guam had occurred in the spring of 1686 after the pirates crossed the Pacific]. He told us that so soon as he came in sight of Guam the governor sent a prow to advise them of our being at an anchor under the island . . . On the news she kept to the southward of the island and came foul of the shoal which we run over, where they struck their rudder off and were three days before they could hang it up again; that their strength consisted more in the countenance of their ship and number of their men than in knowledge, courage, or conduct. They had 50 great guns and but four mounted. They had 300 seamen and 500 passengers and they had 800,000 dollars of merchants' money besides private adventurers' very considerable. He likewise told us it was three months afterwards before they got to the Manila, where they were no sooner arrived but they heard of our being at Mindanao for the General of Mindanao [the independent Muslim sultan] had sent a prow on purpose to give them an account of our strength and condition, desiring their assistance to destroy us (we heard some such thing at Mindanao).[46]

Dampier related events somewhat differently in his published account, with some detail, notably the Guam events, being relegated to other sections of the book:

> The 21st Day we went from hence with the wind at E.N.E. a small gale. The 23d Day [there is no entry for February 22] in the Morning we were fair by the S.E. end of the Island *Luconia* [the modern island of Luzon],[47] the place

that had been so long desired by us. We presently saw a Sail coming from
the northward, and making after her we took her in two Hours time. She
was a *Spanish* Bark, that came from a place called *Pangasanam*, a small Town
on the N. end of *Luconia*, as they told us; probably the same with *Pongassiny*,
which lies on a Bay at the N.W. side of the Island. She was bound to *Manila*,
but had no Goods aboard; and therefore we turned her away. The 23d we
took another *Spanish* Vessel that came from the same place as the other. She
was laden with Rice and Cotton-Cloth, and bound for *Manila* also. These
Goods were purposely for the *Acapulco* Ship: The Rice was for the Men to
live on while they lay there, and in their return: and the Cotton-Cloth was
to make Sail. The Master of this Prize [Dampier later refers to it as "the rice
prize"][48] was Boatswain of the *Acapulco* Ship which escaped us at *Guam*,
and was now at *Manila*. It was this Man that gave us the Relation of what
Strength it had, how they were afraid of us there, and of the accident that
happen'd to them, as is before mentioned in the 10th Chapter [they had run
aground on shoals in Guam]. We took these two Vessels within seven or
eight Leagues of Manila.[49]

A close investigation of the accounts of Ramírez, Dampier, and RAH 9/2668
proves that they were describing the same events, notwithstanding the many
differences in detail.[50] We can examine the evidence by tackling the journalistic
"six honest serving-men" of research, inspired by Rudyard Kipling's *Just So Stories:* What, Why, When, How, Where, and Who.[51] Generally speaking, we know
the "what" and "why" already from the three accounts: pirates pillaged Spanish
ships for plunder near Manila in early 1687. Let us, then, first consider the apparent inconsistency in the exact "when" of these events, a glaring problem which
may be puzzling the reader at this point.

The apparent discrepancy between Ramírez's date (March 4, 1687) and
Dampier's date (February 23, 1687) is only a figment of early modern calendrical and administrative differences. To begin with, as a Catholic subject of the
king of Spain, Ramírez was using the Gregorian calendar promulgated by Pope
Gregory XIII in 1582 to realign Easter festivities with true astronomical time.
Gregory declared that October 4 of that year was to be followed immediately by
October 15, forcing the date forward by ten days. Dampier, however, was natu-
rally enough following English practice, which continued to reject the "Popish"
calendar until 1752, when Parliament officially gave up on the medieval Julian calendar. If we translate Tuesday, March 4, 1687, into the Julian calendar, we come

up with Tuesday, February 22, 1687 (Julian, New Style).[52] This is one day off from Dampier's date of February 23, 1687. Did the capture of the Philippine vessels by the *Cygnet*'s crew occur on Tuesday, February 22, not Wednesday, February 23? What explains this missing day? Were Ramírez and Dampier simply describing different events, or did their memories fail them?[53]

One explanation can easily be discounted. The date was not an error in Dampier's writing. Although he made extensive corrections to the manuscript before it went to print, this date was not corrected.[54] The second possibility relates to the log keeping of early modern navigators. Seamen in the age of sail kept logs of days starting at noon and ending at noon, because that is when they typically "shot" or observed the sun to determine latitude. Dampier himself explained the practice in his diary on May 20. When transferring the logbooks for publication, however, it was their usual practice to change this "naval" time to standard time (the manuscripts and printed versions of Captain James Cook's famous journals of Pacific voyages have confused many a reader on this count).[55] Thus the capture of one of the Spanish barks may have happened sometime before Dampier made his latitude calculation at noon, when February 23 had not yet begun, according to this nautical tradition. Neither one of these explanations is necessary, however. There is a much simpler one, but it requires a preliminary remark about the composition of Dampier's text.

Dampier kept a log of his voyages. This text later became the framework for his famous *A New Voyage round the World*, which he started writing sometime in 1691 and published in 1697. We no longer have the log, but we do have the manuscript on which Dampier wrote editorial corrections for the proofs. It is clear that Dampier, like any good navigator, was meticulous about his record keeping. At the beginning of Chapter 15, which corresponds to his log entry for January 14, 1687, the day the pirate company left the island of Mindanao bound for Manila, Dampier enters into a fairly lengthy explanation of a calendrical problem which baffled him when the *Cygnet* arrived in Mindanao in 1686. The pirates noticed in July 1686 that the Muslims on Mindanao, with whom they spent the better part of half a year, celebrated the Muslim holy day of Friday on Thursday.[56] In fact, Dampier related, "at *Mindanao*, and all other places in the *East-Indies*, we found them reckoning a Day before us, both Natives and *Europeans*... So among the Indian Mahometans here, their *Friday*, the day of their Sultan's going to their Mosques, was *Thursday* with us; though it were *Friday* also with those who came eastward from *Europe*."[57]

What Dampier had encountered, of course, is the famous time difference which modern timekeeping has resolved by creating the imaginary dateline in the middle of the Pacific Ocean. When crossing this line from east to west, as Dampier did, the hour, month, and year remain the same, but the weekday and the date both skip ahead by one: Thursday, for example, becomes Friday and January 1 becomes January 2. There was no dateline in the Pacific in 1687, of course. Like Ferdinand Magellan and others before him, Dampier noted the phenomenon in his journal, correctly assessing its cause: "Having travell'd so far Westward, keeping the same Course with the Sun, we must consequently have gain'd something insensibly in the length of the particular Days, but have lost in the tale, the bulk, or number of the Days or Hours."[58]

How does this resolve the one-day difference between the dates given by Ramírez and Dampier in their accounts of the *Cygnet*'s activities off Manila? Again, we can let Dampier explain: "the *Spaniards of Guam* [were] keeping the same Computation with our selves," that is, the incorrect date and weekday, one day too early.

> The reason of which I take to be, that they settled that Colony [Guam] by a Course westward from *Spain;* the *Spaniards* going first to *America*, and thence to the *Ladrones* and *Philippines*. But how their reckoning was at *Manila*, and the rest of the *Spanish* Colonies in the *Philippine* Islands, I know not; whether they keep it as they brought it, or corrected it by the Accounts of the Natives, and of the *Portugueze, Dutch* and *English*, coming the contrary way from *Europe*.[59]

Dampier's hunch was right. The Spanish colonials in Asia effectively kept Mexican time and would do so until Governor Narciso Clavería changed Philippine time in 1844 to match the time kept by Chinese, British, Dutch, and Portuguese trading partners in Asia, all of whom were one day ahead of Manila.[60] An anonymous Spanish colonial report from 1794 noted how this phenomenon affected watches: Spaniards from New Spain arrived in Macao 16 1/6 hours late for Macao time, whereas Portuguese from Europe invariably arrived 7 5/6 hours early; "the tardiness of the former and the earliness of the latter make up a natural day."[61]

With the Gregorian-Julian conversion plus the missing day caused by Philippine "Mexican time," the Gregorian-Philippine date that Ramírez gave for the capture of his ship off Manila, March 4, 1687, becomes Dampier's

Julian-corrected European date of February 23, 1687. It is reasonable to assume that Dampier began to correct his log entries for the one-day difference at Mindanao in the summer or fall of 1686 in order to be in line with both the Mindanao Muslims he lived with and the "Dutch and English" he expected to meet in Asia. Having dealt with the illusory time discrepancy, we can turn our attention to the "how" and the "where" of these events.

According to Ramírez, the attack happened when he was tacking around the headland near Mariveles known as Cochinos Point,[62] though he did not mention the headland by name. While Dampier related that the *Cygnet*'s crew captured two Spanish barks on the same day (presumably one in the morning and the other in the afternoon) and that they saw no other vessels, Ramírez's account mentions the capture of only one ship: his Spanish bark. Nevertheless, he recalled that the supply convoy consisting of two ships under the command of Caravallo and Gambaldo was in the area. Were three Spanish supply ships near Mariveles channel that day?

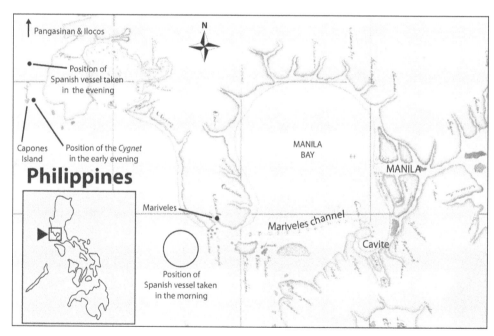

MAP 2.1. Approaches to Manila Bay. Based on *Plano de Manila* (1771). Courtesy Library of Congress Maps Collections. Cartography by Elwood Mills.

Again, archival evidence which has never been used before proves that Ramí-rez's story was a garbled narrative of real events. This evidence comes from some of the many captives whom the *Cygnet* pirates released on two occasions, fifty-two on the morning after Ramírez's capture on Capones Island and a few others several months later on the Babuyán Islands north of Luzon (Dampier's "Bashee Islands"). Both groups were eventually interrogated by Spanish officials in Manila, and their testimony survives in its entirety. Additionally, a soldier who questioned some of the first batch of captives after their ordeal was over provided important details concerning the vessel taken on the morning of March 4. All of this allows us to reconstruct the precise movements of both the *Cygnet* and Ramírez's vessel in great detail on that day and afterward. Ultimately, this evidence reveals at least one of Ramírez's deceptions.

Manila's governor heard the eyewitness accounts of the capture of the two Spanish vessels on March 13 and 14. Five of the captives released on Capones were crew members aboard the *Nuestra Señora de Aránzazu y San Ignacio*, a navy frigate newly built in the Philippine Islands, commanded by Captain Felipe Ferrer. This was the ship captured by the *Cygnet* in the late afternoon of March 4. Three of these witnesses were navy sailors: Bartolomé Luis, José Baltasar, and Luis Angel, all fairly young. Another was Ferrer's lieutenant (*alférez*), Antonio de Guevara. The last witness testifying from what we may call the Capones contingent of fifty-two captives was Miguel Flores, a soldier in the Ilocos garrison carrying dispatches to Manila from the provincial commander there, Don Francisco Ramírez Nieto.[63]

The information they provided was confirmed and expanded a year later, on February 2 and 3, 1688, by the testimony of another eight eyewitnesses released subsequently on Babuyanes Islands. Five of them were also members of Ferrer's crew: Mateo Francisco (thirty-six years of age) and Diego Rendón (twenty-nine), both sailors; Alonso de Luna, an eighteen-year-old cabin boy; Juan del Pilar, the Japanese-Filipino mestizo servant of Ferrer's quartermaster, Francisco de Acosta, who was also taken captive but could not testify due to illness; and Silvestre Moxica, Ferrer's own *mulato* slave. The remaining three eyewitnesses are particularly trustworthy given their identity, but two had been taken prisoners several months after Ramírez's capture and reveal nothing specifically about the March 4 events.[64] The other non-Spanish captive, however, is very important for our analysis: Asam, a Muslim from the kingdom of Jolo, which at the time ruled an empire on the Sulu Archipelago stretching from Borneo to southwestern

Mindanao.[65] Asam's ship was captured by the *Cygnet* between Jolo and Mindanao, probably one of the "two Prows belonging to the Sologues" which Dampier says they "met" near Zamboanga in late January 1687.[66] Apart from Dampier, Asam is our only non-Spanish eyewitness to Ramírez's capture (we shall return to his testimony in the next chapter for important evidence concerning the *Cygnet*'s subsequent adventures).

The sequence of events is remarkably clear and detailed.[67] On the morning of March 4, while sailing with a strong northeast trade wind to their advantage off the entrance to Mariveles channel, the *Cygnet* captured a privately owned sampan under the command of Don Francisco Arsaga, outward bound from Manila to Pangasinan, Ilocos Province. The pirates removed its cargo: "small stuff and assorted passengers," according to Asam; but Arsaga's vessel also contained "valuable property" belonging to a "Captain Alonso del Castillo," which several other witnesses said included a manservant and three of "his" women "with their suckling babies."[68] The pirates took everyone prisoner and sank the sampan. Later that day, farther along the coast as the *Cygnet* headed northward, the pirates espied the *Aránzazu* on a southbound course toward Manila harbor. It had made the return trip from Manila to Pangasinan in forty-three days with a crew of thirteen sailors and ten cabin boys (some witnesses said sixteen and eight), bringing back a cargo of 2,101 baskets of cleaned rice, 2,000 pieces of Ilocos cloth, and some cotton which the governor of Ilocos was sending for the navy. Around four or four-thirty in the afternoon, while due north of Capones Island, the nearly becalmed *Aránzazu* spied the almost equally motionless *Cygnet* to the south, close by the island on its landward side. José Baltasar stated that the Spanish frigate could make no headway because of the slight contrary wind.

At first nothing happened. Then Ferrer's men saw that the *Cygnet* had launched a pirogue, which rowed straight toward them. They "assumed," as Bartolomé Luis later recalled, that the pirate ship "was one of the merchantmen . . . from the port of Cavite" and did not worry. When the pirogue came within calling distance, however, they saw that the thirty men aboard were all armed with shotguns and carbines. Someone on the pirogue shouted out: "Ahoy there! Where have you come from? Where are you sailing to?" Now wary, the *Aránzazu* men responded with an evasive: "From the sea." The pirogue's crew answered by ordering them to "Furl your sails!" (stop their vessel). Captain Ferrer's angry retort of "Come aboard and do it yourselves!" was met with a concentrated barrage of musket and small gun fire from the pirogue, which then pulled behind the frigate's unprotected stern and kept itself athwart the ship.[69]

The battle continued for three hours or slightly more, but as the wind picked up the pirates' tactic of pinning down the Spaniards from the pirogue while the *Cygnet* with its hundred men and cannons moved relentlessly toward the *Aránzazu* began to succeed. Spanish morale eroded. Finally, with four pirates and two Spaniards wounded (including Ferrer's lieutenant), the *Cygnet* came up to the *Aránzazu*. The exact order of events now becomes less clear: confident in their superior numbers and firepower (eighteen cannons), the throng of pirates on the *Cygnet*'s deck began telling the Spaniards to "ease their sheets" and give up the fight. The thirty buccaneers eventually fought their way from the pirogue onto the king's frigate. The exhausted and overwhelmed Spanish crew surrendered. (Bartolomé Luis said the final assault consisted of two pirogues in addition to the *Cygnet*, but all the other witnesses remembered only one pirogue.) The battle ended not long after sunset, which occurred just after 6 p.m. on March 4, 1687. Most of the eyewitnesses placed the last shots fired around 7 or 7:30 p.m.[70]

Ferrer and five sailors, including three of those who testified (Bartolomé Luis, José Baltasar, and Luis Angel), were immediately taken aboard the *Cygnet*. There they found out that the pirate captain who had defeated them was named "Yandrid [John Read]."[71] In the inevitable interrogations which followed, conducted in Spanish, the Spaniards were individually questioned concerning the movements of the Manila galleons, island merchantmen, and local defenses. José Baltasar was asked if Manila's fortifications were as strong as those of Cadiz. The pirates pressed their prisoners to reveal whether the *Aránzazu* carried secret cargo, for "they had come solely looking for silver and gold, not rice." Ferrer's lieutenant heard them say that they were "out corsairing and had no interest in taking captives . . . only silver and gold." As the night progressed, more of the "English, Dutch, and Irish" pirates came aboard the *Aránzazu* and transferred batches of Spanish captives to the *Cygnet*.[72]

From midnight onward on March 5, fifty-two captives from Arsaga's sampan and Ferrer's *Aránzazu* were ferried in small groups from the *Cygnet* and *Aránzazu* to Capones Island and released (including Don Alonso's "women" and babies). Others remained aboard. We do not know who these men were, but most of the eyewitnesses concurred that Captain Ferrer and nine of his sailors were among them (two witnesses said nine sailors plus five cabin boys). José Baltasar heard from one of the people aboard the sampan that its captain, Francisco Arsaga, had been killed in the morning fight, but no one said anything about how many of his crew remained with the pirates. Asam's memory was that most of the fifty-two released prisoners were from Arsaga's sampan and that most of the Spanish sailors from the *Aránzazu* stayed with the pirates. In any case, the following morning, March 6, the *Cygnet* and *Aránzazu* sailed away on a south-southwest course.[73]

The differences between these eyewitness accounts and Ramírez's are striking. To begin with, none of the witnesses testified that anyone aboard the *Aránzazu* mistook the *Cygnet* for Gambaldo's or Caravallo's supply vessel. Not one witness even mentioned them. We can only conclude that participants in both events reported only two ships on a collision course that day with the *Cygnet*, Arsaga's and Ferrer's. Ramírez's narrative of the two-hour fight, furthermore, does not readily match the other witnesses' three-hour battle, especially if we pay close attention to details. His description of the relative positions of the "two" pirate ships "to the windward" of his own vessel, which "continued tacking," clashes with the reports that the *Cygnet* was unaccompanied and both the *Cygnet* and the *Aránzazu* struggled for hours during the afternoon to maneuver under light winds. Unlike all the witnesses except Bartolomé Luis, Ramírez said that "two pirogues" started to paddle toward him as the fight began: even Luis did not go that far, remembering only that two pirogues were involved in the final assault—and here we may doubt his word, given the many testimonies to the contrary. Finally, Ramírez insisted that everything elapsed quickly and that "it was all over" by "six in the afternoon," instead of seven or seven-thirty. His account does not quite jibe with the facts.

Ramírez did not tell Galve and Sigüenza the whole truth about his involvement in that fatal day's events. Nevertheless, we can get closer to it from several key details and one critical discrepancy which he revealed inadvertently in the two versions of the 1687 events that he gave to officials in Mexico in 1690. We need to reread these narratives in light of what we now know about the two prizes taken by the *Cygnet* on March 4. Originally, in January 1690, Ramírez told the Yucatan officials that he was a captain aboard a king's ship. In the version which Sigüenza printed several months later he downgraded this to being in charge of a sampan, a smaller local coastal vessel. Furthermore, on two occasions in *Misfortunes* (Chapters 2 and 3) Ramírez said that the pirates had taken his ship near the "entrance to the Marivelez channel" and "at the mouth of the Marivelez channel." From general information—and more specifically from Dampier's log entries—we know that the trade winds were blowing from the northeast at the time in that area. Ramírez's talk of "tacking" upwind insouciantly heading *toward* the two ships which he took for Gambaldo's and Caravallo's does not suit the conditions under which the battle took place in the afternoon near Capones Island, over sixty kilometers to the north.

This is particularly striking if we consider that the *Aránzazu* and *Cygnet* were clearly struggling to make way for hours because of the wind shadow caused by the coastal ranges leading up to Mount Pinatubo to the east of Capones. In contrast, Ramírez remembered tacking upwind into a dangerous channel opening, a feat which is demanding at the best of times when steady winds are blowing. Clearly, the answer lies in Ramírez's telescoping of the morning and afternoon battles into one event. The sailing conditions and location given by Ramírez *do* fit the conditions and location of Arsaga's sampan, taken in the morning when the *Cygnet* used the weather gauge caused by the rush of wind at the mouth of the Mariveles channel to overtake and capture its victim.[74] That is why Ramírez recalled on at least two occasions that he was taken there, and not at Capones, which, as he himself explained, lay "fourteen leagues" to the northwest. On March 4 Ramírez was not aboard the *Aránzazu*.

The preponderance of the evidence is that Ramírez's muddled accounts conflated the taking of the two ships. His consistent admissions of where he was taken and navigational explanations of how he was taken both place him aboard Arsaga's sampan when it was captured in the morning. The Asian ethnic identity of the crewmates named by Ramírez in Chapter 4 of *Misfortunes* supports this conclusion as well: two sailors were Philippine natives, one Chinese, another of mixed Chinese-Spanish or Chinese-Philippine ancestry, and one East Indian. In Chapter 3 Ramírez also mentioned that his second-in-command or "quartermaster" was a Philippine native, which was more likely on a privately owned coastal sampan than on Ferrer's navy ship. Ramírez was not with the crew who gloriously defended Ferrer's frigate for three hours in the afternoon, though he may have witnessed the entire battle from aboard the *Cygnet*. At the very least, if he was confined below decks after capture, he may have heard about the second encounter after the fact from the *Aránzazu* crew members who shared his fate. This reconstruction of events may shed some light on why Ramírez mentioned the two Spanish officers, Gambaldo and Caravallo, though the evidence is currently inconclusive. Placing our knowledge of the booty and captives taken from the Spanish ships in the context of other archival information about the Spanish navy in Manila at the time suggests a remarkable answer to Kipling's final journalistic question: Who were the other Spaniards caught by the *Cygnet* not named by our eyewitnesses? And was an "Alonso Ramírez" really among them?

Dampier said that the captured supplies were for the Manila galleon, and our eyewitnesses and RAH 9/2668 concur: rice for the crew waiting on land for the commander's order to reboard when it came time to head out for Acapulco and "dungaree" for making sails. It would have been natural for the fleet commander in Manila to give command of the cargo ship carrying the valuable rice and sailcloth to the officer who was regularly in charge of them aboard the *nao*. We already know that this man was either Juan Bautista Gambaldo, the Manila *nao*'s *guardián* in charge of "sails, rigging," and the loading and unloading of all cargoes, or Juan Caravallo, its *despensero*, in charge of foodstuffs.[75] The identity of the *Aránzazu*'s commanding officer who collaborated with the pirates, providing valuable information, is given by Dampier himself, but he fails to name the officer.

The "Master" of the valuable vessel taken in the afternoon, Dampier stated in his book, "was Boatswain of the Acapulco Ship which escaped us at Guam, and was now at Manila." As noted above, the *Cygnet* visited Guam between May 20 and June 2, 1686 (Dampier's dates; Gregorian Philippine dates: May 30–June 12). While there, the pirates had kidnapped a Jesuit priest, Fr. Matthias Kuklein (Matías Cuculino), who had mistaken them for Spaniards. They kept him as a guarantee for Spanish compliance with their demands for food. A few days afterward (too late to do anything about it) the pirates learned that the galleon prize they had chased across the Pacific, Gambaldo's *Santa Rosa*, had actually run aground on a coral reef on the island. Unluckily for the pirates but luckily for the commanding officer, Don Fernando González Zorrilla, it came free after three days' work, with only the rudder damaged. The *Santa Rosa* slipped away from the pirates with 100,000 pesos aboard (an official account: Dampier heard 800,000) and eventually made its delivery of the much-needed funds to the Philippines government and population.[76]

Was Ferrer Dampier's *Santa Rosa* "Boatswain"? Or did Ramírez not lie: were Gambaldo and Caravallo with Ferrer? Apart from González Zorrilla, the galleon's captain general or "commanding officer," we know from the Guam governor's correspondence that "Captain Francisco Lazcano" was the pilot; it would seem logical to assume, as established earlier, that Gambaldo and Caravallo were serving at the time as the galleon's *guardián* and *despensero*. Was either one aboard Ferrer's *Aránzazu* when it was taken?

Pending future archival discoveries, we can only point out the parameters of the interpretive difficulties arising from textual inconsistencies, translation issues, and lack of evidence. Dampier's draft did not state that the "Boatswain" aboard the *Santa Rosa* was the "Commander" of the prize taken in the afternoon but rather that he was the "Master." Although early modern English mercantile tradition often did not distinguish between a captain and a master, naval custom sometimes did. The master could be the navigator or sailing specialist aboard. Furthermore, Spanish terminology on mercantile and navy vessels was not easily translatable into English. Dampier's editorial hesitation in the 1690s may reflect his dim recollection of actual translation difficulties in 1687. Moreover, even in straightforward accounts of his English shipmates, Dampier used "boatswain" and "quartermaster" interchangeably on occasion. If Ferrer served as *contramaestre* (quartermaster) on the *Santa Rosa*, which seems probable given the specific command given to him on the *Aránzazu*, then it would not be fanciful to believe that Gambaldo or Caravallo or both of them were seconded to him as his *guardián* and/or *depensero* while the *Santa Rosa* refitted in Cavite, awaiting Ferrer's return. If that is the case and if Ramírez's claim that he acted as an officer on one of the two ships taken was not unfounded, then "Ramírez" may be a pseudonym.

Perhaps it was devised out of the names of Don Alonso del Castillo, whose valuable cargo of property and humans the pirates stole from the sampan, and Don Francisco Ramírez Nieto, the governor of Pangasinan, Ilocos (one of the sailors who accompanied Ramírez to Yucatan was from there). But this is highly speculative. Gambaldo and Caravallo seem to have disappeared from Spanish naval records; but so did Arsaga, missing in action, and, most compellingly, Ferrer himself. Although negative evidence is notoriously untrustworthy, Ferrer's long-term collaboration with the pirates after they released him later that summer near Cambodia (discussed in the following chapter) and Dampier's memory that it was the *Aránzazu*'s commanding officer who gave the pirates the most sensitive information about Spanish weaknesses add to the suspicion that his disappearance from Spanish records is not accidental. The supposition that "Ramírez" was Ferrer's pseudonym, however, would require a revision of our understanding of Ramírez's actions on March 4, which placed him aboard the sampan, not the *Aránzazu*.

Ramírez's true identity as Ferrer, Arsaga, Caravallo, Gambaldo, or one of their crew members would have presented the imposter with a problem in 1690 when the shipwreck in Yucatan led suspicious authorities to pack him off to Mexico City, an eventuality which might have placed him in the direct path of former crewmates. We know that the *Santa Rosa*'s replacement ship, the *Santo Cristo de*

Burgos, was in Acapulco in the spring of 1690, probably with many of Ramírez's former mates aboard.[77] Luckily for Ramírez, a year had passed since Galve had met with the Jesuit Fr. Antonio Jaramillo, recently arrived from Manila (and quite possibly the author of RAH 9/2668), on April 16, 1689. They talked about Philippine matters on the occasion of the departure of the outgoing viceroy, Melchor Portocarrero Lasso de la Vega, the Count of Monclova, who was bound for his new appointment in Peru.[78] Galve either did not connect Ramírez's story of captivity with Jaramillo's news about pirate attacks off Manila in the spring of 1687 or chose to ignore the confluence of facts (we shall return to this in Chapter 3).

Corroboration of Ramírez's grounds for concern that his collaboration with pirates might be revealed in Mexico can perhaps be found in Dampier's description of how forthcoming the "boatswain" was. The *Cygnet* missed the *Santa Rosa* in May 1686 because no Spaniards divulged its presence. Dampier apparently learned who was serving aboard the galleon not in May 1686 at Guam but rather the following March off Manila, as his account clearly implies. According to Dampier, the information came from the "boatswain" himself, who collaborated with the pirates quite freely by revealing Spanish naval and military strength in Asia. This contrasts sharply with Ramírez's version of events:

> The very first words he [the pirate captain] uttered were a promise of freedom if I revealed to him the names of the wealthiest places on these islands and whether he would find that the inhabitants would put up much resistance. I limited my answer to a confession that I had left Cavite exclusively to travel to the province of Ilocos—from which I was currently returning directly to Cavite—and thus would be unable to comply with his request. Not satisfied, he prodded further, asking whether it would be possible to beach and repair his ships on the island of Caponiz, which lies from northwest to southeast fourteen leagues from Marivelez, and whether the inhabitants might try to prevent him from landing. I calmly answered that the island was uninhabited and that I knew of a bay where he could easily accomplish his desires—my intention being, if they took the bait, to enable not only the natives of the island but also the Spaniards who garrison that island to surprise and capture them.

Apart from his protests of heroic resistance, Ramírez's account here fits what we know of the standard modus operandi of early modern pirates on at least one key point. The very first interaction between the buccaneer captain and the

Spanish captives was "a promise of freedom" in exchange for collaboration. Historians know this moment by its contemporary pirate name: the "Distribution of Justice." Pirate captors typically offered defeated sailors not just freedom from captivity but freedom in Dampier's sense of full participation in a profitable, if criminal, entrepreneurial endeavor. This came with incredibly democratic overtones for any sailors who were tired of excessive merchant or naval discipline: the pirates gave them an unparalleled opportunity to put their officers on trial. Evidence suggests that crews took advantage of this opportunity.[79]

It is difficult to know who collaborated or joined Captain Read's pirate company during those initially tense March days. Inevitably some of the *Aránzazu* and sampan men immediately did; others took longer to decide their future with the pirates, as we shall discover in the next chapter. Three years later Ramírez denied ever having collaborated with the pirates and dedicated one entire chapter to a painfully detailed account of the forced labors, humiliations, and tortures which they meted out to his men and himself between 1687 and 1689. None of our other eyewitnesses described similar treatment, however, and Ramírez's stilted account of how he was ultimately given a frigate as a reward for all his hard "work" for the pirates smacks of deception. Dampier—for obvious reasons— did not reveal the cruel side of "privateering" (his term for the pirates' private war against humanity), so he offers no evidence of captives' collaboration.

Given that Dampier's and Ramírez's versions of their meeting differ, it is appropriate at this juncture to note three pieces of evidence which nevertheless tie Ramírez firmly to the English pirates. Ramírez's linguistic peculiarities were noted by Estelle Irizarry in 1990. In fact, her whole attempt to historicize what most scholars at the time considered a novel was based on a sophisticated analysis of the rhetoric and lexicon in Ramírez's narrative. She demonstrated convincingly that it did not match Sigüenza y Góngora's usual prose style.[80] An important example for our purposes comes from a peculiar nautical term used by Ramírez. At the beginning of Chapter 4 of his narrative Ramírez recalled that one of "Captain Bel"'s officers, Dick, was the *quartamaestre*. As Dampier explained, the quartermaster was the "second Place" aboard a ship, "according to the Law of Privateers."[81] What might not strike the English-speaking scholar as odd should surprise the Spanish-speaking one, because "quartermaster" is invariably *contramaestre*, not *cuartamaestre*, in early modern Spanish usage.[82] The answer can only be that Ramírez picked up the term from an English-speaking crew.

The second piece of evidence is more substantial. The pirates gave Ramírez quite a bit of information about how they had come into the South Seas in 1684

and 1685 around South America's Cape Horn. Admittedly, Ramírez's recollection in 1690 was fragmentary and telescoped secondhand memories already at
least two years old by 1687. It is thus difficult to prove conclusively that his brief
summary of the pirates' two years cruising off Peruvian and Mexican waters corresponds to Dampier's detailed account. Nevertheless, the two accounts contain no insurmountable discrepancies, and on several points Ramírez's memory
jibed closely with Dampier's.

For instance, Ramírez heard that the pirates' "intent of raiding Peru and Chile
was frustrated by a sudden unrelenting storm that bore down on them from the
east with remarkable vehemence." This mirrors Dampier's memory of incessant
storms off Chile. After rounding Cape Horn near 57° S latitude the pirates encountered "a violent Storm" which lasted for two weeks, at first "blowing a fierce
gale of Wind" from the southwest and south. But then the wind veered "to the
Eastward," forcing the ship to sail away from Chile into the Pacific. Later that
summer, winds from land again foiled the pirates' plans against Peru: they could
not approach land easily because of "the Wind" that blew "right in our Teeth."
For the better part of September the pirates "steered towards the Coast of Peru"
in poor weather, occasionally bumping into other ships in the growing pirate
fleet then operating in those waters: "we had *Tornadoes* every Day till we made
Cape St. Francisco, which from *June* to *November* are very common on these
coasts; and we had with the *Tornadoes* very much Thunder, Lightning and Rain."
Captain John Eaton, aboard the *Nicholas*, one of the consort vessels accompanying the *Cygnet*, told Dampier that they had "met with such terrible *Tornadoes* of
Thunder and Lightning, that as he and all his Men related, they had never met
with the like in any Place."[83]

The third piece of evidence is conclusive proof that Ramírez and Dampier
sailed together. At the end of a long explanation of how cruelly he and his companions had suffered at the hands of the heretical English pirates, Ramírez told
his Mexican audience that perfidious Albion was less to be feared than traitor-
ous Spain:

> I suspect that the evil of their manner in treating us was increased by the
> presence of a *Spaniard* in their company, a native of *Seville* whose name was
> *Miguel*. No intolerable task given to us, no occasion for mistreatment or
> hunger enforced on us, no danger to life sent our way ever came without
> his having had a hand in planning and executing it. He gloried in how these
> acts boldly pronounced to the world his godlessness, his abandonment of

his native Catholic faith, and his commitment to living a pirate and dying a heretic. It pained me most—and my company as well—when he would join the Englishmen in praying and reading from their books on their feast days, which were every Sunday in the calendar and Christmas. May God grant him the enlightenment he needs to correct his life and merit the Lord's forgiveness for all the iniquities of his actions.

This elusive, intriguing, and cruel Protestant Sevillian was not a figment of Ramírez's imagination. Several independent witnesses testified to his presence aboard the *Cygnet*.

Dampier wrote that in the late summer of 1686, while the *Cygnet* lay off the Muslim island of Mindanao, "some of our Men were weary and tired with wandring" and deserted, "assisted, as was generally believed by *Raja Laut*," a member of the local anti-Spanish Muslim dynasty. On August 24, 1687, five of these deserters, four English and one Irish, gave themselves up at the Spanish outpost in Dapitan on the northern shores of Mindanao. An investigation began immediately. According to their testimony, 30 or 40 of the *Cygnet*'s crew, a substantial number out of the total of 150 crewmen, had abandoned the piratical company (Dampier, who stayed aboard, clearly misrepresented the seriousness of the desertion).[84] Unfortunately for the five suspects, an embassy from the Mindanao sultan was in Manila at the time. Two of these diplomats and one Spaniard, who had also left the pirate company in the fall of 1686 to work for the sultan, testified against them.

Bernardo de Uriarte, a forty-nine-year-old *vecino* (resident or native citizen) in the mining town of San José del Copal near Guanajuato in Nueva Vizcaya (today's northern Mexico), was questioned on January 16, 1688. He said that he had been taken captive by the pirates in one of their coastal attacks in the winter of 1685–1686. Uriarte testified that before setting sail across the Pacific the pirates had released thirteen of their "Christian" prisoners on the Marías Islands near Puerto Vallarta. They had kept four Spaniards taken in Peru, one from Panama, six Indians, and one young Spaniard from Seville. We know more about this Sevillian from the two Mindanao diplomats, who testified against the five pirate suspects ten days after Uriarte was questioned. They told Spanish authorities all about the *Cygnet*'s protracted stay in Mindanao and said that several non-English subjects were aboard the vessel, including two Spaniards: "Bernardo" from Vizcaya, Spain (in reality, Uriarte from New Vizcaya in Mexico), and "an Andalusian son of Seville by the name of Miguel de Medina."[85] Thus we have the full name of the cruel Protestant called Miguel who so tormented Ramírez aboard the pirate ship. It is inconceivable that another "Miguel" from Seville was aboard a different English ship which also happened to take two Spanish prizes between Mariveles and Capones on March 4, 1687. The crew who captured Ramírez on that day came from Dampier's *Cygnet*.

One final observation should be made about their fateful meeting. The incredibly tense moment of the "Distribution of Justice" described above did not always occur quickly; it could be played out slowly, as crews kidnapped sailors and worked on convincing them to sign up as active participants in piracy. The more sailors feared going home, of course, the more an opportunity for wealth and freedom might appeal to them. In considering the case of Ramírez and his shipmates' collusion with the crew aboard the *Cygnet*, it is therefore important to realize that they may have had a good reason to join Dampier's mates in 1687. In 1685 and 1686 Manila's naval docks had been flooded with hundreds of unemployed sailors from the *San Telmo*, the *Santa Rosa*'s sister galleon, which Governor Curuzeláegui had decided to have dismantled at the Royal Arsenal at Sorsogón (Bagatao). He happily reported to Madrid that forty tons of iron had been extracted from its hulk for the construction of a new vessel, the *Santo Cristo de Burgos*. However, it would not be launched until 1688. Unemployment undoubtedly constituted both part of the great savings which Curuzeláegui celebrated in his report on May 21, 1686, and a serious motivation for some of the Spanish captives aboard the *Cygnet*.[86]

The issue of economic incentives brings us to a consideration of how the loot which these pirates acquired after March 4, 1689, in Asia ended up on an American shore and why the viceroy of New Spain legalized what was evidently an illegal cargo brought to Yucatan by a carpenter making dubious claims. It will also take us to more archival evidence which links Ramírez—and Ferrer—to yet another pirate "company."

CHAPTER 3

Siamese Treasure, Mexican Merchants, and the Law

Their dim comprehension of higher things—put bluntly—is fastened
with pins, for they are solely attached to material things.

FRANCISCAN MISSIONARY FR. FRANCISCO DE SAN ANTONIO,
bemoaning the materialist shortcomings of islanders in the western Pacific (1738)

A T LEAST ONE OF THE PIRATES' SHIPS ended up on the Yucatan coast in late 1689 as Ramírez's shipwrecked frigate. But which one, and when was it taken? From whose ships was its cargo stolen? These are questions which became significant as soon as Ramírez found himself back in the part of the world ruled by European laws. Good evidence indicates that the appeal of the frigate's valuable cargo, mostly Siamese treasure, explains why Galve protected Ramírez; but this ultimately required complex legal reasoning concerning the true ownership of goods stolen by maritime predators. Furthermore, Ramírez's adventures with pirates became even more complicated when the *Cygnet* reached what is today the coast of Vietnam, though it is quite likely that the viceroy never realized—or chose to ignore—just how incriminating those adventures had really been. Greed and need controlled the actions of Ramírez and Galve to one degree or another. It was not only Pacific islanders who were obsessed with "material things."

Ramírez's cargo could not have come at a better time for Galve. In 1690 he was planning the following year's major expedition against the French and the buccaneers on Tortuga, even as Madrid ministers instructed him to keep

American expenses down in order to ship more bullion to Spain. The war with France was putting incredible pressure on American resources. On June 26, for example, Galve was told to garrison forts with "the smallest possible number of soldiers," because "90 out of every 100 men who enter the army in Spain to serve in the Indies have no intention of remaining soldiers." Additionally, he was instructed not to make "great assignments . . . to be paid in the Indies" before Spain's European financial needs were met. An even more elemental problem in the early winter of 1689–1690 was the short supply of bronze to forge cannons, copper for fittings, and iron for armaments. Ramírez appeared on the scene in early 1690 at the exact moment when Galve had extra need: he had just shipped twelve of his best cannons from Mexico City to increase Yucatan defenses.[1] Rough iron was available in New Spain, but the high-quality iron used by military and naval foundries in the colonial New World was imported from Europe.[2] These were expensive items, and Galve's letters at the time prove that he was dealing with a budget crunch.[3] Galve's increasingly acrimonious responses to Madrid councillors' unreasonable expectations for bullion shipments that winter prove that he clearly disagreed with their prioritization of the monarchy's European needs over its American and Asian ones. His promise to his brother on July 11, 1689, that he would not let "scruples" prevent him from finding the resources necessary to meet everyone's needs was becoming a painful reality by December. He ranted that metropolitan impediments to direct rule were diminishing the success of his policies: "over there [meaning Spain] every effort is being made to hinder me." He begged Infantado to convince the king directly to accept a restructuring of New Spain's finances, particularly in terms of naval matters, which would allow critical decisions to be made without prior approval from Madrid's councils. The crescendo of frustration culminated during the summer months when Galve commissioned Sigüenza to transcribe Ramírez's account: "for there to be Indies," with all the necessary revenue they produced, the viceroy fulminated, councillors in Madrid needed to think less of Europe and more of "preserving" America.[4]

The dissemination of Ramírez's pirate-victim narrative was intended to justify the costs of his antipirate initiatives to government officials like the Marquis of Vélez. At that very moment they were intent on curtailing spending in the colonies, even searching for privatization alternatives and "offshoring" contracts to defray crown costs (the collision course between Vélez's council style of government and the brothers' behind-the-scenes military-aristocratic style exploded in 1691).[5] Ramírez's frigate offered a partial but practical solution to Galve's immediate need: the cargo could supply the viceroy with relatively cheap military supplies. What was Ramírez's cargo and where did it come from? Answering these two questions helps us understand the brief but odd 1690 alliance between a Spanish pirate and a Spanish viceroy.

We know quite a bit about the frigate and its cargo because Ramírez described them for Sigüenza a few months after the shipwreck:

> [The ship] was—or I should say she is, for she may still be there—sixty-two feet along the keel, triple-planked, all her masts and yardarms of the most excellent pine to be had, and her entire design of a lovely cut, so much so that with a fresh wind she would easily do eighty leagues in a day's run. We left nine iron pieces of artillery aboard her and on the beach, with more than two thousand four-, six-, and ten-pound shot, all lead, as well as at least a hundred hundredweights of this metal, fifty bars of tin, fifteen hundred pounds of iron, eighty bars of Japanese copper, a great quantity of China, seven elephant tusks, three barrels of powder, forty musket barrels, ten matchlocks, a medicine chest, and numerous surgeon's instruments.

Undoubtedly Ramírez provided a detailed list for one reason: to publicize that the viceregal government recognized all this as his property. Ramírez's cargo, if it was as large as he claimed, was worth a fortune, especially in the New World during a time of war. The 500 pesos that he was offered by a local Yucatan resident did not even begin to cover its value.[6] The quantity of lead that Ramírez claimed to have had on board amounted to roughly one-tenth of the lead sold annually by the Dutch at that time on the entire coast of Coromandel.[7] Furthermore, what we know of the activities of Ramírez and Dampier following their meeting off the Philippine Islands confirms that they had preyed on Siamese-Japanese shipping. Galve's official recognition that Ramírez had been the victim of pirates and was not a pirate himself exonerated him from further prosecution, but it also provided Galve with valuable supplies.

SIAMESE TREASURE

The origin of this peculiar combination of cargo items seems clear. Iron, copper, tin, and lead were staples of the southeast Asian coastal trade, appearing on both European and Chinese ships. Siam's importance in such trade was reaching its apogee in the 1680s. We can link Ramírez's cargo to typical Siamese trade goods with a certain degree of assurance, especially in terms of the metals he listed. Even ivory, more generally available in markets from Africa to Asia, was a major

Siamese trade good.[8] One English East India Company man with "12 years experience" in the kingdom noted in 1699 that Siam dominated ivory exports in the region, which is confirmed by Chinese evidence.[9]

Ramírez's metals are even more clearly linked to Siam. When the French allies of Siam were kicked out in 1688–1689, for example, the directors of the French East India Company noted that they would have to look for new sources of "lead, tin, and copper." Siamese copper and tin figured prominently in Spanish Philippine imports as well.[10] Siam's prime minister, an expatriate Greek-speaking native of the Venetian island of Cephallonia by the name of Constantine Phaulkon, explained to King Louis XIV in a 1685 letter that Siam's wealth derived from its "tin, iron, and copper" trade.[11] Tin was one of King Narai's principal state monopolies, supplying Batavia's Dutch with much of their trade.[12] According to one French missionary at the time, Narai had cornered the southeast Asia distribution of "tin, saltpetre, [and] elephant's teeth."[13] Siam's "strong, white tin" looked as fine, said one Cantonese magistrate at the time, as anything "made from silver."[14]

Siam thus not only produced metals found in Ramírez's cargo but dominated the Asian coastal trade in them. Although northern Vietnam, Burma, and Siam all produced lead, for example, Siam regularly acted as the go-between for Chinese importers of all southeast Asian lead.[15] Chinese ships based in Siam also served as intermediaries for copper from Japan, from whose ports Europeans were banned in 1603.[16] Ships flying the Siamese flag with mostly Chinese crews (nicknamed Patani ships after one of Siam's principal ports) regularly carried Japanese copper to Siam, where European merchants could buy it openly. Dutch agents were specifically instructed to visit Siam, which Batavia considered "the door for China and Japan," to load articles unavailable due to trade restrictions elsewhere.[17] It was through Chinese merchants, wrote one Frenchman who knew Siam personally, "that [the king of Siam] continues to carry on trade with the Japanese," sending "every year . . . several of his ships manned by Chinese, accompanied by a few Siamese mandarins, who keep their eyes open for everything around them."[18]

Contemporaries knew the value of this annual Siamese copper fleet traveling to Japan, both for private merchants and for the king of Siam. Port records from Nagasaki show that the king directly owned 57 percent of all the Siamese ships that docked there between 1689 and 1715.[19] The king of Siam depended on the annual Japan and China fleets for his income, just as the king of Spain needed New World shipments of gold and silver. Salaries in the Siamese navy, the prime minister once told the French admiral in charge of it, could not regularly be paid without the income from the trade fleet.[20] It was also Siamese trade which prompted Louis XIV to send several economic, political, and religious missions, which created a Siamese-French alliance in 1685. But it began to unravel in 1687 and ended disastrously for the French—and Phaulkon—in 1688 (as we shall see, Ramírez had heard of some of the early episodes in the disintegration of the Franco-Siamese alliance).

The economic evidence suggests that Ramírez's cargo had a southeast Asian origin. Although he claimed that the frigate he shipwrecked off Yucatan was taken in the straits of Singapore, much of its cargo had originated in ships operating in Siamese and Chinese waters. Evidence indicates that Ramirez and the pirates he traveled with encountered and took ships carrying a cargo of Japanese copper and Siamese tin there in 1687 or 1688, but this can only be understood properly within the context of events in southeast Asia between the fall of 1686 and the summer of 1687.

The central concern for ambitious sea captains in the area was how an Anglo-Siamese war affected their ability to profit as commissioned agents of belligerent states. With commissions or patents (also known as "letters of marque") captains could capture enemy ships and have them adjudicated as "fair prizes" by the commissioning state. This allowed captains to sell loot in legal markets at prices higher than on the black market; without patents, "privateers" were just "pirates" under the law, acting violently for personal gain. By October 1686 tensions in southern Asia over prizes taken by the Siamese king's ships and English East India Company merchantmen combined with the king's unpaid debts to the company to stir up a *de facto* state of war.

According to Asian gossip, Siam's prime minister Constantine Phaulkon was desperately pleading with the East India Company headquarters in Fort St. George, India (Madras), but to no effect. The company instead followed its agents' requests to publish orders "to pursue the King of Siam with open war until he has satisfied us for the injuries formerly done us." Commissions were issued against Siamese vessels "to be adjudged and condemned as prize ships and goods by our Court of Admiralty."[21] One East India officer called Phaulkon "that notorious, ungrateful, naughty man," and a French rival described him as a man of "boundless ambition" and "insatiable avarice." Undeniably skillful, Phaulkon stalled for time by appealing above the company's head, sending a lengthy missive directly to the king of England in which he praised the "amity" between King James II and King Narai: "if my demerits were such as to require pardon," he wrote, "I would beg it of his Majesty of Great Britain, the head, and not of the Company." But Phaulkon's bid for time failed. Furthermore, the alliance with France which Narai had courted since 1683 was breaking down, and the French navy would end up fighting Siam instead of protecting its shipping.[22]

Both the East India Company and James II recognized the official state of war in early summer. On July 11, 1686, the king even made it illegal for private Englishmen to serve the Siamese government. The East India Company issued similar instructions on October 22, ordering its agents to pursue Siamese ships with open war: they were also to sentence "all the English by martial law whom you shall find in the said King of Siam's service." Late in the summer the company's ship *Curtana*, under Captain Anthony Weltden, arrived in Mergui, Siam's Indian Ocean port. Weltden was ready to take the town and create a fort if Narai refused to pay the £40,000 he owed and another £65,000 in damages. King Narai countered by declaring war on the East India Company on August 11, 1687. Englishmen who served Siam were now considered criminals, common traitors, and pirates: "hanging some," wrote a group of company agents in February 1687, "may clearly do great good."[23] We shall return to this when discussing Dampier's recollection of his activities with the pirates in 1687.

Beginning in late 1686, then, captains could take advantage of any Siamese ships which did not yet know that East India Company commissions had been issued against Siam. In May 1687, for example, a company official in Fort St. George wrote to Captain John Gladman, an English merchant setting off from India for China, that the company thought "it best not to make public our design against the King, but carry it as close as may be till it be published by your laying hold of a good rich prize, which we heartily wish."[24] News of this type of warfare prompted one Spanish observer in Manila to write to Galve that the East India Company men were nothing but "English pirates."[25] The situation dragged on. Because Phaulkon pinned his hopes on resolving the conflict diplomatically through the authority of the king of England, Siam was reluctant to pursue open war; Siam's August declaration still stressed that it intended to attack the "English Company and all those in its service," but not all English ships, "until such time as his Majesty of Great Britain by his authority over the aforesaid Company puts an end to this strife."[26]

Very early in 1687 Asian and European captains began to take advantage of the open season on Siamese shipping, like the two buccaneer ships "from Jamaica" which Dutch reports announced were roaming the islands.[27] As far as sailors were concerned, this privateering war offered easy pickings for months, at least until news of the massacre of Europeans in Mergui on July 14, 1687, was received abroad. (The massacre was a result of the machinations of Captain Weldten and an agent of the king of Siam: a notoriously corrupt ex–East India Company Englishman by the name of Samuel White.) One English sailor in those waters at the time wrote that this event heralded "the first beginning" of total war.[28] We do not know the names of all the Siamese prizes taken before knowledge of the Mergui massacre became public. According to Dutch correspondence from Batavia, however, five of the king of Siam's ships and one Portuguese vessel containing jewels belonging to the king and Phaulkon had been captured by "the English" before open war had been declared. Spanish reports also noted that "English pirates" had taken Dutch and Portuguese merchantmen as well as one of the king of Siam's ships "on the coast of Tonquin." Dampier's and Ramírez's prizes may have been some of these.[29]

The possibility that pirates could have East India Company courts adjudicate Siamese ships as "good" prizes in 1687 explains why Dampier's companions on Mindanao split into two companies on January 14, 1687. Spanish as well as English evidence tells us much about this split, although Dampier as usual downplayed his participation in the arguments.[30] After several months' sojourn with the sultan of Mindanao, the pirates learned that he had received a letter from an English merchant (Thomas Bowrey in Sumatra) enquiring about mutually beneficial trade agreements. Other information contained in this letter, however, triggered the final break among the quarreling buccaneers. "The main Division," wrote Dampier, "was between those that had Money and those that had none." Captain Swan's refusal to act on the news of the availability of East India Company letters of marque against Siam made this "General Disaffection" worse, particularly since some of the pirate company suspected others of conspiring with the sultan; and Dampier reported that the sultan was plotting with the Spanish authorities to send troops down from Manila "to destroy us," as we saw in the previous chapter. The anti-Swan group was driven by the hunger for "Action." Recriminations exploded on January 14. Some of the men refused to engage in any further maritime predation and chose to stay ashore with Captain Swan, hoping to find jobs with the local officials or a way back home. Dampier did not recall how many stayed ashore or "absconded" with the assistance of "Raja Laut," the sultan's brother.[31]

The trial of four of these pirates, who eventually turned themselves in to Spanish authorities in Manila in 1687, provides us with hitherto unpublished evidence concerning the split. According to John Fitzgerald, a twenty-eight-year-old Irishman from Limerick, about thirty men refused to continue pirating. Michael Shillito, a forty-year-old Yorkshireman, concurred. Thomas Baggs, one of the *Cygnet*'s carpenters, recalled that Swan's men had begun to break with their crewmates around September, but things had gone from bad to worse. Antonio Marqués Toribio, "a black creole [*negro criollo*]" from Callao who had been captured by the pirates in Peru but who escaped in September 1687 off the northern end of the Philippine Islands, confirmed that the split was about future pirating. Bernardo de Uriarte, another Spanish captive taken in 1685 on Mexico's Pacific coast (whom we have already met), gave even clearer indications of how the pirates were desperately negotiating the line between pirating and privateering, seeking some kind of governmental support for their predatory actions.[32]

Uriarte asserted that the sultan had formally agreed in public to allow the English to use his capital as a pirate base for an annual fee of 6,000 pesos. This would have provided them with legal open markets to sell their loot, thus raising their profit margins. The Mindanao diplomats "Campo" and "Manso" confirmed the arrangement but said that it was only to cost 1,000 pesos and was eventually scrapped because of internal Mindanao disagreement, no doubt adding to internal dissent among the pirate haves and have-nots. Dampier did not recall any of these negotiations. Fitzgerald's testimony, however, confirmed Uriarte's information that by the fall of 1686 everyone in Mindanao knew (from two ships arriving from Borneo in 1685 and 1686) that English commissions had been issued. At least one of these commissions was to set up a factory in Mindanao (clearly a "free" or noncompany factory). Undoubtedly the East India Company–Siam rift was announced to the pirates in conjunction with this news, offering new legal markets for future loot. Dampier would later recall that the 1686 letter sent to Mindanao was actually written by a Captain Bowrey he met two years later at Achin, Sumatra, who knew that "the Siamers were now at Wars with the English."[33]

The trigger may have come in November when Barent Brouwer, an agent of the Dutch East India Company (VOC), traveled from Amboina to Mindanao because he had heard of possible English competitors there. Brouwer wrote to the Batavia governors that he had met up with "an English corsairing ship . . . named *The Swan*," adding with surprise that "the captain who came on it was also named Swan, *Charles Swan*." Brouwer also reported to the VOC's governor general that the ship he encountered "carried 14 guns and about 140 men" and was well stocked with weapons, "having by her side [as tender] a large bark, which they had taken from the Spaniards." Brouwer undoubtedly confirmed the

English company's war on Siam to the pirates, sealing the fate of the recalcitrant pirate Captain Swan.[34] Thus one of the major causes of the January 1687 split among the pirate company was the chance for Siamese prizes, even if the "Golden projects" of seizing the Manila galleons failed.[35] At least thirty men stayed behind on Mindanao; the rest, including Dampier, sailed off aboard the *Cygnet.*

Timing is everything in piracy. The *Cygnet*'s crew members were betting on being able to prey on Siamese shipping with some degree of indemnity under English law because of the company's war on King Narai's ships. They also knew that late winter and spring were ideal times "to go on account" in the Gulf of Siam: Narai's annual China, Japan, and Philippine merchant fleets usually returned to port by February and began sailing outbound in April or May, following the veering of the monsoon winds.[36] "These are the winds," wrote one Chinese official, "which the foreign galleons observe carefully with an eye to their voyages."[37] To protect his fleets, King Narai had asked two French commanders based in Bangkok (the port for his capital, Ayutthaya) to patrol the gulf, which they did until late July–early August 1687. Dampier and Ramírez were lucky that the French were more interested in safeguarding Louis XIV's position in Bangkok than in catching anti-Siamese pirates.[38]

THE TRUE IDENTITY OF RAMÍREZ'S PIRATES

Having established how the political and economic context of 1686–1687 explains the pirates' motivation, we can now turn to our two eyewitnesses and additional archival evidence to reconstruct actual events. Two points become clear. First, the prizes taken by this pirate company were undoubtedly linked to the diplomatic, economic, and religious relationships of Siam, Portuguese Macao, and the Jesuits. Second, the ultimate form that Ramírez's and Dampier's memory of events took was inspired by their disparate fortunes in the 1690s. This alone, however, does not explain the increasing divergence between their accounts.

Both men recalled that after Ramírez's capture in March 1687 the pirates headed to the island of Pulo Condore. Strategically located at the mouth of the Gulf of Siam, this was the ideal spot to hunt for Siam-China-Japan merchantmen "until the western monsoon came" and they could return to seek out the Manila galleons.[39] Both Ramírez and Dampier pruriently described how the crew's wait was made pleasant by the islanders' sexual freedom, a favorite topic of seventeenth-century European travelogues. "Mothers would bring daughters and husbands would deliver their own wives," Ramírez noted; he condemned the pirates' promiscuity as "the most unashamed vice I have ever seen." Dampier also remembered how the natives were "so free with their Women," but he stressed pragmatic self-interest, not morality, and minimized the violence of the situation, unlike Ramírez. At the end of this stay, Dampier's memory was that the pirates did not pillage the island. They "left the Spanish Prize taken at Manila"; Ramírez, in stark contrast yet again, said that they destroyed it. But was this true? The question is an important one: sailors without a boat have fewer options than those with one. We can tell whether Ramírez or Dampier lied by referring again to the eyewitnesses from the *Aránzazu* crew who later testified to Spanish authorities about their captivity aboard the *Cygnet*.

Only six were with Dampier and Ramírez on Pulo Condore: Mateo Francisco, Diego Rendón, Alonso de Luna, Juan del Pilar, Silvestre Moxica, and Asam. The other five either had been released earlier on Capones Island (as part of the fifty-two set free on March 5 and 6) or were not captured until later that summer, near Canton (Enco and Chingco). Except for Asam, all of them, like Ramírez, stated categorically that the pirates burned the *Aránzazu* at Pulo Condore. Asam, however, did not, agreeing with Dampier. In fact the testimony of Francisco, Rendón, Luna, Pilar, and Moxica (given in that order) was suspiciously identical except for nautical details, which the last three could not master. This is a sign that they had months to memorize statements in the (accurate) conviction that they would immediately be suspected of collusion with the pirates. After all, they had remained on board much longer than the fifty-two landed on Capones and admitted under interrogation that others had subsequently left the pirate company at Pulo Condore, months before they did. Given his age (thirty-nine, versus twenty-nine, eighteen, eighteen, and twenty-nine), seniority, and experience, Francisco was probably the group's leader, which is why the Manila authorities questioned him first; the other four were, respectively, a more junior sailor, a cabin boy, the quartermaster's servant, and captain Ferrer's slave, ideal recruits for a pirate company. We can conclude that Francisco's little group hid from authorities that the *Aránzazu*, the most valuable item stolen by the pirates from the Spanish, was abandoned *but not destroyed* at Pulo Condore just as Dampier said and Asam (our most reliable witness) corroborated.

What is more, the group testified that their former captain, Ferrer, and eighteen other captives were released on the same island when the *Cygnet* first visited it, between March 24 and April 26, according to Dampier's log (adjusted Gregorian calendar). In contrast, Ramírez did not recall this at all but did state in Chapter 3 that eight of his men were released later during the pirates' brief stay on Pulo Ubi (May 1 to 4), before they set off for the Bay of Siam. On their return voyage out of the bay both Dampier and Francisco's group remembered that the pirates stopped again at Pulo Condore between June 3 and 14. However, the testimony of the group added important details regarding this second visit that are absent from Dampier's account (but not necessarily irreconcilable with it—or with Ramírez's). Captain Ferrer was apparently still there and came aboard the *Cygnet* (implicitly, from the *Aránzazu*): perhaps surprisingly, the former captives and captors then traded on friendly terms in silks, tobacco, and other "small stuff" before the two groups went their separate ways, Ferrer's men back to the island and the *Cygnet* off to China. In Ramírez's version of events the pirates never revisited Pulo Condore; consequently, the friendly trading scene there had never occurred. After pillaging Siamese shipping, he said, the pirates had set off directly from Pulo Ubi into more southern waters with him and his men as captives.[40]

According to Ramírez, they made their biggest captures while based on this island: three ships, one belonging to the king of Siam and the other two Portuguese, from Macao. The king's vessel carried fabulous wealth and a Siamese ambassador to Manila. One of the Portuguese ships carried another ambassador, part of a Portuguese delegation to Siam on a sensitive political mission of reconciliation.[41] Dampier, in contrast, said that very few ships were taken near Pulo Condore and Pulo Ubi, with hardly any worthwhile cargo; and the month-long Bay of Siam cruise was equally disappointing: "We met with nothing of remark in the Bay; therefore I shall be silent in such of our actions as can neither be profitable nor divertive."[42] The discrepancies between the two men's accounts by early summer 1687 cannot be ignored. Once again, evidence from an unexpected source comes to our aid.

On May 12 a small English ketch called the *Good Hope*, moored off Bengal, was taken over by a group of pirates stranded in India. Its captain, Samuel Heron, was deposed and his mate, Duncan Mackintosh, was made captain. Most of Heron's men joined the pirates. Amazingly, these were none other than old cruising partners of Dampier and the *Cygnet* from South American buccaneering days in 1683 and 1684: Captain Eaton's men from the *Nicholas*. Separating from the *Cygnet* near today's Ecuador in 1684, Eaton had traversed the Pacific in 1685 on almost exactly the same route taken by the *Cygnet* the following year. His buccaneer company, however, had imploded in the South China Sea in December 1685 soon after visiting Borneo (to which we shall return). Eaton jumped ship "when the crew became exceedingly mutinous," according to an eyewitness, and then most of the crew ended up for the next year and a half on the fringes of employment in English and Mughal India.[43]

Now, under Mackintosh's leadership, the old *Nicholas* crew had a new lease on life, cruising past Burma and the Malay Peninsula and through the Malacca strait into their old "Pyratting" grounds, the South China Sea. They captured four ships along the way "under the King of England's colours." Eyewitnesses aboard the *Good Hope* noted two years later in their testimony to East India Company officials in Fort St. George that they had then sailed to Pulo Condore, "to wait the coming of the ships," which everyone knew inevitably passed by the strategic spot: "they remained" there "until the time of the year served for the coming of shipping from China, Japan, and Manila, then went out a-cruising to windward" into the Bay of Siam, "having first made the ketch into a pink by putting another mast in her." Like the *Cygnet*, the *Good Hope* sailed to Pulo Ubi before entering the Bay, but "fearing they should fall so deep" that the southwest summer monsoon would prevent them from exiting it (it veered by the end of May), they returned mostly empty-handed to Pulo Condore, "where they cruised a considerable time." Afterward they set a southerly course, no doubt when the northeast monsoon winds kicked up in the fall of 1687. The *Good Hope*'s subsequent course matches Ramírez's account exactly, as we shall see.[44]

The coincidence can be explained by comparing the names of the pirates mentioned by Ramírez to the roster of Mackintosh's crew and reconsidering Ramírez's story of a mutiny among the pirates led by two Dutch sailors. Two years after these events and their escape from the *Good Hope*, our eyewitnesses reconstructed Mackintosh's 1687 crew roster with East India Company officials in Fort St. George. The resulting list in descending order of command, in characteristic naval fashion, was as follows: "Captain Heron's mate turned rogue, Dunkin Mackintosh, hanged in Guinea; Walter Beard, hanged in Guinea; Nicholas Burton, Richard Web," and fifteen others named individually.[45]

This remarkable piece of evidence confirms Ramírez's connection to Captain Mackintosh's crew (and, again, to Dampier). Ramírez named the chief pirate officers at the beginning of his Chapters 3 and 4 as "an Englishman they called Master Bel," who "governed" the principal ship or *capitana* (to which Ramírez's twenty-five men were transferred on March 5); the "owner of the other ship," in charge of a smaller crew, Captain Donkin; the "Master Gunner, Nicpat"; and "Dick, the Quartermaster."[46] Once allowance has been made for the way in which the Spanish-speaking Ramírez heard English names, the parallel is convincing: Captain "Donkin" was Duncan Mackintosh;[47] "Nicpat," Nick Burton; and "Dick," Bel's "Quartermaster," Dick Web (their ranks, as given by Ramírez, can be reconciled with the nautical ordering of officers in the English evidence).

But what of Ramírez's mysterious second captain, the man who "governed" the ship he was put on when captured? Who was the not-so-friendly "Captain Bel," as Ramírez calls him in Chapter 4, who opposed his more compassionate pirate mates and on more than one occasion apparently forced Ramírez and his comrades to drink his excrement as "medicine"? The answer comes not from equating "Bel" with "Beard" but from rereading a familiar source, the draft of Dampier's book. We may recall that Captain Read's pirates took the *Cygnet* and their prize, the *Aránzazu*, from Capones Island to Pulo Condore. Dampier tells us exactly who was the captain of the "rice prize" which, according to Ramírez, carried the Spanish captives during this two-week cruise: before leaving Capones, Dampier states, the pirates "constrained me to take charge of and carry" it to Pulo Condore, putting "ten men besides myself into her and all the prisoners."[48]

All this clarifies why Ramírez told Sigüenza and Galve that he was taken captive by two English pirate ships on March 4 when we know the *Cygnet* operated alone that day. The simple answer is that he told the truth but lied about the context. Between 1687 and 1689 he *had* been aboard two English pirate ships: Captain "Bill" Dampier's *Aránzazu*, left at Pulo Condore, and Captain Duncan Mackintosh's *Good Hope*, from Pulo Condore onward.[49] The tense episode in Chapter 4 describing Ramírez's release by the pirates may quite likely conflate two moments: the first "release," when Ferrer and his eighteen men were freed at Pulo Condore (and given the *Aránzazu*); and a second "release" when Ramírez and his mostly Asian crew parted company with Mackintosh (and were given the "frigate"). Two facts confirm Ramírez's voyage with Mackintosh: the *Good Hope*'s course *after* cruising in Siamese waters matches Ramírez's exactly and—even more significantly—Ramírez's memory of a mutiny against Mackintosh led by two Dutch pirates is corroborated by our *Good Hope* eyewitnesses.

Ramírez related in Chapter 4 that at some point during the cruise in the South China Sea, while escape "to Manila" was still possible, a certain "Cornelio" confided in him that he was planning to lead a mutiny against Mackintosh. Here Ramírez came closest to admitting that he had lived among the pirates as one of them, asserting that Cornelio accused him of "planning to kill" the captain. From then on, the crew "began to live with greater vigilance," suspecting all the Spanish on board. After a sound whipping, Ramírez revealed to the captain that it was Cornelio who had planned the mutiny. The captain ordered a severe whipping for Cornelio and his accomplices (presumably as named by Ramírez), one of whom, "Enrique [Henry]," subsequently jumped ship with a lot of treasure at an island (in Madagascar, according to Ramírez). This episode of double-dealing is confirmed by our *Good Hope* eyewitnesses, but their version of events ironically reveals that at times there is no honor among conspirators. Dr. Henry Watson said that it was he who planned the mutiny and then "persuaded seven or eight" of the crew to join him. However, "the night it was to be put into execution, the Carpenter, a Dutchman, one as deeply engaged by oath as anyone in that enterprise, discovered it." The plot was crushed. Watson and the other mutineers were immediately marooned as punishment but eventually were rescued. They named the conspiring carpenter and his chief accomplice as "Cornelius Petterson, a Dutchman," and "Hendrick," also "a Dutchman."[50]

If we now return to the critical issue of how Ramírez's frigate and its cargo are connected to the ships that he said were taken by these pirate companies during the spring and summer of 1687, several possibilities exist. Our witnesses to the movement and activities of the *Cygnet, Aránzazu,* and *Good Hope* between Pulo Condore and the Bay of Siam do not agree on the number or identity of the prizes attacked or taken.[51] Nevertheless, the number of prizes between April 26 and June 14 that Dampier listed in his manuscript matches Ramírez's count, although Dampier underplayed their importance (he diminished it even further in the printed book).[52] On June 14 Dampier and the *Cygnet* left on a course to China. Ramírez probably stayed with Ferrer and the *Aránzazu* at Pulo Condore; then he and his sampan colleagues joined Mackintosh's *Good Hope* at some point during the "considerable time" it was based on that strategic island before the fall monsoon kicked in around late September or October. Perhaps Ferrer and his men did more than just trade with Dampier's shipmates on the *Cygnet's* second visit, consorting with them in attacking the three ships mentioned by Ramírez; perhaps Dampier's three prizes were different from Ramírez's prizes, which might have been taken by the *Aránzazu* alone, before Ramírez joined Mackintosh's crew. It is even possible, given the extreme similarity of their routes through the Bay of Siam, that the *Good Hope* and *Cygnet* consorted before June 14. We simply do not have enough data concerning the *Good Hope* or the *Aránzazu* to describe their activities conclusively.[53] In any case, independent Portuguese evidence concerning the economic, religious, and political relations between Siam and Macao corroborates the importance of the three prizes in Ramírez's story, which he said were taken in those waters during that summer's monsoon season.[54]

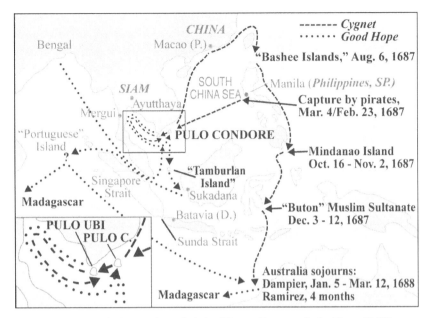

MAP 3.1. Ramírez's Course through Asian Waters. Cartography by Elwood Mills.

RAMÍREZ AND SIAMESE-PORTUGUESE DIPLOMACY

To begin with, Siam and Macao were involved in a lengthy loan negotiation. In 1669 the capital-strapped port of Macao had secured a loan from the king of Siam for "605 *cates* of silver and other products." But Macao began to default on its regularly expected interest payments soon thereafter (it was paying 1 percent yearly in the 1680s). The Portuguese port also failed to satisfy Siam's expectations of diplomatic tribute gifts (Portuguese *saguates*) and trade privileges for royal Siamese cargoes. These cost-cutting measures were forced by the new Qing dynasty's policy of increasing Chinese customs duties and promoting Canton as a competitor. This, one Macao official wrote, was "the time of our greatest vexations."[55] Exasperated with this dilatoriness (the loan would not be paid off completely until 1722),[56] in 1678 King Narai appealed to a higher power: the Portuguese viceroy at Goa, in charge of all Portuguese possessions in India. But Goa procrastinated. An embassy to Portugal under the leadership of Ok-khun Chamnan was shipwrecked off Cape Agulhas in South Africa on April 27, 1686.[57]

The years 1684–1687 marked one of the low points in the amortization of the loan, a direct result of Chinese pressure on Macao.[58] Siam chose the Flemish Jesuit Fr. Jean-Baptiste Maldonado to take over from the ineffective merchant who had tried to improve relations with Macao directly until 1684.[59] With eleven years' experience as head of the Portuguese Jesuits in Siam, Maldonado confidently left Ayutthaya for Macao on July 21, 1684, charged by Narai with renegotiating the loan.

Maldonado's mission, however, was also motivated by Jesuit concerns over the encroaching power of the "apostolic vicars." These missionaries were loyal to the pope but were seen by many as instruments of the Asian ambitions of Louis XIV and enemies of the Portuguese king's *padroado* (control of his church in Asia).[60] The apostolic vicars formed part of the contingent of French Jesuits traveling with the secular French delegation sent out by Louis XIV in the 1680s. The members of this delegation were part of his "Siamese" initiative to oust the English and Dutch mercantile companies and set up a French protectorate over the kingdom of Siam. They came armed with powerful papal bulls issued between 1669 and 1678, which had cut back on the king of Portugal's *padroado* in incremental steps. A French defamation campaign tarred Asian Jesuits with the usual brush of being "greedy merchants" instead of generous missionaries, but this was a response to the political reality that Asian Jesuits were recognized as the leaders of local resistance to the apostolic vicars. In their turn Maldonado and Phaulkon reported to the pope that the French apostolic vicars themselves were acting like "merchants." Their leader, François Pallu, bishop of Heliopolis, had set up shop in Siam like the head factor in a Dutch "Kantoor" or "trading post."[61]

Maldonado and his companion, Father Manoel Soares, traveled repeatedly between Macao and Siam on the society's and Phaulkon's business during the late 1680s. They assuaged Siamese-Macao tensions and worked behind the scenes to foil French interests by building animosity toward the French military presence in southeast Asia among local elites.[62] After Phaulkon's conversion to Catholicism in 1682, Fr. Maldonado officiated at his marriage to Portuguese-Japanese Siamese resident Maria Guyomar da Pinha; thereafter Maldonado served Phaulkon as confessor and French interpreter during the visits of Louis XIV's ambassadors in 1687 and 1688.[63] In a letter to the pope written in late 1687 or early 1688, Phaulkon stated that Maldonado had been his staunch collaborator for many years in matters religious and political. The old-style Jesuit missions in Asia were founded on the accommodationism of Francis Xavier and Allessandro Valignano (becoming "all things to all men in order to win all to Jesus Christ").[64] Phaulkon and Maldonado shared a profound conviction that those missions were preferable to the new-styled missions instituted by the French-inspired apostolic vicars. Phaulkon considered them not only corruptible but also lacking "in all philosophy and theology." The church in Asia, he said, needed men with "more patience, more virtue, better letters, and greater circumspection and obedience."[65] These Jesuit Siamese delegations, quite likely led by Maldonado himself, constitute the most probable candidates for the Siamese ambassadors encountered by Ramírez and Dampier in 1687.

Ramírez recalled three years later in Mexico that the embassy was bound for Manila as well as Macao (the Siam-China-Japan triangle trade included Manila).[66] Although it is not possible to confirm this, we do have quite specific archival evidence corroborating Ramírez's memory that the pirates encountered two Portuguese ships connected to Siam in the spring of 1687. In fact, we know their names and the reason for their voyage through the Gulf of Siam.[67]

In mid-1686 the Siamese royal vessel *Aguia Real* and its consort, *Nossa Senhora do Rosário*, arrived in Macao with substantial cargo and a letter from Phaulkon to the city council requesting that it exempt the king's merchandise from all customs dues. Macao's council denied the request on August 28.[68] Like most ships on the China-Japan-Siam triangle trade, the two ships probably waited until later that fall for the summer monsoon to end in order to catch more favorable northeasterly winds on their homeward voyage to Siam, a crossing which Chinese sources say could take as little as ten days.[69]

When they finally arrived in Siam, the *Aguia Real* and its consort brought King Narai and Phaulkon new confirmation that Macao was refusing to honor the 1669 loan terms.[70] Narai responded by sending out his two ships again in early 1687 with more strongly worded complaints against Macao. But on June 20 the two ships hobbled into Macao's harbor, badly damaged. Their captains told Portuguese authorities that their supplementary instructions to destroy "Chinese pirates" active near Cambodia had led to an encounter with pirates.[71] There can be little doubt that the *Aguia Real* and *Nossa Senhora do Rosário* had fallen afoul of the pirates we have been pursuing.

Ramírez's memory of events, befuddled as it was by time, was nevertheless close to the record of Siam and Macao's relations in the 1680s on other counts. Ramírez's narrative provides two remarkable examples of this in Chapter 3: a distorted version of a recent rebellion in Siam and a description of the odd bejeweled "ambassador's column" which the pirates stole from the Siamese embassy. The reader should now be able to sort out some of the historic truth behind his words:

A Genoese individual—the circumstances of whose presence in that country I do not know—managed not only to become a favorite of the King of Siam but also to be named his royal representative in the principal port.[72] Becoming over-proud with such high titles, this Genoese had the hands of two Portuguese gentlemen living there cut off for a minor offense. The Viceroy in Goa had been informed and was now requesting satisfaction, even asking that the Genoese be turned over to him for punishment. Because a demand such as this one exceeded the bounds of probability, the gift mentioned before was being sent to garner the King's goodwill. I myself saw and touched it; it was in the shape of a tower or castle, a fathom long, made of pure gold embedded with diamonds and other precious stones. Although not as valuable, the other objects were equally marvelous: silver jewelry, quantities of camphor, amber, and musk, not taking into account the rest of the ship's cargo intended for trade or sale.

The odd object referred to here was the typical "palanquin of state" or "vehicle" which Siamese ambassadors carried to house the king's letters and to symbolize ambassadorial authority. We know what they looked like in the 1680s from a contemporary depiction of a Siamese embassy to Louis XIV's court (see the illustrations at the end of the Introductory Study).[73] Understanding where the story about Phaulkon cutting off two Portuguese gentlemen's hands "for a minor offense" came from requires a wider search for evidence. But once again Ramírez's muddled retelling had a historic basis: this time, gossip about a Portuguese Creole revolt in Bangkok which had happened a year earlier. Ramírez probably picked up the news from Portuguese sailors aboard the *Aguia Real* or *Nossa Senhora do Rosário.*

Count Claude Forbin (the French officer who was King Narai's new "Admiral and General of the King of Siam's Armies and Governor of Bangkok") said that the mutiny occurred between October 30, 1685, and July 1686, when the existing "Portuguese-Creolian" soldiers garrisoned in Bangkok heard that they were to be replaced by commissioned French soldiers.[74] When Phaulkon himself spoke to the rebellious Portuguese, "they answered one and all that they would not have a Frenchman as their commander," spurred on by the sermons of a Portuguese priest who reminded the rebels that "the Portuguese nation has always been predominant in the Indies." The soldiers' mutiny was unsuccessful, however. Although Forbin claimed the victory, it was probably Phaulkon's command of Portuguese which turned the tide of rebellion. "He sallied out of the fort absolutely resolute and intrepid," wrote Forbin, and began to negotiate with them personally. Suddenly one of the mutineers, drawing his sword, rushed Phaulkon. After a scuffle Phaulkon "managed to take his sword away." Further negotiations ended the rebellion without bloodshed, but the Portuguese "colonel was arrested, as were the soldiers and officers who had organized the conspiracy." Forbin's retelling of what happened next is the grain of historic truth behind Ramírez's story that Phaulkon cut two Portuguese men's hands off "for a minor offense":

> By order of Monsieur Constance, I called a council of war . . . where we condemned the soldier who had laid his hand upon the hilt of his sword to have his hand cut off. Two others, who were convicted of having been the heads of the conspiracy, were sentenced to death; some of the officers were banished, and the remaining soldiers were condemned to the galleys [after being forced] to finish building the new fortifications.[75]

Ramírez's version thus telescoped, distorted, and misrepresented the events. Phaulkon was not Genoese, but he had been a subject of another Italian naval power: Venice. And Ramírez's claim that the Siamese embassy he met in the Gulf of Siam was a response to the corporal punishment meted out to a Portuguese delinquent belies the facts. As we have seen, Portugal's colony in Macao and King Narai were involved in much more serious financial and jurisdictional disputes. But these inaccuracies are exactly what we would expect of second-hand information received from Portuguese sailors on the *Aguia Real* and *Nossa Senhora do Rosário*, whose sympathies probably lay with the mutinous soldiers. Importantly, although Galve (and perhaps Sigüenza) had heard of some of these Siamese events by February 1690 through the Jesuit, Dominican, and Franciscan reports which he had received, none of them mentioned the story of the Bangkok rebellion.[76] If the *Aguia Real* and *Nossa Senhora do Rosário* were the two large junks which Dampier said the pirates took in these waters, then why did he not tell his readers about their diplomatic and economic importance, unlike Ramírez?

In retelling their stories "back home," the two men shared a fear of prosecution for piracy, but they found that British and Spanish antipiracy policies, which were converging for the first time in the 1680s, affected them differently. Real bureaucratic collaboration between New Spain and Jamaica in the 1680s and 1690s coupled with metropolitan legislation from both sides which encouraged the colonies to sentence and execute pirates without shipping suspects to Europe was changing the traditional tacit English acceptance of predation "beyond the line." As regular trade became more profitable, moreover, English colonial businessmen were shying away from pirate black markets.[77] The differences in Dampier's and Ramírez's description of prizes taken in Asia reflect the unique circumstances of their reinsertion into civil society, beyond the differences in their personalities and ambitions.[78] In crafting narratives about the recent past neither man wanted to incriminate himself. Ramírez returned to Spanish territories with a shipload of pirate cargo and no logbook, but he ultimately garnered viceregal approval. Dampier, in contrast, returned to England without a cargo and with his logbook intact, but he struggled to find patronage between 1691 and 1695, when show trials of pirates initiated by the East India Company were denouncing Englishmen's criminal escapades in Asia as no longer tolerable.

It became increasingly dangerous to blur the legal line between the "right of all Englishmen to trade to the East Indies" and privateers' interpretation that this included pillaging non-Christians or nonallies as free agents. As Dampier edited his manuscript for publication in 1696, we know that he watched former shipmates from Captain Henry Every's crew being sentenced to death in London for piracy. He must have listened with great trepidation as Sir Charles Hedges, chief judge of the High Court of Admiralty, instructed the jury to find Every's crew guilty. If they did not, he said, then "the barbarous Nations will reproach us as being a Harbour, Receptacle, and a Nest of Pirates." To make matters worse, the letters of marque which the *Cygnet* had relied on against Siamese shipping in 1687 might have condemned Dampier himself in 1696—and Siam's negotiations with England were continuing. Too much honesty would have placed him in the middle of a "battlefield between supporters and opponents of the East India Company." Additionally, Dampier's publisher must have been worrying about the negative swell in public opinion against maritime predation, as he watched pundits celebrating the June 7, 1692, earthquake which destroyed the Jamaica buccaneering capital of Port Royal—Dampier's old home—as God's judgment on hypocritically criminal Englishmen: "a short representation of the great Day of Tryal."[79] Ramírez, in contrast, knew that Spanish laws treated those who worked for pirate captains much more leniently than their leaders; in the long run, even that fear evaporated because Galve decided to protect him.[80] Thus Dampier distanced himself rhetorically from the gruesome reality of piracy while Ramírez emphasized graphic depictions of English pirate cruelty which served his and, more importantly, Galve's purposes perfectly.

Less precise but equally important examples indicate that Ramírez subsequently telescoped, simplified, and distorted the truth. His story of being given a frigate and its contents by pirates off Brazil as recompense for years of good service is scarcely credible as told. It is more convincing as the description of a pirate company splitting into two groups, but our evidence is sketchy from midsummer of 1687 until Ramírez shipwrecked on the Yucatan coast. Tantalizingly, we can glimpse the movement of Mackintosh's *Good Hope* from East India Company correspondence and sea captains' logs. Ramírez recalled that they voyaged south to "Tamburlan" Island, a cruise which is corroborated by our other witnesses aboard the *Good Hope:* Dr. Watson said that he and his co-conspirators were marooned on that island ("Tymbolan") by Mackintosh.[81] Unfortunately, this leaves us with no independent reliable eyewitnesses for what happened next, according to Ramírez: the savage sack of Sukadana, an important diamond-exporting port on the west coast of Borneo.[82] But we are not completely without evidence to comprehend why Mackintosh's pirates headed there.

We know from Ambrose Cowley's manuscript log describing Captain Eaton's doomed voyage through the South China Sea that his ship, the *Nicholas*, spent time along the northern shores of Borneo between October and November 1685. We should recall that Eaton's men made up the bulk of the pirates who seized the *Good Hope* and made Mackintosh their pirate captain in 1687. The men of "Captain Donkin," as Ramírez called him, thus had extensive experience of Borneo. Like Cowley, they would have remembered the ambassadors from the king of all Borneo whom they met there, with "a commission written to our sight in characters or like China letters" (Ramírez likewise believed that the entire island was ruled by one Muslim sultan). What drew Mackintosh to Borneo was being told by his men, based on their interaction with the 1685 embassy, that the Borneo king was a formal ally of Spain. This explains Ramírez's memory that the pirates were pleasantly surprised to find that the local governor in Sukadana welcomed them as "Englishmen" because Anglo-Borneo trade relations had been set up in the meantime and that they did not need to repeat the 1685 subterfuge of pretending to be Spaniards. Most significantly, Mackintosh's men told him, like Cowley, that "this island affords diamonds, [and] camphor, the best" in the East Indies.[83]

This is all we can say about Ramírez and Mackintosh's voyage between southeast Asia and Africa with any certainty. According to Ramírez, the pirates set an awkward course west after Sukadana through the straits of Malacca to a mysterious "Portuguese island," only to reverse their direction once in the Indian Ocean, heading southeast to Australia (New Holland). There their course may have coincided with Dampier's aboard the *Cygnet*, which could explain some of the similarities between Dampier's and Ramírez's descriptions of Australia.[84] The next stop in Ramírez's text, Madagascar, agrees with archival evidence demonstrating that both the *Good Hope* and *Cygnet* (now under Captain Josiah Teat's command and renamed the *Little England*) were operating from pirate bases (at St. Mary's on the northeast coast and St. Augustine on the southwest coast) between late 1688 and June 1689.

In an English shipwreck narrative also entitled *Misfortunes* by its protagonist, we find news of both ships from 1689, which is confirmed by secondhand information given to Dampier in later years. In early June, near the Comoros Islands between northwestern Madagascar and the Mozambique mainland, Captain William Freke of the *Anne* encountered "the *Little England*, formerly Capt. Swann, sent out to the Spanish South Seas about 6 years since by Sir John Buckworth." It was full of plunder from two Portuguese ships seized between Sofala and the Comoros. Its consort at the time, "which they [had] met at St. Augustine Bay," was a New England ship commanded by Captain John Knight, not the *Good Hope* (although, like Mackintosh's crew, Knight's belonged to the old 1683–1684 buccaneer fleet which had pillaged Spanish America). Freke also told the East India company officials, however, that sometime before April 24 (Old Style) a Captain William Deerrow returning from Sofala had "touched at St. Augustine's Bay, where he met up with the Right Honourable English East India Company ketch *Good Hope*, belonging to Bengal, that was run away with, turned into a ship, the mate of which was commander, going by the name of Thompson, but his true name's Duncan Mackantrash [sic]; Capt. Deerrow told me he had store of gold and diamonds aboard but very few men." The *Cygnet* and *Good Hope* thus seem to have parted company in St. Augustine, Madagascar, by June 1689.[85]

Shortly thereafter (no earlier than late April and no later than late May) a London ship heading east met a vessel returning to New York (called the *New York*) loaded "with negroes" at St. Helena island in the South Atlantic. The slaver belonged to New York's Frederick Philipse (1626–1702), the principal merchant sending agents to Madagascar in the 1680s and 1690s to buy stolen goods from pirates. The news they heard from the slaver, which John Ovington, a passenger, recorded and then published, corroborates and expands on Freke's and Dampier's information and perhaps links directly to Ramírez's. The slaver had left "three pirates . . . rendezvousing in St. Augustine's Bay . . . so richly laden with store of silks . . . that they were prodigal in the expenses of their unjust gain," buying liquor "at any rate" and boasting that for lack of canvas they had made sails from silk. If Ramírez's memory of a merchantman (at the end of Chapter 3) fending off Captain Bel's "skills in thieving and avarice" at Madagascar refers to this same episode, then it was Philipse's captain who skillfully defended his ship and cargo with "vigilance and sagacity." On a more introspective note, Ovington repeated his informants' belief that the pirates were "so frank both in distributing their goods and guzzling down the noble wine, as if they were both wearied with the profession of their rapine and willing to stifle all the melancholy reflections concerning it."[86]

Although this evidence is inconclusive concerning Ramírez, it places his former cruising mates from the *Cygnet* and *Good Hope* in occasional consortship in Madagascar, roughly two years after their escapades in the East Indies.[87] Nothing, however, proves that Ramírez was still with the *Cygnet* or *Good Hope*, although there is a slim chance that Ovington's third "pirate" at St. Augustine was Ramírez's frigate (perhaps the *Aránzazu*). This is suggested by the testimony of Dampier's informant John Humes, the surgeon's mate on Freke's *Anne*, who joined Knight's pirate crew at the Comoros during the first week of June 1689. He told Dampier at Achin, Sumatra (between April and September 1689), that Knight arrived in Madagascar "soon *after*" (emphasis added) the "New York ship" left. This would mean that Ovington's report of three pirate ships at St. Augustine, which he received from the *New York* slaver, could not refer to Knight's ship but, most likely, to the *Cygnet*, the *Good Hope*, and a mysterious third ship, perhaps Ramírez's frigate (unless it was Deerrow's ship, the *John and Mary*).

However, Ramírez's description of the pirates' passage from Madagascar round the Cape of Good Hope as a difficult five-day voyage (at the end of Chapter 3) both confirms and contradicts this scenario. It places their departure on the southern tip of Madagascar, which fits the slaver's information because of St. Augustine's location; but a five-day struggle against headwinds around the cape matches winter weather patterns, not summer conditions, when fierce west or northwest winds around the cape clash with the southeasterly flowing Agulhas current. For Ramírez to be in the Atlantic in 1689 (necessary timing for his Caribbean shipwreck in the late fall), the pirates would have had to make this crossing between the fall of 1688 and spring of 1689, making Ramírez's presence in St. Augustine in the spring of 1689 impossible.[88]

Nonetheless, at a more impressionistic level, Ovington's description of the three pirate crews' "melancholy" does conjure up a pathos reminiscent of the sentiment ascribed to Captain Donkin in Chapter 4 of *Misfortunes*, when describing how Donkin pleaded with his shipmates for Ramírez's release: "It is enough . . . that we have become degenerate, robbing the Orient of its best, in unholy ways. Are not the many innocents, the fruits of whose sweat and toil we took, and whose lives we stole, not clamoring to the Heavens?" We can say nothing more at this time about this stage of Ramírez's voyage, pending archival discoveries that might flesh out our evidence that Mackintosh and at least one of his men were caught and executed for piracy "in Guinea" sometime before 1690.

No evidence suggests that Galve ever disbelieved Ramírez's version of events or suspected him of collusion with the pirates: in any case, what would have been the point? No matter how the goods had been acquired, they were now in New Spain's possession and could contribute significantly to Galve's counterattacks on the French and their Caribbean pirate allies. We can understand the excitement of New Spain's viceroy when he discovered that Ramírez's frigate contained an unexpected supply of the necessities for war: lead, tin, copper, and iron. All Galve had to do was offer Ramírez viceregal patronage; in exchange he would have relatively cheap access to the goods. But this had not been Ramírez's original plan.

THE CRIMINAL INVESTIGATION OF A YUCATAN CASTAWAY

Ramírez had not counted on needing to throw himself on the mercy of the viceroy of New Spain. His principal goal had to be to get his cargo to market, but fencing stolen goods always presented pirates with difficulties. Who could Ramírez trust in Asian, Indian Ocean, or Atlantic ports? Dealing with Philipse's New York agents in Madagascar, for example, would have exposed Ramírez to the risk of their denouncing him as a Spaniard to Spanish authorities in the Americas in exchange for a reward. Ramírez needed fellow subjects of the crown of Spain who would give him higher prices for his stolen cargo because as similarly vulnerable Spanish subjects they would be more tractable business partners. We cannot corroborate most of his movements between the Indian Ocean crossing just discussed and the fall of 1689, when his frigate fell afoul of the Yucatan coast. Strong evidence suggests that the "twenty vessels" flying "English colors" that Ramírez remembered spotting off Trinidad were the fleet of Captain Thomas Hewetson, cruising for French vessels exactly in those waters at that very moment.[89] Ramírez's brief interaction with the French governor of Guadeloupe in August 1689 seems to indicate that he preferred to work with fellow Spanish subjects, but the governor's correspondence reveals nothing.[90] We have no immediate reason to suspect that Ramírez lied about his basic route from Madagascar around the Cape of Good Hope to America. But we have only his word for the improbable story that the pirates gave him the frigate and its cargo somewhere off Brazil, an uncharacteristically generous act that Ramírez was at pains to explain. Nevertheless, we can deduce from internal evidence in his narrative and what we have established about the origins of his cargo that his return to the New World was motivated by a decision to maximize the chances for profit. Ramírez had no legal paperwork for the frigate or its cargo, so he chose to head for familiar territory, one of those nominally Spanish coasts that were nevertheless "effective vacuums of sovereign authority," preferred by smugglers and pirates.[91]

True to piratical intent, Ramírez never aimed to land his suspiciously acquired cargo in Puerto Rico, contrary to what he told authorities in Yucatan in January 1690. He selected the dangerous eastern coastline of Yucatan because of the mercantile contacts he had previously made in the region. Until 1682 Ramírez had worked for an itinerant merchant based in Oaxaca, trading into what today is Belize, Guatemala, and Honduras (*Misfortunes*, Chapter 1). Yucatan's maritime frontier remained Spanish America's most porous and profitable

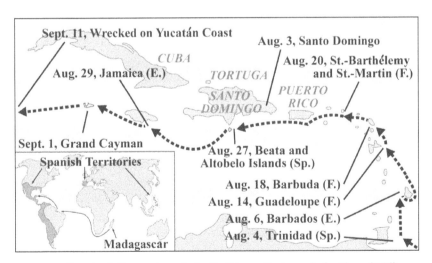

MAP 3.2. Ramírez's Course through the Caribbean. Cartography by Elwood Mills.

border well into recent history. This was due to three factors: shallow waters with extensive mangrove swamps that were difficult to patrol; a location near the island bases of English, French, and Dutch smugglers; and, most importantly, proximity to major Spanish urban centers, whose consumer demands dominated illegal Caribbean trade.[92] The viceroy's correspondence stressed the scope of the problems he faced in trying to close this border to smuggling. Despairing, Galve described the coasts of Yucatan to the king on February 1, 1690, as "nothing more than a robber's roost . . . an open door through which enemies can and regularly do enter." It was a lumpenproletariat dumping ground: "the common den of thieves from all the Nations of Europe."[93] His strenuous efforts to maintain an expensive coastguard fleet of frigates and large canoes, financed in part by elite Yucatan merchants (one ship was a former chocolate freighter), had produced limited success since 1689. The 350 men of the Windward Fleet, upped to 850 in June 1690, were simply not enough, he wrote to the king, to deal with "the numerous pirates who traffic in these seas." We can deduce from Dampier's testimony that Ramírez had been in contact with pirates aboard the *Cygnet* and *Good Hope* with knowledge of the Bacalar coast. "Many" of them had been there, wrote Dampier, including Captain Read. Based on his own experience, Dampier recommended such "low" coasts as ideal anchorages and stated that "our traders had . . . found the way of trading with the Spaniards in the Bay of Honduras" by the 1690s. He knew of at least one buccaneer who had smuggled goods through there as early as 1679.[94]

Galve did not confide in the three isolated and poorly garrisoned coastal forts as a deterrence: the forts at San Felipe de Bacalar (near modern Chetumal, Mexico), Puerto Caballos in Honduras (the modern Puerto Cortés), and the even smaller fort between them at San Felipe del Golfo Dulce, Guatemala, were too far apart. This left 180 miles of difficult mangrove coast separating Bacalar from Puerto Caballos and another 100 miles of poorly defended shore stretching north of Bacalar toward Cozumel. Both Spanish and English officials recognized that the poor Spanish settlements and coastal Indians eluded government control and acted as a conduit for goods. Reports noted that smugglers traded "quite openly with the provincials of Honduras and Guatemala" and suggested that pirates were even acquiring arms from suppliers in the Spanish inland cities through the Maya. To preclude smuggling along such coasts Galve recommended to the king (precisely in February 1690) that the new governor of Campeche, a western Yucatan region with similar problems, should be a military man, not a merchant "who might despoil it."[95]

Furthermore, through Juan López, his former commercial partner based in Oaxaca, Ramírez had commercial contacts who traded with Indians south into Maya territories. Although López had died before Ramírez left New Spain for Asia in 1682, he had apparently not parted with López's family on very good terms.[96] Nevertheless, he may have been betting on a better relationship now that he had valuable cargo to trade.[97] The trade network of López and Ramírez had extended from the tribes north and west of Oaxaca (Ramírez's "Cuicateca" and "Mixe" Indians) to areas far to the east and south of the city. It included the province of Soconusco, the mountains surrounding Chiapa de Indios (near modern Tuxtla Gutiérrez), and the highlands leading into Guatemala and Honduras, where the "Chontal" peoples lived.[98] Ramírez headed for the nearby Yucatan coastline, hoping that his former partners would help him launder his stolen goods in legal markets.

Along his Caribbean course, Ramírez carefully bypassed Spanish possessions, most remarkably his native island of Puerto Rico, but not for the flimsy reasons he gave Galve (*Misfortunes*, Chapter 5). He needed to find trusted allies to pawn a pirate prize—in keeping with the historic truism that buccaneers' greatest challenge was not thieving and robbing but rather selling and pawning. Unfortunately for Ramírez, his frigate was shipwrecked as a result of choosing a very dangerous course, dictated by desire to maximize profits. The shipwreck dashed his plans. As his crew struggled to stay alive on a deserted beach, he must have pondered the future. Perhaps he thought along the lines of one of his wily contemporaries, the Cadiz-based merchant Raimundo Lantéry, who noted in his journal: "Only adaptable plans are wise ones [*Sapiens est mutare concilium*]."[99] To survive, Ramírez would have to seek help from the locals, which would expose him to official scrutiny. But he had no other way out of his predicament. Bowing to the authority of Spanish officials was now a necessity.

Patronage, however, can trump officialdom. Ramírez first befriended important people like the priest of Tijosuco, the educated but obscure Don Cristóbal de Muros, and the powerful *encomendero* Don Melchor Pacheco (who knew the Pobletes, Ramírez's former family by marriage in Mexico City).[100] Nonetheless, some law enforcement officials in Valladolid immediately smelled a rat. The Valladolid magistrate, Ceferino de Castro (alcalde and acting *fiel ejecutor* [royal market inspector]), began taking note of the gossip that Ramírez was a collaborator of "corsairs" involved in smuggling and piracy.[101] He opened up an investigation, apparently independently of senior alcalde Don Francisco Zealerún, who held ultimate authority over Castro, the junior alcalde (Ramírez notes quite

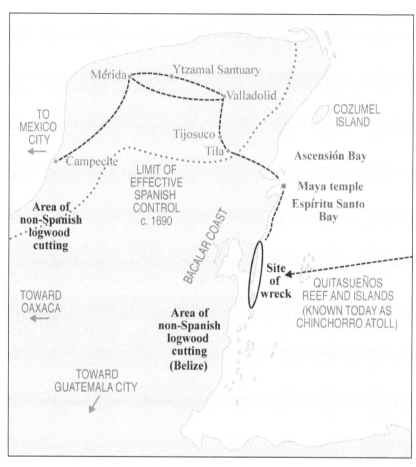

MAP 3.3. Ramírez in Yucatan. Based on Antonio de Herrera y Tordesillas, *Historia general de los hechos de los castellanos en las islas, y tierra-firme de el mar océano* (1725) and García Bernal, *Economía, política y sociedad en el Yucatán colonial.* Courtesy Santa Clara University Library Special Collections. Cartography by Elwood Mills.

precisely that Valladolid's senior alcalde had recently been granted the civil rank of "teniente [de capitán general]," which included the military authority of a captain ["capitán de guerra"]). By the 1680s the mixed civil-military enhancement of the power vested in Valladolid's senior alcalde was leading to jurisdictional disputes with the Yucatan governor, which may have played a role in the way Castro's investigation of Ramírez was "managed up" to the viceroy in Mexico City.[102]

Castro's official capacity as market inspector logically led to suspicions when he heard that people were bidding for Ramírez's frigate full of undocumented goods (as Ramírez himself relates). But perhaps it was the news that Ramírez had made a gift of a rare Malayan kris to Don Melchor Pacheco, presumably as a thank-you gift, which made Castro suspect that the castaway had not just been a victim of pirates (see the illustrations at the end of the Introductory Study). A precious weapon, after all, would be an odd gift from a pirate to a supposed "slave." Interestingly, the gift deepens our appreciation of how much the half-dozen years that Ramírez spent in southeast Asia (1682–1687/1688) influenced him. Krisses were "secreted and venerated family heirlooms," according to David van Duuren, the curator of the world-renowned collection in Amsterdam's Tropenmuseum; "for many generations" they were "passed down from father to son." These "sacral weapons" were considered "powerfully protective amulets" with magical yet dangerous powers, closely tied to noble status, political clout, and southeast Asia's peculiar maritime empires. Grateful survivors sometimes gave expensively decorated krisses as gifts to their benefactors, like the world's oldest one, given by a Javanese prince to the Dutch physician Charles Knaud in the late 1800s for having cured his son. The most valuable of all were made from an extremely rare nickeliferous iron found in only a few places in today's Malaysia and Indonesia. This fact relates materially to Ramírez's *Misfortunes*, because the principal carriers of this rare nickeliferous iron were the Buginese merchant-warriors that he reported meeting during his many travels throughout the southeast Asian archipelagos (in Chapter 2): "the coastal regions of Borneo," like Sukadana, had especially "large Buginese communities."[103] We do not know when, where, or how Ramírez acquired Pacheco's kris, but he arguably fulfilled Malay and Buginese customs with this gift and demonstrated a deep knowledge of kris lore in his narrative (see note 88 in the translation). However, this peculiarly southeast Asian gesture cemented the junior alcalde's suspicions.

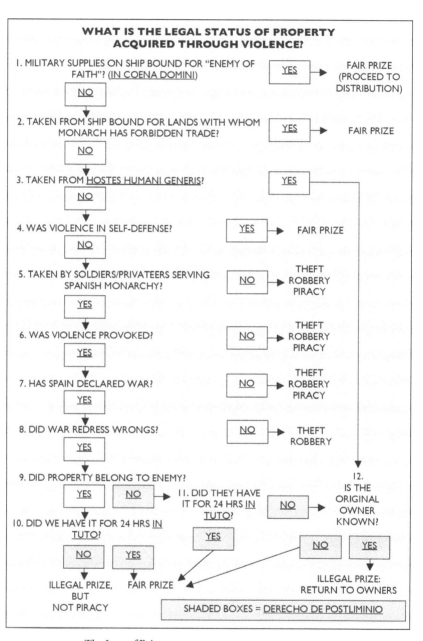

DIAGRAM 3.1. The Law of Prizes

Castro began exploring how canon laws governing war against non-Christians, the Bulls of the Santa Cruzada (Holy Crusade), might be applied to impound Ramírez's frigate. At Castro's command, Antonio Zapata, his subordinate in Tila, prevented Ramírez from returning to the shipwrecked frigate. Ramírez did not give up: it is clear from his account that he consistently maintained throughout his ordeal that he had never performed any piratical acts himself, taking advantage of the protection that the law provided to those who found themselves working aboard pirate vessels but had never exercised any command.[104] He wrote that "the encouragement and support" of the priest Don Cristóbal de Muros led him to seek help elsewhere. The priest probably also suggested how another papal bull, *In Coena Domini*, might be used to counter Castro's use of the Cruzada laws.[105] When Ramírez returned to Yucatan's capital city, Merida, however, the governor forcibly packed him off to Mexico City. He was obeying the viceroy's order that the troubling case should be heard at the highest colonial level.

THE LAW OF PRIZES AND SHIPWRECKS

Who owned the frigate and its contents? In order to appreciate how the viceroy's court assessed Ramírez's case, we must understand how property captured through violence, war, or shipwreck was adjudicated in courts of law. They followed a complex understanding of Roman imperial codes, canon law, and royal statutes. The salient questions of the law governing the legal capture of ships and cargo and their distribution as "fair prizes" to soldiers, commanders, and investors are summarized in Diagram 3.1.[106] Several points are immediately evident. Proving that a ship and its cargo were a fair prize was a complicated issue. After extensive litigation both might have to be returned to the original owners. Juridical opinion agreed on most issues, but questions 1 and 2, for example, were disputed, particularly by early modern northern European Protestant jurists who rejected medieval papal authority. Questions 9 through 12 were also controversial, even within Spanish circles. Some fine points of law were fairly recent additions in 1690, and other minor applications of rules were affected by local custom.

This is clear from the definitive seventeenth-century explanation of the law of prizes, published in 1658 (and republished in 1683). It was written by the ex-president of the Audiencia of Santo Domingo or Caribbean Supreme Court, Don Juan Francisco de Montemayor (1620–1685), who had extensive experience as a soldier, litigation lawyer, and judge in Europe and the Americas. Some principles were simple: for example, as enemies of humankind (*hostes humani generis*), pirates could never acquire property rights over stolen goods. "Pirating," Montemayor explained, is different from soldiers looting after a victory. Pirates do not violently acquire property as part of redressing wrongs committed against them; nor do they do so at the behest of a sovereign who has previously declared war on an enemy and stated clearly which wrongs need redressing ("just cause"). In this vein, the English under William Penn and Robert Venables who invaded Santo Domingo and Jamaica in 1655 without their sovereign having declared war properly were criminals in Montemayor's estimation. Any property acquired by them in either engagement constituted the proceeds of "piracy."[107] Other principles, however, were more involved.

Between 1607 and 1633 Spain added criteria for the proper acquisition of prizes and their distribution: for instance, changing how original owners' rights over property taken from them were protected during wartime. This right (*derecho de postliminio*) is illustrated in questions 9 through 12. In the sixteenth century the ships and property of pirates and illegal immigrants entering the monarchy's waters were legal prizes to be distributed among their captors, but more and more limitations were placed on this practice. After 1570 ships and cargo captured by the king's fleets or duly commissioned privateers were considered "fair prizes" or legal captures only if twenty-four hours had elapsed since they had been taken to a secure "safe place" (*in tuto*). Some jurists interpreted this as a home port, while others thought the victorious fleet itself fulfilled the requirement (Montemayor sided with the former). Otherwise, prizes were illegal and had to be returned to the original owners. This had the unfortunate effect of discouraging attacks on the monarchy's enemies by duly commissioned sea captains.

The 1633 Royal Naval Ordinance built on a 1624 legislative attempt to encourage attacks on pirates by specifying that any navy vessels taken automatically belonged to the king, along with all militarily "useful" items such as artillery and munitions and all pearls, jewels, gold, and silver on board. More dramatically, Spanish navy ships and privateers could now also keep Spanish property recovered from an enemy instead of returning it to its original owners (contrary to a 1584 statute) as long as the *in tuto* principle applied. It also allowed the confiscation of the same articles on *any* enemy or pirate ships traveling from the East or West Indies (a point which may have influenced Galve's judgment of Ramírez's case).[108] The new legal measures encouraged attacks on pirates, but the ultimate effects on public morale were mixed, as courts struggled to establish who owned what.

In March 1682, for example, a royal official in Cartagena argued that the new laws subverted the Windward Fleet's purpose by encouraging personal lucre instead of returning property to the victims of attacks. The following year Veracruz residents were understandably upset when "their" slaves, taken by people they considered pirates, were put up on the public block by Windward Fleet officers. In 1685 the inhabitants of Campeche were astonished to see that the property which had been stolen from them by "pirates" was for sale in local markets set up by the fleet's officers. One of Galve's successors, José Sarmiento y Valladares, the Count of Moctezuma, bemoaned in 1698 how such scenes perversely altered "the mission" of the Windward Fleet from "fighting" to carrying profitable cargo.[109] The problems arising from the real-life application of the law of prizes increased as Spain's diplomats struck deals with allies like England or Holland or enemies like France. Signing alliances ensuring amnesty for prior acts of violence or peace agreements ending wars usually vitiated the original owners' claims for recovery.

How did Ramírez's frigate and cargo fare according to this complex law of prizes? As in the port disputes just discussed, the general principles of the law were easier to apply than the more specific injunctions. Contemporaries argued about how far the king's sovereignty extended out into the ocean (at the shoreline, a cannon-shot out into the water, or as far as his navy dominated coastal seas?).[110] But it was indisputable that the shipwrecked frigate and its contents, originating in Asia, now lay physically on a beach within Spanish jurisdiction. Ramírez did not argue that the pirates or he himself had a letter of marque to cover the capture of the frigate or its contents (though many blank patents were available at the time in the Caribbean, particularly from local French governors).[111] Moreover, even if the pirates had indeed given Ramírez the frigate in the manner he related (and Castro was right to suspect otherwise), they could not legally dispose of goods that they had acquired criminally (question 3). At no time did Ramírez state that he intended to return the goods. Some courts provided up to a year and a day after the theft of stolen goods for the original owners to claim them (question 12). Hence Ramírez might have been forced to wait until no one responded to announcements for his title to be confirmed.[112] Finally, even if Ramírez did have legal ownership, any cargo brought into Spanish territory without due registration papers was to be impounded by law: Ramírez seems to have had no papers.[113]

Things were not as bleak for Ramírez's claim as they might seem, however. Castro prohibited Ramírez from salvaging anything on the grounds that the ship and its cargo belonged to the crown by reason of the Cruzada Bulls. These papal bulls, periodically reissued, recognized the Castilian monarchs' almost permanent crusading against Muslims by granting them special revenues from their subjects (originally voluntary but by 1690 obligatory), which were to be used in crusading. In 1601 Pope Clement VIII extended the Cruzada Bulls to wars against all heretics, schismatics, and enemies of the church, thereby implicitly broadening their application to wars against heathen pirates in the New World. Innocent X confirmed this royal prerogative in 1650. During the 1690–1692 financial reordering of the state, some ministers in Madrid even suggested—though without success—that the Cruzada Bulls could be used in a similar fashion to fight the perfidious Louis XIV. Over the centuries, income from the Cruzada grew. Revenues claimed by its officials in the 1600s included "escheated goods or waif property [*mostrencos abintestatos*]" and any property whose title remained unsubstantiated in court. By extension this might include flotsam or a shipwrecked frigate like Ramírez's, especially due to its association with heretical pirates.[114] We can perhaps infer that the "helping hand" which the bishop of Mérida gave Ramírez included valuable information about the Cruzada: among his many talents, Bishop Juan Cano y Sandoval at one point also acted as the administrator of the Cruzada for Yucatan (*comisario sub-delegado general*).[115]

Thus piety may not be the only reason for Ramírez's protracted worship at the sanctuary of Our Lady in Ytzamal during Holy Week in the spring of 1690. His piety could have been intended to weigh against Castro's legal arguments. Any sailor who paid the Santa Cruzada *limosna* (effectively a biannual tax) and who, according to one senior official, "prayed before any suitable holy image" was automatically granted "all of the indulgences conceded" by the Santa Cruzada Bulls.[116] Ramírez may have been trying to strengthen his credibility against Castro by claiming higher moral ground. This is supported by Ramírez's smirking description of the alacrity of the constables who took him in December 1689 directly from Valladolid to Mérida, specifically preventing him from stopping at the shrine of Our Lady of Ytzamal: "with as much haste as I had been in the habit of using whenever I caught sight of English ships on the seas." Like pirates, the local police fled from everything that was true. Moreover, Castro's game was not altogether altruistic, and this may have led Galve eventually to side with Ramírez. When the Tribunal of the Santa Cruzada was created in 1573 in the New World, it was given complete financial jurisdiction over all properties attached to it. Had Castro pressed the issue successfully, the wreck might have fallen to the Cruzada Tribunal. Significantly, Castro stood to be paid one-sixth of its total value if Ramírez was found guilty of contraband in the process.[117] But other laws which applied to shipwrecks must have influenced Galve's decision to accept Ramírez's version of things publicly.

It was important that Ramírez's vessel had run aground accidentally in a tempest. Canon law rewarded salvagers' efforts with one-fourth of the value of objects recovered which still legally belonged to others, similar to the *postliminio* returning of illegal prizes (inspired by Roman law), which required original owners to reimburse the costs of recovery. On unclaimed goods, the king's lot might run as high as two-thirds. More in Ramírez's favor, however, was the maritime tradition which extended greater legal latitude to seamen suffering shipwreck than to those arriving safely in port. Judges routinely considered several factors in weighing who got to keep goods salvaged from wrecked pirate or enemy ships (this was analogous to the prize courts' consideration of *postliminio* in questions 9–12). Were they "derelict"—that is, did the original owner abandon the goods or give them away? Was the salvager's own property (say, a boat) "imperiled" in the act? Did he "expose himself to the danger of death in saving them?"[118] In this light, narrative details such as the account of the pirates giving Ramírez the frigate or Ramírez's heroic attempts to save his crewmates on the reef carried legal as well as dramatic import.

As prescient readers will already have realized, Ramírez's strongest argument in law was the one undoubtedly suggested to him by Cristóbal de Muros, the humble priest he met in 1690 in Tijosuco, Yucatan. Uncharacteristically for a parish priest, Muros had a university degree and quite probably pointed out to Ramírez how another bull, *In Coena Domini*, applied to his situation. This bull stemmed from a medieval pope's decision that he exercised jurisdiction over the part of the Mediterranean Sea near Rome and thus could "excommunicate and anathematize all Pirates, Rovers, and Robbers" upon his seas and adjudicate their possessions.[119] Not surprisingly, proponents of royal sovereignty disliked *In Coena Domini*. Philip II once expelled a papal nuncio for publishing it, outlawing its application in his realms in 1582. But the bull made its way back in the 1600s and, "in spite of the opposition of princes, it was known to the faithful through diocesan rituals, provincial chapters of monks, and the promulgation of jubilees." In addition, "confessors were often ordered to have a copy of it in their possession." By mid-century we find the Supreme Court in Santo Domingo applying the bull in its investigation of a shipwreck, warning survivors to reveal any hidden "gold, silver, pearls, merchandise, silk, [or] chinchilla." Otherwise they would suffer *In Coena Domini*'s punishment of "excommunication for all persons without exception or reservation" who were found in illegal possession of property removed from a shipwreck. Well into the eighteenth century *In Coena Domini* continued to be cited in court to establish that pirates were nothing but criminals whom "any private person can take prisoner or kill, as alien to and unworthy of the protection afforded by Law." The papal bull held awesome authority as a favorite lawyer's strategy to argue against problematic statutes. In the 1600s the Spanish equivalent of the English "Throw the book at him!" was "Throw the Bulls at him!"[120] If we are right, then Muros's advice to Ramírez in 1690 may have been to throw *In Coena Domini* at Castro.

LEGAL THEORIES VERSUS THE CONTEXT OF IMPERIAL NEEDS

The possibility that *In Coena Domini*'s antipirate sanctions were suggested to Ramírez by Muros is supported by another archival piece of information. Moreover, it demonstrates the degree to which the monarchy's defensive concerns and religion-oriented patriotism could be shared by a local priest and a handful of shipwrecked sailors from Asia led by a Spaniard from Puerto Rico. Muros fed Ramírez and his companions for eight days and gave them confession on Saint Catherine's day in 1690. But apart from tending to their physical and spiritual needs, Muros had a personal interest in their stories about pirates' depredations against Spanish subjects from the Pacific to the Mediterranean. In April of the previous year Muros had donated twenty pesos to the fund organized by the Merida chaplain, Don Nicolás de Salazar, to strengthen "His Majesty's defense" against "the piratical enemy infesting the provinces of the South Seas," in light of "the extremely urgent necessity to aid in maintaining this war against infidels and Turks" (in Salazar's words). That priests in Yucatan, which bore the brunt of piracy between 1650 and 1700, made substantial donations to fighting pirates everywhere in the monarchy speaks volumes about the global solidarity of the Spanish elite. Ramírez's account of his suffering at the hands of heretical pirates was contrasted to the gentleness of his reception among the people in Yucatan. This corroborated locals' animosity toward the "tyrannical oppression" which characterized the non-Catholic world beyond the boundaries of the monarchy, a predatory world which mocked all morality and coveted the goods of the subjects of the Spanish king.[121] Symbolically, *In Coena Domini* canonically enshrined their communal hatred of those who terrorized their shores.

Thus Ramírez wielded this papal bull as both a moral and legal argument which the viceroy, with his own Catholic suspicions of Protestant English cupidity, might readily accept. The shipwrecked frigate fell under *In Coena Domini* if the viceroy chose to believe that it was the one taken from Malayans, well known for being Muslim, in the straits of Malacca (Ramírez explicitly suggested this). The militarily useful supplies listed by Ramírez supposedly originated in Malayan cargo. Even if some of the loot originated in the attack on Sukadana, as a Muslim sultanate, this could also be justified in similar fashion ("Moors" were stereotyped as "pirates" in any case).[122] According to some interpretations of the 1633 *Ordenanzas*, however, military cargo automatically became the king's and not Ramírez's. If the viceroy's answer to question 1 about being bound for an "enemy of the faith" was "no," *In Coena Domini* could not be applied. He would then be forced to move on to questions 2 and 3. Despite Ramírez's own repeated statements that he was entitled to the frigate and its cargo, the problem with all three questions was that, on his own admission, he had not *taken* them as prizes but had been given them by pirates. Furthermore, because the pirates had never legally owned them, question 12 applied: "Is the original owner known?"

Ramírez's account gave no explicit indication of the answer to this question about a third party, notwithstanding the evidence that much if not all of the cargo originated in Siamese trade and his suggestion that the frigate had belonged to Malayans. Spanish treaties with Holland in 1650 and England in 1667 had set out what happened to the property of third parties. Even friendly ships could be boarded during war, and the goods of an ally of Spain's enemies aboard them could be confiscated and considered legitimate prizes. Ramírez's cargo might fit that description quite easily if the viceroy chose to accept that the cargo was mostly Siamese in origin. Siam was effectively an ally of France in 1687, Spain's key enemy in 1690. Spanish law could treat Ramírez quite leniently, even if he had been associated with pirates for over two years. He had acted under duress (extensively described in his account) and had risked his life to bring the cargo to Spanish jurisdiction and then to bring some of it ashore in Yucatan. Even if Ramírez's ownership was questionable, the *in tuto* rule could be applied to argue that the prize did not have to be returned to its original owners because much more than twenty-four hours had elapsed since its capture. In the final analysis—as far as we can go at the moment—the law as it stood in 1690 advised magistrates to apply the ancient Roman principle of privileging redress over profits (*de damno vitando* versus *de lucro captando*). After duly considering the facts and points of law affecting a particular prize case, they were always to favor those who needed to reverse harm done to them in the final distribution of the moneys.[123] The pathos of Ramírez's experiences eminently suited this consideration.

Although the motives of Galve and Ramírez are mostly clear, the reconstruction of the legal reasoning behind Galve's acceptance of Ramírez's claims must remain speculative until more documents are discovered which shed further light on the various legal interpretations discussed here. But the details show-ing how the publication of Ramírez's account meshed with the Count of Galve's need for military supplies confirm Montemayor's 1655 juristic quip about justice versus legal fact: in "the chess game" of rights, what matters is convincing the right person.[124] The viceroy's decision to favor Ramírez was questionable, as is evident from the problematic way in which the law of prizes applied to the facts of his case (as far as they were known by Galve's court in Mexico City). Political expediency led all early modern states at one point or another simply to ignore or bend maritime laws, so Galve's method was neither self-interestedly cynical nor unethical.[125] As the highest judicial authority in New Spain, he was acting within his rights and duties. He was in fact rebuked by the king for exceeding them in 1694, but Ramírez's case did not form part of the royal criticisms.[126] As a well-known attorney general in Peru stated in 1647, illegal imports "can be legal-ly registered . . . on the discretion of the viceroy, for it is his charge to determine what is most convenient to the king's interests."[127] And it was only in 1690 that the king finally set up a Committee of Reprisals (Junta de Represalias) to sort out all the confusing legislation and begin judging cases of unregistered, unofficial landings of ships. Ramírez's case just squeezed in under the line.[128]

Our assessment of the true conviction behind Ramírez's own expressions of Catholic and Spanish patriotism remains inconclusive without further corrobo-rating documentary evidence, although analysis has revealed his deep complicity with pirates. But one man's law, after all, can be another man's piracy, as Mon-temayor noted when positing that the Dutch legal expert Hugo Grotius overex-tended sound principles simply to defend his compatriots' piratical predations on Spanish people and their property.[129] Ramírez's account contains evidence that there was indeed honesty among thieves: the careful list of his crewmates which he provided had legal weight with financial consequences. In the divi-sion of fair prizes, each man's identity was to be documented formally, "name by name" according to the law of prizes, even when they were merely common sailors with equal shares. Compensation for work actually done and wounds suf-fered was to be meted out equitably.[130] Ramírez had made sure that he kept to this principle.

The point in all this, borrowing Lauren Benton's advice from a different context, is not to get too bogged down in reconstructing "the law" which per-tained to Ramírez's case "as either transparently political or a mask for deeper processes defining hegemony" or, in Ramírez's case, a different form of power struggle: subterfuge.[131] Rather, Galve's decision to accept Ramírez's improbable story and promulgate it in book form demonstrates that Galve believed it was useful for the interests of God, the monarch, and the subjects of the king, over whom he exercised custodial responsibility. Merchants railed against officials who "discover laws to fit the king's desires," but few would argue against Galve's emergency measures during the heyday of piratical attacks on Spanish America. The context of an unprecedented and diplomatically complicated world war against Louis XIV's France must have made legalistic quibbling in such a case tantamount to unpatriotic wickedness and foolishness. Colonial distances had contributed to make legitimating *faits accomplis* the norm, and it is a fact that Madrid retroactively approved Galve's 1690 antipiracy initiatives.[132]

This deep ideological concern was shared with others, from Muros down to locals who suffered attacks and depredations on the fringes of the empire and up to the economic and social elites who worried about their fortunes. Galve protected Ramírez from local prosecution for piracy and contraband because he cared more for the fortunes of the king of Spain's monarchy than for the legalities of the king of Siam's treasure. Such accommodationism seems to have characterized the mature form of early modern Spanish bureaucracy. Tolerance of the paralegal behavior of local elites functioned as an institutionalized negotiation which ensured their investment in the project of state maintenance.[133] Galve needed bronze for guns to fight terrorists, so he saved a Puerto Rican who collaborated with pirates from a legal downfall for a higher purpose.

CHAPTER 4

Conclusions

There never was a sailor's story that wasn't a damn lie.
MARITIME NOVELIST KENNETH ROBERTS,
warning readers never to fall for sea stories

HIS STUDY LEAVES MANY QUESTIONS for further research. After an in-depth study of the historic facts behind the text of *Misfortunes*, it is clear that Ramírez and his stories keep what the literary historian Jean-Pierre Poussou recently characterized as the "permanent ambiguity" of these kinds of apologetic autobiographical accounts.[1] Sigüenza's literary embellishments without doubt altered what was already Ramírez's distorted picture of events. The historic nature of *Misfortunes* should not blind us to its fictional qualities, but these arose more from the carpenter's self-promotion than from the cosmographer's skill. I leave it to literary scholars to analyze how our appreciation of *Misfortunes* as a text molded by Sigüenza's genius is affected by the historicity of Alonso Ramírez's story. Undoubtedly, Ramírez's *Misfortunes* to some degree already constituted a sailor's "lie" before Sigüenza's pen ever touched paper, but as such it nevertheless reveals many historic truths, as we have seen, some specific, others broad.

The historical existence of Ramírez and the reality of his adventures are now incontrovertibly proven (documented lying, after all, is as historic as documented truth-telling). More broadly speaking, this study shows that the historical investigation of early modern societies is particularly profitable if pursued on the high seas. The myriad unofficial connections linking far-flung ports and beaches were the result not just of imposed empire but also of tremendously diverse, legal and illegal, ethical and unethical uses of the early modern world's "most complicated machine," the sailing ship.[2] Our modern environment continues to rely on this same maritime habitat. Despite airplanes, cell phones, and satellites, containerized shipping still carries the wherewithal of modern civilization. And yet it is equally important that the high seas are still beyond the law's reach, even in the twenty-first century. The contemporary continuation of these early modern dilemmas has notable historiographical consequences.

With no central privileged vantage point for our analysis, we must literally journey along with the people and objects traveling in time and space in order to study them. The maritime interconnectedness of the early modern world imposes a methodology because our reconstruction of realities is a slave to multifaceted subjectivities. The historian must ship aboard in order to follow the perspective from the ship, but without losing sight of the perspective of the peoples left ashore. In this difficult task, maritime historians are assisted—as I have been—by the remarkable survival of minute pieces of evidence in archives created by the people who owned, managed, and used most of those ships. The silences created by these extremely detailed but selective sources tell a tale of European and Neo-European state and capitalist dominance and predation which frustrates those who search for total visions. The voices of Pulo Ubi, Sukadana, and the dozens of villages in the Americas sacked by pirates are as elusive as those of the pirates themselves. When interrogated, most humans prefer to conceal rather than reveal. Though this study glimpses many details of the real Ramírez's occasionally predatory circumnavigation of the globe between 1682 and 1689, his cameo in the history books will remain momentary and open-ended. Ramírez will continue to elude the grasp of final judgment, and this, in an important way, is how he would have wanted it. Nevertheless, we can reach specific conclusions concerning his interactions with others in specific moments.

Galve bent Spanish law in Ramírez's favor, but no one blamed him. Manuela Cristina García Bernal has explained that in the province of Yucatan, "as in many other American ones, laws were not applied, perhaps because of the reasoning used" by one official in the eighteenth century that "royal laws are obeyed insofar as they can be adapted to the time and the place; to which end the *law of experience* corrects them when observing them would seriously harm or perniciously affect the common good."[3] Retroactive approval for a viceroy's decisions was a routine bureaucratic procedure necessitated by colonial distances and hierarchical due process. At one point it took Galve over two years to receive approval for a decision made in 1691. Contraband had become so accepted in the seventeenth-century Pacific trade networks linking Asia through the Philippines to Mexico and South America that officials simply allowed it in exchange for regular payments of negotiated *indultos* (amnesties). On one occasion the price negotiated was 74,000 pesos per Manila galleon arriving in Acapulco.[4] No evil consequences arose from such situations as long as the members of the Council of the Indies were convinced that the king's reputation, interests, and coffers had not been diminished and the common good had been protected.[5] Although Galve returned to Spain with great wealth, the mandatory investigation of his term in office (*residencia*) found no proof of serious wrongdoing.[6] He had done his duty by accepting Ramírez's story. No one bothered with details when Ramírez's militarily valuable cargo and *Misfortunes* had become part of the resources wielded to gain an important victory against pirates and Louis XIV in 1691.

Ramírez's real identity remains a mystery, despite the possible identifications suggested by his interaction with Spanish sailors and English and Scottish pirates.[7] Ramírez disappears from the historical record in the company of Carlos de Sigüenza y Góngora's friend Juan Enríquez Barroto, a captain of artillery in the Windward Fleet. They were traveling together in the summer of 1690 down to the Veracruz naval depot, bound for the attack on French and buccaneer Caribbean bases. Ramírez joined the fleet on the viceroy's order, probably within one of the *compañías sueltas* (loose companies) which were the bane of fleet commanders at the time.[8] Ramírez may have been one of the twenty-six subaltern officers (sergeants and ensigns) appointed on July 18, 1690, the day before the fleet set sail. Or perhaps he sailed with Captain Blas Miguel, a privateer commissioned at the same time.[9] If so, then in the end Ramírez contributed to the severe rebuke that Madrid meted out to New Spain's officials on October 19, 1690, for expanding colonial budgets by issuing commissions in the navy without the king's approval.[10]

In the long run Ramírez succeeded, in pirate terms: he disappeared from governmental notice and achieved anonymity, to the great loss of historical analysis but clearly to his own benefit (we can speculate that he would not have been at all pleased with the results of this investigation). Others were not so lucky. Dampier did not disappear from the radar; mutinies under his command and accusations of illegal doings in later years besmirched the façade of respectability that he so carefully constructed during the mid-1690s. Visitors to the National Portrait Gallery in London are still haunted by the aura of guilt which emanates from his portrait.

Somewhere between Dampier's failure and Ramírez's success lies the fate of Ramírez's "Captain Donkin," Duncan Mackintosh. Under the alias of "Thompson" he was apparently hanged in Guinea in 1689 or 1690, but this disappearance from the historical record is problematized by a rather surprising though inconclusive piece of French evidence.

In 1702 the disgraced ex-mayor of Tacuba, New Spain, Don Francisco de Seijas y Lobera, was in self-exile in Paris. This virulent critic of Galve's administration told Louis XIV's court that year that Galve had used private ships to ferry the ill-gotten American proceeds of his corrupt regime. The only captain whose name Seijas wrote down was "Thomas Donkin."[11] Were Ramírez's Donkin and Seijas's Donkin one and the same? We may never know, but Captain Deerrow's casual remark to Captain Freke in 1689 that Mackintosh used the alias "Thompson" is intriguing.

At a larger remove, understanding the historical context of *Misfortunes* is a lesson in the strength of Spain's imperial fabric. Aristocrats in late seventeenth-century Spain benefited from its diffuse and complexly articulated governmental structure, known as polysynody: rule through advisory and executive councils. At the very least, their financial ties to the monarch allowed for the exercise of consultative authority. The dynasty's recruitment of ambassadors, viceroys, and council members from their ranks (like Galve, Infantado, and Vélez) assured them continuing political importance. "The government might ignore the councils on specific issues, but could never afford to ignore the political élite represented on them."[12]

A dialectical tension between a centrifugally predisposed oligarchy and a centripetally driven system of king's favorites, the *valido* system studied by Francisco Tomás y Valiente, characterized early modern Spanish political life.[13] Both oligarchs and *validos* saw themselves as monarchists, but the former tended to be wary of change which upset the court traditions of the Spanish Habsburgs as defined by the three Philips between 1555 and 1665.[14] When the helm of state was not in the hands of someone like Don Juan de Austria (the upstart bastard son of Philip IV, whom R. A. Stradling calls modern Spain's "first military dictator"),[15] high politics seemed to reside in aristocratic machinations. These intrigues, however, were far from haphazard or motivated purely by self-interest.[16] As long as Infantado acted as Carlos II's *valido* from behind the scenes and Galve made sure that Spain's overseas enemies were kept at bay while bullion flowed steadily to Europe, the fragile balance which kept the empire going at its highest level was assured. This was a system with ample opportunities for regional elites below the highest levels. It was not yet characterized by the eighteenth-century Bourbon regime's heavy-handed and systematic preference for Europeans, which Mark Burkholder and D. S. Chandler have credited with undermining Spain's control of the New World.[17]

The monarchy's officials in the 1680s and 1690s repeatedly stated that they ruled "for the benefit of the King's service, but also for the common good of the provinces and their peoples."[18] It is hard to dismiss this offhand when reading how one viceroy in 1690 helped a carpenter launder pirate goods into Mexico in order to support an attack on pirates who terrorized civilian populations and French enemies who threatened the state's integrity. We are encouraged to consider the probability that repeated instances of this sort of commitment to the negotiated body politic over the centuries contributed significantly to the longevity of the Spanish empire. In creating *Misfortunes*, Sigüenza, Galve, and Ramírez proved that political fortunes often rely on turning individuals' misfortunes to a common purpose.

Don Gaspar de la Cerda Sandoval Silva y Mendoza (1653–1697), Count of Galve, viceroy of New Spain (1688–1696). Courtesy Museo Nacional de Historia, Mexico City.

Don Gregorio María de Silva y Mendoza (1649–1693), Duke of Infantado, member of the Council of War and Council of State, Head Gentleman of the Bedchamber, and Groom of the Stool for King Carlos II (r. 1665–1700). Courtesy Museo del Prado, Madrid.

Don Fernando Joaquín Fajardo de Toledo (d. 1693), Marquis of Los Vélez, viceroy of Sardinia (1673–1675), viceroy of Naples (1675–1683), head of the Council of Indies, and Spain's chief naval minister (1683–1693). Courtesy Biblioteca Nacional, Madrid.

Don Carlos de Sigüenza y Góngora (1645–1700), royal cosmographer and author of the published text of *The Misfortunes of Alonso Ramírez* (1690). Courtesy Nettie Lee Benson Latin American Collection, University of Texas at Austin.

William Dampier (1651–1715), buccaneer, privateer, naturalist, and English Royal Navy officer. Courtesy National Portrait Gallery, London.

Louis XIV receiving the ambassadors from Siam in the Palace of Versailles, 1686. The right side of the image shows the type of ambassadorial column which Ramírez described seeing in 1687. Antoine Coypel (1661–1722). Louvre Museum, Paris. Courtesy Réunion des Musées Nationaux/Art Resource, New York.

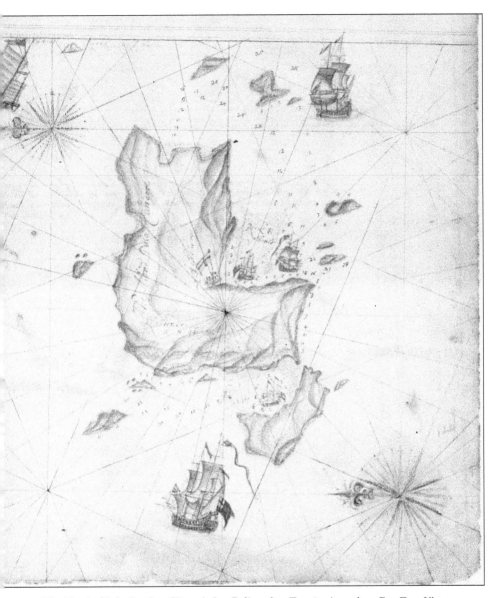

The island of Pulo Condore (Dampier) or Pulicondon (Ramírez), modern Con Dao, Vietnam, where Ramírez transferred from one pirate ship to another. Edward Barlow, "Barlow's Journal, His Life at Sea in East and West Indiamen, 1659–1703." Courtesy National Maritime Museum, Greenwich.

The type of weapon, known as a kris, which Ramírez gave to his Yucatan benefactor, Don Melchor Pacheco, in 1690. Indonesia; Java or Sumatra, approx. 1600–1800. Steel, gold, wood, enamel, and paste stones. Gift of the Christensen Fund, F1988.6.53. © Asian Art Museum, San Francisco. Used by permission.

The Misfortunes of Alonso Ramírez

A CRITICAL TRANSLATION

The Misfortunes which Alonso Ramirez, a Native of the
City of San Juan in Puerto Rico, Suffered, both while under the
Power of English Pirates who captured him in the Philippine Islands,
and while Sailing on His Own, without a Course, until He Ran
Aground on the Coast of Yucatan: In this Manner
Circumnavigating the World

* * *

As described by Don Carlos de Siguenza y Gongora,
Cosmographer and Professor of Mathematics in the Mexican
Academy by Appointment of His Majesty, Our King

* * *

With License in Mexico, [printed] by the Heirs of the Widow of
Bernardo Calderon, on St. Agustin Street, in the Year 1690.

DEDICATORY EPISTLE

To His Excellency Don Gaspar de Sandoval Cerda Sylva y Mendoza, Count of Galve, Gentleman in the service of His Majesty's Chamber, Knight Commander of Salamea and Seclavin in the Order and Knightly Company of Alcantara, Perpetual Governor of the Royal Mansions, Gates, and Bridges of the City of Toledo and of the Castle and Towers of Leon, Lord of the towns of Tortola and Sacedon, Viceroy, Governor, and Captain General of New Spain, and President of the Royal Chancillery of Mexico, etc.[1]

I have often heard it said that temerities can end in success and errors will find their pardon, which truths motivated in me an abundant hope that my presumption in seeking asylum in the church of Your Excellency's presence[2] would not be counterbalanced by the many favors that Your comprehension, delicate and beyond discreet, has already granted to my book *Astronomical and Philosophical Balance*,[3] a book I sent to press sheltered in the shadow of Your patronage this very year. And since Your Excellency was graciously pleased to hear the original sufferer of these hardships recite them in brief to You in person, I cannot but be assured that my longer recital will meet with equal favor. It was in Mexico that Alonso Ramirez closed the cycle of his hardships,[4] which amounted, in the course of being captured by English pirates in the Philippines and then stranded on the shores of Yucatan, to a circumnavigation of the globe. And given how Your Excellency pitied the sufferer of these tribulations when he related them to

You, no one could doubt that Your munificence will continue to favor him in the future except one who refuses to acknowledge how Your Excellency, in tempering commiseration with grandeur, reconciles them so reciprocally that they are matched equally. The combination is so perfect that I can say that no mind, no matter how perspicacious or lynx-like, will be able to discern which comes first in Your Excellency, the greatness inherited from Your most excellent ancestors or the native-born pious pity[5] of Your compassion, which never denies succor to the pitiful tears of those toiling under the injury of their misfortune. Encouraged by the real proof of these qualities which I daily witness in Your presence, and trusting that Your Excellency's Palace doors are never closed to the destitute men whose narrative you entrusted me to write,[6] I offer up on the altar of Your Excellency's beneficence this lamentable pilgrimage, confident, for my part, that it will garner both patronage and esteem from Your Excellency's astounding judgment in hydrographic and geographical matters.

Placing himself at the feet of Your Excellency,
Don Carlos de Siguenza y Gongora.

Granted by Licenciado Don Francisco de Ayerra Santa Maria, Chaplain of Our King's Royal Convent of Jesus and Mary in Mexico City.[7]

I committed myself to reading this work in the spirit of obedience to Your Lordship's decree, which commanded me to examine *The Misfortunes of Alonso Ramirez*—a compatriot of mine—whose account has been recently described by Don Carlos de Siguenza y Gongora, the King's cosmographer and His Professor in Mathematics in this Royal University. But in addition to obedience, the delightful novelty promised by its subject matter compelled me to read it. Though at first I began it under the force of obligation and curiosity, as I progressed into it, the variety of its events, the disposition of its elements, and the structure of its story seemed so pleasing to me that it turned what I had originally thought would be a studious task into an inestimable favor. The central subject of this narrative can count himself a happy man, for his misfortunes are now in two ways fortunate: first, because having gloriously suffered them they are now over and, in the words which the Mantuan Muse issued through the mouth of Aeneas when on a similar occasion he spoke to his Trojan companions, *Forsan et haec olim meminisse iuvabit*;[8] and second, because it was his fortune to have found such a Homer (the hope Anthony harbored for his Caesar, *Romanusque tibi contingat Homerus*),[9] who infused the embryo of an ill-fated confusion of events with the life of seasoned discourse and teased the golden thread out of a labyrinthine tangle of detours, thereby crowning himself with our applause. It is no surprise, considering this Author's exquisite pieces and laborious work, that he achieves happily everything he undertakes with diligence, and since in the account books of hydrography and geography he has earned so much credit, I do not wonder that this book has emerged so fully formed, for with such beginnings his work was already half done. It was enough for the material to have body so that he might shape it with the chisel of his labors. Nor was this an occasion for spoken words to suffice, but rather one that called for them to be written down so that others might consider them at a remove, for the written word survives but the vicissitudes of time make one forget the former and a case as unprecedented as this one deserved to be printed for the sake of future memory. *Quis mihi tribuat, ut scribantur sermones mei. [sic] Quis mihi det, ut exarentur in libro stylo ferreo, vel saltem sculpantur in scilice?*[10] To make his words immortal Job wanted someone to write them down, and he was not satisfied with anything less than sculpting every detail of what he had known how to endure with a chisel into rock: *dura, quae sustinet; non vult per silentium tegi* (so says the Gloss), *sed exemplo ad notitiam pertrahi* . . . [11] And the subject of this story has seen that desire of Job, *Quis mihi tribuat*, fulfilled in having this author write a narrative which, for the general notice and usefulness of the public, not seeing anything censurable in it, I recommend print should make immortal.

And this is my view, etc. . . .

Mexico, June 26, 1690
Don Francisco de Ayerra Santa Maria

By order of his Most Excellent Lord Viceroy Count of Galve, etc., on June 26, 1690, and by virtue of the decision which Señor Doctor Don Diego de la Sierra, etc., Diocesan Judge and General Vicar of this Archbishopric, issued on the same day, the printing of this account was licensed.

CHAPTER I

Motives which induced Alonso Ramirez to leave his native land.[12]
Occupation and voyages in New Spain. His stay in Mexico
until his travels from there to the Philippine Islands

My desire in writing is for the curious reader who might peruse this narrative to be entertained for a few hours with an account of what caused the grave tribulations which beset me for so many years. In daily life one can often deduce maxims and aphorisms from stories that exist only in the minds of those who counterfeit them but are lessons that in the passing delight of an enjoyable tale cultivate our reason. However, such is not my intent here; my aim is rather to solicit compassionate tears. Though belated, they will in no small way make the memory of my burdens tolerable and, with their company, comfort me as I recall those I shed when I was in the midst of these tribulations. Having said this, let not my honest and plain confession make me a vile coward in your estimation, for I would not have it so and have omitted minor details from my narrative which might have spurred others less unfortunate than myself to register many more claims on your compassion. I have related simply the first things I remembered from the long series of events that happened to me, and these remain the most notable.

My name is Alonso Ramirez and my native land is the city of San Juan in Puerto Rico, the capital of the island which today is known by that name but in antiquity was called Borriquen and which separates the realms of the Atlantic Ocean from those of the Gulf of Mexico.[13] It is celebrated as a stopping point for its delightful waters, which refresh those who, thirsty for New Spain, voyage from the Old in search of the New. It is famous for the beauty of its bay and the unparalleled grandeur of its Morro, which safeguards its security with curtains of walls and bastions crowned with artillery. The privilege of being protected from the ravages of corsair[14] attacks, though, is due less to these fortifications, for, after all, other parts of the Indies[15] possess similar ones, than to the spirit that the sons of this fertile island are given by the genius of a place without need. Native islanders repay the debt which these merits impose with a sense of due honor and loyalty, despite the alterations of time. For the riches it was named after[16] have vanished; the veins of gold that could be found throughout the island are no longer mined for lack of the original natives to work them; tempestuous hurricanes razed the chocolate trees which came in due time to supplant gold as a means of trafficking in life's necessities; and thus, in the case of islanders born in recent years, yesterday's riches have become today's penury.

Among those this poverty took upon itself to harbor in its bosom were my parents, even though their recommendations did not merit such attention;[17] but we all know that such is today a typical burden in the Indies. My father's name was Lucas de Villanueva and, although I do not know his place of birth, I am nevertheless certain of the fact—because I overheard him say it on many occasions—that he was Andalusian.[18] My mother I know unquestionably was born in the same city in Puerto Rico as I was, and her name is Ana Ramírez.[19] To her Christianity I, in my childhood, owe the one thing that the poor can give their offspring, the advice needed to incline them toward virtue. My father was a ship's carpenter and imposed on me, when my age permitted it, the same employment. But such work not being continuously gainful and fearing a life always full of the inconveniences which already, though I was but a youth, forced themselves upon me, I determined to steal myself from my own land[20] to seek more convenience in foreign ones.

I took advantage of an opportunity which presented itself to me in the shape of a fly-boat[21] belonging to Captain Juan del Corcho [Juan of the Cork],[22] which was to sail from our port bound for La Habana in that year of 1675. I was less than thirteen and so was given the post of cabin boy.[23] It did not seem a particularly burdensome occupation to me, considering that I was finally living in liberty and freed from the promise of cutting wood all day, but I must confess I doubted whether anything good was to come of it. Perhaps it presaged future calamities that I had begun my search for fortune by taking to the sea on a cork! And who will deny that my doubts had merit, if they but consider the events that followed from such a beginning? Leaving the port of La Habana, well known among the Windward Islands[24] as much for the conveniences endowed by nature as for the fortifications which man's art and painstaking work have given it, we voyaged to San Juan de Ulua on the mainland of New Spain,²⁵ where, separating myself from my employer, I came up to the city of La Puebla de los Angeles. I suffered not a few discomforts on the way there, due in equal degree to the rough tracks that rise from Jalapa up to the mountain pass at Perote and to the cold which, unaccustomed as I was, seemed to me intense beyond belief. Those who live in La Puebla say that it is second only to Mexico City in the area it encompasses, in the cheerful openness of its streets, and in the magnificence of its temples, as well as in every other possible point of comparison. It appeared to me—for I had not seen anything comparable before—that in a city that large I would have no problem finding great conveniences; and so I decided on the spot, without any further discourse or thought, to stay, applying myself to serve as a carpenter's helper to eke out a living, biding my time until another means of becoming rich might present itself to me.²⁶

However, during the six months' time that I wasted there, I experienced even greater hunger than back home in Puerto Rico. Cursing my unbusinesslike resolution²⁷ to abandon my home for a land where generous liberality is not always forthcoming, I proceeded to add myself to a group of traveling mule drivers and, without too much trouble, landed in Mexico [City].²⁸ It is a great pity that the magnificent splendors of such a proud city are not published throughout the world, graven like diamond-cut images on gold plate. Whatever I had learned back in Puebla about urban grandeur was struck from my memory in an instant the moment I stepped on Mexico's causeway. It lies on the southern approach and opens up a welcoming passage for foreigners across the enormous lagoon in which its foundations lie. I will be the first to praise the magnanimity of the inhabitants of this metropolis, a magnanimity bolstered by a natural abundance of all things necessary for a life of ease; unfortunately, then, I can only attribute it to my fatal star that I was once again forced to take up my profession to make ends meet.²⁹ Christoval de Medina, master builder and architect, took me on at a middling salary and put me to work on construction projects as they arose, in which occupation I spent roughly a year.³⁰

I was motivated to leave Mexico for the city of Oaxaca by the news I received that Don Luis Ramirez exercised the office of councilman there, and, because he was a relative on my mother's side, I trusted that he would at least lend me somewhat of a hand up the ladder of life, even if I did not dare hope for a boost disproportionate to the foundations of my merit. But the only compensation I received for a trip of eighty leagues³¹ was to have him deny our relations with many foul words, which left me to apply myself to strangers, not being willing to suffer the indifference of relatives, the more hurtfully lamentable as they were unexpected.[32] And so I applied to serve a traveling merchant by the name of Juan Lopez, who was occupied in trafficking Castilian articles to the Mixe, Chontal, and Cuicateca Indians, for whatever they were lacking, trading in exchange those locally produced, namely, cotton, capes, vanilla, chocolate, and cochineal.[33] What can I say of the things one endures while traversing these rough Sierra mountains? In order to engage in this trade, you are forced to cross and recross the mountains on foot repeatedly, and your life amounts to nothing but an unending fear of falling from the narrow paths down precipices into the horrifying depths of ravines, amid constant rains and arduous obstructions of all kinds; to which terrors you may add two more, the innumerable mosquitoes which flourish in the unbearably hot constricted valleys and, everywhere you go, *sabandijas*, little animals which make themselves abominable to all living things with their fatal venom.[34]

But the quickening desire to find riches tramples on all of one's troubles, and so I put up with these things alongside my master, persuaded as I was that my toil would find its reward in equal measure. We made for Chiapa de Indios[35] and from there to different places in the provinces of Soconusco and Guatemala, but, it being the common fare of human activities for the happy day of prosperity to be interrupted by the sad night of heavy sorrow, my master became ill on our way back to Huaxaca[36] in the village of Talistaca,[37] to such an extreme that he was administered last rites in preparation for death. I began to lament greatly that his work now became mine and equally lamented that mine still had to be done; so I spent my time laboriously trying to devise an occupation that would ensure that I enjoyed the rest of my life in greater ease. But the sudden recovery of Juan Lopez calmed the storm that afflicted me, and it gave way to a sense of tranquillity, though this turned out to be only temporary; for on the following trip no remedy sufficed when he took ill with the same condition and passed away in the town of Cuicatlan. I was paid the compensation that his heirs were willing to part with as payment for my assistance to the trader and, indignant and despairing of both myself and my fortune, headed back to Mexico; but before going there I wanted to have at least some reales in my pocket,[38] so I determined to work in Puebla to try to get some. I found no master builder willing to take me on, however, and, fearing a relapse into the hunger that I had previously suffered there, I pressed on without delay toward Mexico.

The dedication with which I worked as assistant over the course of a year to master builder Christoval de Medina,[39] a dedication recalled by those who knew me, prompted them to encourage me to take up official residence in Mexico. This I achieved by marrying Francisca Xavier, a maiden orphaned daughter of Doña Maria de Poblete, sister to the Venerable Señor Don Juan de Poblete, Dean of the Metropolitan Church, who renounced an archbishop's miter in Manila so that he might die like a Phoenix in the nest that gave him birth and who was a living example to those who would eternalize his memory with the rectitude of their conduct.[40] I am well aware that to invoke his name is to compass all possible nobility and outstanding virtue, and so let me say no more, for, reluctantly, I do not want to be prolific in narrating the many things that my gratitude reminds me I owe him.

I found in my wife much virtue and in my esteem for her she deemed me worthy of tender love. But this joy was but like a dream of only eleven months' duration, for the fact is that, on the very first occasion of giving birth to our child, she gave up her life. I was left by such an unexpected and deeply felt blow close to losing my own [life] and as an escape from it all I came back to the city of Puebla, where I settled down to being a journeyman for Estevan Gutierrez, master carpenter. But since my master was barely making ends meet, imagine how miserably his employee survived life's needs. I despaired of ever turning myself into a person of consequence, and finding that in the tribunal of my conscience I had not only accused but condemned myself for being useless, my determination became to receive the sentence meted out to delinquents in Mexico, namely, exile in the Philippine Islands.[41] Consequently, I crossed over to them by taking a berth in the galleon *Santa Rosa*, which, under General Antonio Nieto, left the port of Acapulco piloted by Admiral Leandro Coello and made way for El Cavite in the year 1682.[42]

This port of Acapulco lies at 16° and 40' latitude north of the Equator and offers vessels making themselves secure in its harbor as much beauty and safety as it gives its inhabitants discomforts and distress. These inhabitants number but a few, given the bad temper of the place, its infertility, the lack of drinking water, and even life's necessities, which must perforce be brought to it from adjoining areas. Add to this the intolerable heat and the ravines and precipices along its pathways, and you will see how this port incites you to leave it at once.[43]

CHAPTER 2

He leaves Acapulco for the Philippines; the route normally
taken is laid out and a description is given of what he
did with his time until his capture by the English

To clear Acapulco harbor it is best to catch the sea breezes that blow toward land
out of the west-northwest or northwest, which at that time of year arise at the
eleventh hour of the day; but as it is more ordinary for it to blow from the southwest or veering to the south and south-southwest, it is necessary to await the
third hour in order to avoid working to windward, because after the sun crosses
the Meridian the wind veers aft to the west-northwest and northwest and you can
stand out to sea without hauling upon the wind. From there the ship runs south,
working to windward with the sea breezes I mentioned above and not worrying
too much whether they vary by a point or so or turn from the Meridian, until 12°
is reached, or somewhat less. Here the winds veer northeast or north, indicating that you have made the northeast and east trade winds,[44] and you must set a
course west-southwest, then west one point northwest bearing off 500 leagues
from the Meridian. It is convenient at this point to run at 13° latitude.

Once on this line, the compass needle begins to decline steadily to the northeast, and upon attaining 18° variation you know that you have sailed, in addition
to the 500 leagues already noted, another 1,100. Keeping to 13°, and watching
for the moment when the needle declines only 10°, which will be when the ship
is 1,775 leagues away from the meridian of Acapulco, within a day's run more or
less you will come to the south headland of one of the Mariana Islands, which is
called Guan,[45] and lies from 13° 5' to 13° 25'. Once you pass a small island which
adjoins it, you should close haul for 100 leagues, coming to anchor in the bay of

Humata, which opens up immediately in front; and, keeping a reef that lies west of this small island one cannon-shot's length away, you can anchor in the road in twenty fathoms[46] or whatever you desire, for it is a smooth, easy bottom.

In order to seek out San Bernardino channel, the vessel should stand west one point southwest, taking care to steer a course as the needle points. After 295 leagues you come to Espiritu Santo Cape, which lies at 12° 45'. If you can lay a course for it at fewer degrees then it is to be preferred, for if the usual storms arrive early and blow in from the south-southwest or from the southwest, it is imperative to be to the windward, under the cover of the island of Palapa and of the said Cape.

Once the breezes get up you can sail along the coastline of this island for twenty leagues, heading west-northwest, sheering to west because the needle steadies here; once east of San Bernardino Key, you direct your course for the island of Capul, which lies four leagues to the southwest. From this place you should take a westerly course for six leagues until you reach the island of Ticao then run down the coast northwest five leagues to the headland at the north end of it, veering west-southwest, plotting your course to the straits between Burias and Masbate Islands. The separation between these two is not quite one league wide, Burias lying to the north. These straits lie about four leagues from the Ticao headland.

Beyond the narrows, the pilot should steer west-northwest in the direction of the straits between the islands of Marinduque and Banton, of which the latter lies three-fourths of a league south of the former, and the distance to Burias from both is seventeen leagues. Northwest one point west the course lies toward the small islands of Mindoro, Lobo, and Galvam.[47] Once through the narrows between Isla Verde and Mindoro, you stand west eleven or twelve leagues, until nearing the Island of Ambil, fetching fourteen leagues northwest, then north, and finally northeast from this place to Marivelez, which lies at 14° and 30' latitude. From Marivelez, the course of some five leagues runs first northeast veering to east-northeast and then east to the port of Cavite, staying clear of a bank lying east-northeast of Marivelez, which bottoms out at four and a half fathoms.

Once I found myself on this voyage I became disabused of the illusion that I would ever ascend beyond the level of my social sphere, although I still resented that many men with fewer merits to their name were able to reach the highest ones.[48] I gave up on the many plans that had so encumbered my imagination in previous years. There is much abundance in those islands, and you can especially enjoy those offered by the city of Manila. Whatever you desire for sustenance and raiment is easily available there for a moderate price, due to the solicitude with which the *sangleyes*,[49] eager to enrich themselves, conduct commerce in Parian, this being the place outside the walls where the Spaniards allowed them to settle. These delights, coupled with the city's beautiful and fortified location, and compounded by the amenity of its river, the surrounding gardens, and all the other things which make Manila famous among the colonies[50] that Europeans possess in the Orient, oblige those who live there to live at ease. Trade is ordinarily of the high-seas sort, for which cause navigation crosses back and forth almost continuously, and so I applied myself to the life of a sailor, taking lodging in Cavite.

Through this occupation, I not only trafficked in profitable commerce which promised great returns in the future but also saw many cities and ports in the East Indies on my several voyages.[51] I visited Madrastapatan,[52] which is the ancient city of Calamina or Meliapor where the apostle Saint Thomas[53] died, a great city in Portuguese times, now reduced to ruins from the violent devastation wreaked by the French and Dutch in their attempts to conquer it. I was also in Malacca, the key to all the East Indies and its entire commerce by reason of its position astride the Singapore strait, to whose governor all who navigate it pay an anchorage toll. Of all these places and many more the Dutch are now the owners, and under their yoke the helpless Catholics who are left in those parts suffer much and are not allowed to practice the real religion, while the Moors and gentiles who are Dutch vassals are permitted to carry out their ritual sacrifices.

I visited Batavia, a most famous city which the Dutch possess in Java Major and where the Governor and Captain General representing the States of Holland resides. Batavia's walls, bastions, and fortifications are admirable.[54] The concourse of Malay, Macassar, Sianes [*sic*],[55] *Bugises*,[56] Chinese, Armenian, French, English, Danish, Portuguese, and Castillian ships is innumerable. Any European manufacture may be found in this emporium as well as those which Asia sends back in exchange. And excellent weapons are produced there for anyone who might care to purchase them. I might say to sum up that the entire World is encompassed in this city.[57] I also traveled to Macan,[58] fortified by the Portuguese who still possess it, but its inhabitants are nevertheless not immune to the treacheries of the Tartars, who dominate greater China.

More as a means for my benefit than as an idle pleasure did I engage in these activities, but there were times when I carried out the same tasks in order to obey those who were entitled to command me. It was just such an occasion that set in motion the fateful series of events I now find myself in and which began as follows: we had need of provisions in the presidio at Cavite; General Don Gabriel de Cuzalaegui, who was Governor over all the Philippine Islands,[59] ordered that a single-deck frigate[60] be dispatched to Ilocos Province to fetch them, as was usual from time to time. The men who shipped on this vessel were regular seamen, and I was given command of both her and all twenty-five of them. Out of the Royal Armory I was given *four pikes and two muskets* for the ship's defense, but since the serpentines were broken we needed to keep our fuses constantly lit to be able to shoot the muskets. They also gave me *two handfuls of bullets and five pounds of powder.*

Supplied with these arms and munitions, but without ordnance or mortars, even though my vessel had ports for six pieces, I set sail. It took six days to reach Ilocos, after which we spent nine or ten in trading for and loading the items we needed. Upon the fifth day of our return passage, beating upwind to gain entrance to the Marivelez channel and reach port, around four in the afternoon we spied two vessels on the landward side. I, assuming along with my crew that they were the ships given to Captains Juan Bautista and Juan de Caravallo to go to Pangazinan and Panay to seek rice and other necessaries for the presidio in Cavite and the surrounding area, continued tacking even though they stood to windward of me, under no apprehensions whatsoever, for there was no reason for any.

My state of mind could not but be changed as soon as I beheld, within a short compass of time, two pirogues paddling at full speed toward us, and it gave me an extreme shock to recognize them, upon their close approach, as enemies. I disposed my ship as best I could for defense with my two muskets and four pikes, but bullets began to rain down on us from the shotguns and muskets from the men aboard their pirogues; however, they did not immediately board us, and we answered their shots with our muskets from time to time, one man aiming while the other fired; in the meantime some of us were engaged in cutting our bullets in half with a knife so that, by doubling our munitions, we might prolong our ridiculous resistance. Almost without delay, the two larger vessels which we had seen before and from which the pirogues had been sent[61] came upon us, and we struck our topsail flags and main, requesting to be given quarter just as the fifty Englishmen boarded my frigate with cutlasses drawn; it was all over in a trice. Having made themselves masters of the quarterdeck, they beat us toward the forecastle, celebrating what was left of our stock of guns and ammunition with laughter and jeers. They mocked us even more resoundingly when they found out that the frigate belonged to the King and that the munitions had come from his armory. It was six in the afternoon on the fourth of March in the year 1687.

CHAPTER 3

Wherein are listed the pirates' robberies and cruelties on the
high seas and on land until they reached America

Knowing that I commanded the vessel they had just captured, they transferred
me onto the larger of their two ships, to which their captain welcomed me with
deceitful amiability. The very first words he uttered were a promise of freedom if
I revealed to him the names of the wealthiest places on these islands and whether
he would find that the inhabitants would put up much resistance.[62] I limited my
answer to a confession that I had left Cavite exclusively to travel to the province
of Ilocos—from which I was currently returning directly to Cavite—and thus
would be unable to comply with his request. Not satisfied, he prodded further,
asking whether it would be possible to beach and repair his ships on the island of
Caponiz, which lies from northwest to southeast fourteen leagues from Marivelez,[63] and whether the inhabitants might try to prevent him from landing. I
calmly answered that the island was uninhabited and that I knew of a bay where
he could easily accomplish his desires—my intention being, if they took the bait,
to enable not only the natives of the island but also the Spaniards who garrison
that island [Caponiz] to surprise and capture them. Around 10 o'clock at night
they cast anchors at a location which they deemed suited their purposes and
whiled away the rest of the night by questioning me further along these lines.

Before weighing anchor,[64] the twenty-five men from my ship were brought
on board their principal vessel.[65] An Englishman they called Master Bel governed this ship, which carried eighty men, twenty-four guns, and eight mortars,
all bronze. The owner[66] of their second ship was Captain Donkin, who had

under him seventy men, twenty guns, and eight mortars. Both vessels were well supplied with muskets, cutlasses, axes, grappling irons, grenades, and several cauldrons full of pestiferous ingredients.[67] No matter how many times I tried to figure out which port they had shipped from, I never managed it; I did, however, gather that they had entered the South Seas by way of the Mayre Strait[68] and that their intent of raiding Peru and Chile had been frustrated by a sudden unrelenting storm that bore down on them from the east with remarkable vehemence. Lasting eleven days, it drove them more than 500 leagues from their meridian; so, judging it not easy to go back to the coast, they had taken counsel to make the best of the distance covered and set their course for the East Indies, where plunder was in any case more lucrative. I also discovered that they had spent some time in the Mariana Islands, after which, battling tempests and heavy seas, they had managed to come round Cape Engaño and Cape Boxeador and, after successfully taking several Indian and Chinese junks and sampans[69] as prizes, had happened upon my ship at the mouth of the Marivelez channel.

The following morning the pirates steered their frigates with mine in tow toward Caponiz and proceeded, pistols and broadswords in hand, to renew their interrogation, this time cruelly adding torture to their questioning. They lashed me and one of my companions tight to the main mast, but finding us unwilling to respond to repeated queries about where they might find silver and gold, they grabbed hold of Francisco de la Cruz, another of my companions, who was a *sangley mestizo*,[70] and with unceasingly cruel flogging laid him out unconscious and almost lifeless on the ship's waist. The rest of us were put into the hold, from whence I then heard bloodcurdling cries followed by a blunderbuss shot.[71] A little while later they brought me back up and showed me all the blood that had been spilled, explaining that it came from one of my men whom they had just killed; they warned me that I should expect the same treatment if I did not satisfy all of their questions. In my humblest voice I confessed that they could do with me whatever they wished but that I would add nothing to what I already had told them. From that point on, I took pains to learn which one of my companions had been killed, but, finding the number of my men unchanged, I was puzzled for a long time. Finally, at a later date, I found out by chance that the blood I had seen came from a dog and the deceit was ended.

Unsatisfied with my previous responses, they renewed their attentions by questioning my quartermaster with kid gloves, from whom, because he was an Indian, I never expected anything good would result.[72] Whereas I had told them that Caponiz was uninhabited, he quickly informed them that the island was indeed peopled and garrisoned. This piece of news, buttressed by the fact that we were running along Caponiz and the pirates had already seen two horsemen on the beach, revealed all of my lies, including having stated that I had never left Cavite except for this one voyage to Ilocos and that I had misrepresented what they would find at Caponiz Bay. The shame of having been fooled becoming unbearable, the pirates retaliated by raising a great cry, hurling insults in my face, and coming at me with their broadswords in their hands. I have never been more terrified at the prospect of death than at that very instant. But the sentence was commuted to kicks and blows that rained down on me about the head so badly that I was incapable of moving thereafter for many days. They anchored on the road far from where the islanders might offer them any injury and marooned the Indian owners of one of the junks they had taken as a prize on the day before the fateful occasion of my capture.[73] Then they steered a course for Pulicondon, an island inhabited by Cochin Chinese on the coast of Camboja,[74] where, coming to an anchor, they carried over to their two ships anything of value from my frigate and then set fire to it.

After this, they armed several canoes with men sufficient to land and found—much to their surprise—that the inhabitants received them with open arms. Our captors communicated to them that they simply wanted provisions, a place to careen their vessels, and a chance to barter with them for whatever fruits of the land they might be in need of.[75] From fear, or some other motive unknown to me at the time, the poor barbarians consented to their requests and received clothes which our captors had stolen from previous prizes, in exchange for tar, lard, salted turtle meat, and other such things. It must be due to the lack of shelter on that island or the desire they have to do what in other parts is reserved for private moments, but it is a fact that their nakedness or their curiosity impelled them to commit the most unashamed vice I have ever seen, for mothers would bring daughters and husbands would deliver their own wives, recommending their beauty to the Englishmen in exchange for a cloak or some other equally cheap trinket.[76]

The stay of four months was thus made tolerable for our captors with such a repulsive convenience; however, life for them was not worth living unless they were thieving. So, once their ships were ready, they loaded up all the supplies needed to set sail from the island. But before setting out, they first made counsel to decide on a suitable payment to the Pulicondones for their hospitality; and, setting the payment thereof for the day they headed out to sea, they attacked them in the morning as they lay asleep, unsuspecting, and slit the throats of the very women they had made pregnant. Then they set fire to most of the town and came on board, with flags waving, greatly rejoicing. I was not present at such notorious acts of cruelty, for I was kept always on their flagship,[77] but I feared that I might eventually suffer the same fate as I heard the shots of muskets and witnessed the fires.

It would matter little to sentence this abominable victory to silence had they celebrated it as they usually did, simply emptying bottles of liquor into their gullets;[78] but the final outrage I saw with my own eyes cannot be silenced. I would fail my conscience and would leave myself nothing but pain and unconscionable qualms if I failed to relate it to the reader. Among the booty they brought with them from the town, which included everything the townspeople had received in exchange for their women and articles of trade, they also carried away the human arm of one of the defenders who had perished in the flames. Of this each one cut off a slice, and, praising the taste of such delicate meat, they made short shrift of it while repeatedly wishing each other good health. As I looked on in horror and anguish at such a bestial deed, one of them approached me with a piece and pressed me with badgering gestures to eat it. To my natural repulsion and rejection, he answered: That being Spanish, and consequently cowardly, I had best not be too fussy if I ever wanted to aspire to their courage. But he gave up on importuning me, as another toast drew him away.

On the third day they sighted the coastline of Camboja and, veering continuously from one tack to the other, managed to seize a sampan full of pepper. They did to those who sailed it what they had done to me and, relieving the vessel of its silver and of anything it carried of value, ignoring its cargo of pepper, they removed its rudder and sails and, in order to destroy it, pointed it away and set it adrift. The people of this sampan they cast ashore on the mainland, then drew near the uninhabited island of Puliubi,[79] where coconuts and yams are to be found in abundance.[80] Secure in the knowledge that there was no way for my men or me to escape from this place, they took us out of the ships to work on splicing a cable. The material from which we made the splice was a green rattan;[81] their insistence that we finish it in a short number of days was the cause of our almost having lost the use of our hands for many more.

They took great prizes at this place, though they were only three in number; one of them belonged to the King of Siam and the other two to the Portuguese in Macan[82] and Goa. Aboard the first of these ships traveled the King's ambassador to the Manila Governor, carrying priceless jewels and many fruits as well as precious goods of that country. The latter were of greater interest than the former, as they amounted to nothing less than extremely rich Chinese silks and a quantity of gold filigree,[83] which they typically were sending to Europe via Goa. The third vessel belonged to the Viceroy in Goa, and in command was an ambassador he was sending to the King of Siam for the following reason.

A Genoese individual—the circumstances of whose presence in that country I do not know—managed not only to become a favorite of the King of Siam but also to be named his royal representative[84] in the principal port. Becoming over-proud with such high titles, this Genoese had the hands of two Portuguese gentlemen living there cut off for a minor offense. The Viceroy in Goa had been informed and was now requesting satisfaction, even asking that the Genoese be turned over to him for punishment. Because a demand such as this one exceeded the bounds of probability, the gift mentioned before was being sent to garner the King's goodwill. I myself saw and touched it; it was in the shape of a tower or castle, a fathom long, made of pure gold embedded with diamonds and other precious stones. Although not as valuable, the other objects were equally marvelous: silver jewelry, quantities of camphor, amber, and musk, not taking into account the rest of the ship's cargo intended for trade or sale.[85]

Once this last ship was unburdened of its cargo—and the others of theirs— the pirates set them all ablaze, marooning Portuguese as well as Siamese and eight of my men on that deserted isle. They then set sail for the islands of Ciantan,[86] inhabited by Malays who clothe themselves only to the waist and carry krisses as weapons.[87] They traded with them for some goats, coconuts, and the oil which is used for *lantia*[88] and other refreshments and then set upon these unfortunate barbarians and raided them. Having killed some and robbed all, they veered, bearing off out to sea in search of Tamburlan island,[89] in which people of the Macassar nation dwell. Not finding there what they had elsewhere, however, the Englishmen set fire to their houses while the inhabitants slept and then proceeded to set sail toward the large island of Borney,[90] but they made little headway, tacking for fourteen days to the windward along the west coast, and found nothing to pillage until they approached the port of Cicudana[91] on said island.

There are many gems in the land surrounding this place, especially diamonds of brilliant depth. It happened that not many months before we arrived greed to trade for and acquire some of these diamonds inspired the English who live in India to request from the King of Borney—in the person of his Governor in Cicudana—permission to build a factory in that location.[92] When the pirates arrived, they sounded the river's bar in pirogues with a view to bringing their larger vessels into the channel while reconnoitering the locale for potential prey.

In this they were interrupted by a local sampan from landward, sent by the Governor to inspect them, but they answered that they were Englishmen come to trade their cargo of exquisite and worthy merchandise for diamonds. The pirates were granted a commercial license by the local authorities, who trusted in the previous experience of friendly relations that they had enjoyed with this nation and in the evidence before their eyes, that is, the samples of rich wares which the pirates had taken off their Puliubi prizes. In exchange for a considerable gift to the Governor, the pirates received permission to travel up the river to the town, a distance from the marina of a quarter of a league, whenever they pleased.

The three days we were there were sufficient to confirm that the town was undefended and open in all directions, and so they proposed to the Cicudana townspeople that they should gather whatever diamonds they wanted to exchange in the Governor's mansion, where they intended on holding the trade fair, alleging that they could not be detained for too long. Leaving us prisoners on board with guards sufficient to the purpose, on the midnight hour they ascended the river, well armed, and came suddenly into the town, going directly to the Governor's mansion. They sacked it of all the diamonds they could find, as well as other precious stones gathered there, and proceeded to do likewise to many other houses before setting fire to them in addition to several boats they found. On board the ship we could hear the screams and musket fire from the town. Afterward they brazenly boasted of the slaughter; this execrable treason was accomplished with little risk to themselves. Dragging the Governor and other principal citizens along as captives, they came on board with great hurry, raised the anchor, and set sail seaward with great speed.[93]

No pillaging ever compared to this one either in the ease of execution or in the exceeding value of the prizes it gave them. Who knows how much it amounted to? I myself witnessed Captain Bel heaping the hollow of his hat full *just with diamonds*. We came to the island of Baturiñan[94] after six days' sailing but abandoned it as worthless and eventually came to a mooring on Pulitiman,[95] where we took on water and wood. Here they marooned the Governor and principal citizens of Cicudana, who had suffered great mistreatment and hunger, and then veered their course toward the coast of Bengala,[96] spurred on by the greater number of vessels in those waters; and indeed in a few days' time they took two large ships belonging to black Moors,[97] loaded with damasks,[98] elephant tusks, gauzes, and *sarampares*.[99] Stripping the ships of the most precious of these items and setting them ablaze, they cut down some of the Moors in cold blood and left the rest to fend for themselves on the small boats from their own ships.

Until now the pirates had not encountered any man-of-war capable of opposing them, but it was at this place that they espied four men-of-war, Dutch in appearance, well provisioned with ordnance, an event occasioned either by the contingency of chance or by the spreading of news concerning such notorious robbers to the places from whence, I assume, these ships had been sent out to punish them. The men-of-war made way to leeward while the pirates tried to keep the weather gauge as much as possible until finally, aided by the approaching darkness of night, the pirates escaped by altering course and made land on Pulilaor,[100] where they took on provisions and water. But they no longer considered themselves to be safe in any port, fearful that the incalculable wealth in their possession might be taken from them, and so determined to leave the archipelago.

In doubt over whether it was best to disembogue[101] through the straits of Sunda or Sincapura,[102] they chose the latter as being closer to their position, though it made for far more difficult and treacherous sailing and the former was a shorter and easier transit; in truth, Sunda was much more frequented by men-of-war going to and from the new Batavia, as mentioned earlier.[103] Trusting to a local pilot they already had on board with them and depending on the aid of breezes and currents—not to mention the immeasurable assistance of the Dutch flags they flew—the pirates waited for a night that would be dark enough and entered into the strait with desperate resolution and with arms at the ready. They ran it almost completely without coming upon any vessels other than a lone ship on the second day, a frigate of sixty-two feet along the keel[104] carrying rice and a fruit they call *bonga*.[105] In keeping with their thieving customs, even when fleeing, the pirates attacked her, at which point the Malay sailors immediately jumped overboard and swam off, reaching land and thus saving their lives.

The pirates rejoiced upon the occasion of acquiring another vessel that would alleviate the heavy burden of their cargo. They immediately transferred seven people with all their arms and ten pieces of ordnance with all requisite tools and munitions from each of their ships into the new one.[106] They then continued on their way and came out of the strait around five in the afternoon on that very same day. At that moment five of my men disappeared; I presume that, availing themselves of the proximity of land, they gained their liberty by swimming to it.[107] After twenty-five days of voyaging we sighted an island (whose name I do not recall). Because it was inhabited by Portuguese, as they thought or presumed,[108] we avoided it and from thence set course for New Holland, a territory which has not been sufficiently discovered by Europeans and still belongs, apparently, to barbarians. At length, after more than three months' sailing, we came upon it.[109]

Those sent to land in pirogues disembarked on the coast and found signs of people having once lived at this location, but the winds were contrary and vehement and the roadstead wild, so more commodious mooring was sought. It was found on a flat island which provided not only a sea-break and shelter from the wind for the ships but a creek of good sweet water, many turtles, and no people, and so they determined to careen their ships there in order to make their way homeward after a while. They occupied themselves in this task while my men and I mended sails and made jerky.[110] Roughly four months later, or a bit longer, we were ready to make for the sea again, and so we stood to sea for the island of Madagascar, or San Lorenzo, twenty-eight days in the offing, and running before fresh east winds made our way there. Trade with the blacks who live there brought in many chickens, goats, and cattle; and, having received notice that an English merchantman was expected in port at any time to engage in commerce with the blacks, they decided to wait for it and did so.[111]

It turned out, however, that my inference from their actions and discussions was wrong and that they intended to try to capture it. As the vessel came to an anchor, it became clear that it was too well prepared with artillery and sufficient men, and so welcoming salvos were shot repeatedly on both sides and there was reciprocal amity. The merchants gave the pirates spirits[112] and wine, and they corresponded with an abundance of things selected from the many articles they had stolen. Despite not being able forcibly to take possession of the merchantman, Captain Bel made all diligence to this effect in whatever way possible; Bel's skills in thieving and avarice, however, were matched by the merchantman captain's vigilance and sagacity, and thus he never came aboard our ships, notwithstanding the insistence with which invitations aimed to accomplish this very trick were proffered. Rejecting all of them, the merchant captain never acted except with the greatest care possible. No less care was taken by Bel and Donkin to conceal from the merchants that they had gone "on the account,"[113] and to achieve this end with greater security they commanded my men and myself, of whom alone they were suspicious, on pain of death not to speak with any of the men on the merchantman and, if spoken to, to say that we were voluntary sailors and members of the crew, regularly paid. Two of my companions contravened this order by speaking to a Portuguese who came with these merchants, but the pirates showed mercy in sentencing them not to death but rather to receive four lashes from each crew member. As there were one hundred and fifty men, the number of lashes amounted in the end to nine hundred;[114] furthermore, they used a special whip and applied it with such violence that all four poor souls were dead by dawn on the following day.

They attempted to leave me and the few companions I had left from my company on that island. But, considering the barbarity of the black Moors that lived there, I got down on my knees and, kissing their feet in great submission, reminded them of the many labors I had endured in their service. Offering to assist them on their voyage as if I was a slave, I managed to have them take me with them when they left. As they had many times before, they proposed that I take an oath to join them forever, in which case they would give me arms.[115] I thanked them for their graciousness; but thinking upon the obligations of my birth, I responded with feigned humility that I would settle much more willingly into a life of serving them than into one of fighting others, for, I explained, I had a great fear of being shot. Thereupon they began to jeer at my being a Spanish coward and chicken and not worthy of being part of their company, which would honor and raise me to too high a level, and so gave up on importuning me any longer.

The pirates took their leave of the merchants, charged their ships with the needed provisions, and stood to sea, making for the Cape of Good Hope on the African coast. After two months of sailing, the first five days of which they had to spend beating to windward, they rounded the cape. From thence we coasted an extensive parcel of mainland for a month and a half until we arrived on an island which they call the Island of Rocks,[116] where we took on water and wood, after which, setting our course westward and making good headway reaching with a large wind,[117] we raised the coast of Brasil in twenty-five days. We sailed the length of the coast, tacking and diminishing our distance from the line, during which period of two weeks they twice sent six men in a canoe to land who spoke with some Portuguese—I do not know who they were—and traded with them for refreshments. This course lasted until at last they came to an extremely wide river at whose mouth they anchored in five fathoms, a body of water which, I presume, was the Amazon, if I am not much mistaken.[118]

CHAPTER 4

He is given his freedom by the pirates and remembers
his sufferings while imprisoned

I should note, before recounting what I endured and suffered, working and undergoing much hardship over the course of so many years, that in all that time I experienced compassion and solace from my constant travails only in the persons of Master Gunner[119] Nicpat and Dick, the quartermaster for Captain Bel, who both helped me materially in moments of extreme necessity behind their mates' backs and proffered kind words encouraging me to be patient.[120] I am convinced the Master Gunner was Catholic. Having set up a counsel at this place, the pirates' discussion revolved around no other topic than what they were to do with me and the seven companions left from my crew. They voted, and the majority were for cutting our throats, while others, not as cruel, cast their vote for marooning. The Master Gunner, the Quartermaster, and Captain Donkin and his immediate mates[121] were all opposed to both groups' plans, reproaching the crew for conceiving of actions so unworthy of English generosity.[122]

"It is enough," the latter noted, "that we have become degenerate, robbing the Orient of its best, in unholy ways. Are not the many innocents, the fruits of whose sweat and toil we took, and whose lives we stole, not clamoring to the Heavens? Think now, what has this poor Spaniard done to deserve losing his? He has served us as a slave, grateful even for what we have done with him since his capture. To leave him on this river where, I believe, only barbarous Indians live is ingratitude; to cut his throat, as some of you advise, would be worse than impiety. Lest his innocent blood cry out to the entire world, I and those who stand with me are now prepared to become their protectors."[123] The dispute raged on until they were ready to take up arms against each other in order to decide the matter, but just then it was resolved that they would give me the frigate that they had taken in the strait of Syncapura, and with the ship freedom, so that I might dispose of myself and my companions as I thought best. I, being a eyewitness to all these goings-on, ask readers to imagine themselves in my place and ponder how altered my mind became with fear and how afflicted my spirits with despair.

Emptied of all its contents, which were transferred into their holds, the frigate[124] now became mine, but I was required to express my gratitude to each individual member of the pirate crew for the compassion they were showing me and for the liberty they were granting, which requirement I duly carried out. They gave me, besides the ship, an astrolabe, a compass, a Dutch waggoner,[125] only one vat of water,[126] and a rice sack, two-thirds full. When, however, the Master Gunner embraced me in a farewell gesture, he whispered that he had hidden on my frigate a bit of salt, some cured beef, four barrels of powder, a good supply of cannon shot, a medicine box, and diverse other useful things, without telling any of his mates. Finally, they enjoined on me threateningly (jotting down the names of eyewitnesses) that if they should ever catch me again upon that coast they would immediately put me to death, saving God's own intervention in my favor, and that, to avoid this end, I should put my helm steady on a course between west and northwest, where I would without fail come upon Spaniards who might aid me. Thereupon they made me weigh anchor, wished me a speedy voyage—all the while mocking and jeering at me—and let me go.

Let me praise all those who seek liberty, even when they might lose their lives in pursuing it, for it is the only thing worthy of our esteem, though we be but brute animals. Such an unexpected and happy event immediately set free copious tears from all our eyes, and I judge that my companions and I now felt them running down our faces with the greater pleasure precisely because we had repressed them for so long in our hidden pains. An unforeseen joy will often in normal life impede our ability to comprehend it, and so it happened with us at that point, for we felt it was all a dream: it took us much reflection before we could openly believe that we were truly free. And then our immediate action was to raise our voices in united gratitude to Heaven, exalting divine compassion at the top of our voices to the best of our abilities, remembering also to thank the one being who had been our lone guiding star in that immense ocean full of so many trying storms. For I believe my liberty would not have been possible had I not kept continuously in my memory and affection Our Most Holy Mary of Guadalupe of Mexico, whose indebted slave I declare I will always remain.[127] I have, throughout my life, carried her portrait with me, and so when I was captured I greatly feared that the heretic pirates would profane her, given the way they had violently torn rosaries from our necks and, swearing at us for our heathenish superstition, cast them into the water; as best I could I managed to conceal her from their sight and on the first occasion when I was sent aloft to the masthead I hid her there.[128]

Here are the names of those from the original twenty-five in my company who were freed at this place, excepting the eight who were marooned on the deserted island of Puliubi, five who fled in Syncapura, two dead by lashing in Madagascar, and another three who suffered the same fate on different occasions: Juan de Casas, a Spaniard born in Puebla de los Angeles in New Spain;[129] Juan Pinto and Marcos de la Cruz, the former a Pangasinan Indian and the latter a Pampanpango Indian;[130] Francisco de la Cruz and Antonio Gonzalez, *sangleyes*; Juan Diaz, a Malabar Indian;[131] and Pedro, a black boy from Mozambique who was my slave.[132] Following quickly on the tears of happiness caused by our freedom came tears which might have been made of blood, heartfelt expressions stemming from the instant anguish evoked by inescapably casting our minds onto the memory of our past travails,[133] which I sum up in the following.

In addition to the threats with which they menaced us on the isle of Caponiz in order to extract confessions which might give them the information they sought concerning the vessels set to sail from Manila, whether they were well armed, and which locales were the richest, they added the injury of almost breaking our fingers by placing them in the matchlocks of their carbines and guns. Afterward, needing to make candles and paying no heed to the stains that the blood streaming from our fingers caused, they forced us to form balls of cotton thread out of the tangled masses they had on board. This exercise became a regular feature of our shipboard life throughout our voyage whenever candles were needed, and every day we were set to scrubbing and swabbing the decks and hulls, inside and out. We were never allowed to be absent from these labors for any reason. Another of our commonly assigned tasks was to clean the cutlasses, cannons, and carbine matchlocks with Chinese ceramic shards, ground every three days. At other times we were put to twisting ropes, making sheets, halyards,[134] and counter-braces as well as turning rope-yarns into cables, robands, and anchor-seizing lines.[135] They added to our work at times by putting us at the helm and at others by having us hull their rice, a meal they ate continuously, soaking it first and then making it into flour.[136] There were occasions when each one of us was given a day to clean eleven fifty-pound sacks[137] of rice, failing which we many times had to put up with the whippings they meted out as punishment.

Never during the storms we experienced on this lengthy voyage did they themselves reef the sails, for we were always the ones sent above, the lash being the ordinary reward we earned for exposing ourselves to such cruel dangers, either for not having accomplished the task quickly enough or because the sails ripped, a not altogether uncommon accident in such circumstances. The only sustenance afforded us as a group in these constant labors to ensure that our strength would not fail was a paltry *ganta* of rice, which is about one *almud*'s worth,[138] which we parboiled in whatever manner we could manage, using seawater in place of salt—which they had in abundance but never gave us. A little less than a pint of fresh water was shared out to each man every day. None of their victuals, whether it be meat, wine, spirits, *bonga*, or anything else, reached our mouths, and even though they had an endless supply of coconuts they would only throw us the dry shells with which they intended for us to make *bonote* for them, which is formed by cleaning and preparing the coconut shell fibers like oakum to caulk the ship's seams;[139] when at anchor, they used to take the fresh coconuts, drink their milk, and then toss them into the sea before our very eyes.

In the last year of our imprisonment, they put us in charge of the galley, in which activity they ensured that every piece of meat given to us was counted and individually weighed so that we would not eat any of it: a miserly, noteworthy piece of cruelty on their part, but incomparable to the following example! They occupied us also in fashioning sailcloth shoes and sewing shirts and undergarments for them, for which they made sure they gave us only precut, premeasured filaments of thread. If we should ever miss a backstitch, which they always wanted done very close together, we got twenty-five lashes for each stitch that had to be redone. They forced one job on me from which my companions were excepted: becoming ship's barber. They kept me at this barbering every Saturday without fail or rest of even the smallest duration during the entire day, and for every time I misapplied the razor—a not infrequent occurrence given my lack of scientific knowledge of how to handle it—I was slapped and cudgeled mercilessly. Everything I have related so far of our life happened while we were aboard, for we were never allowed to land saving on two occasions, on Puliubi and on the deserted island off New Holland, where they sent us ashore to fetch water and wood and to fashion a new cable from reeds.[140]

If I were to enlarge upon the particulars of our experiences, I would extend the discourse overly, while offering one or two examples will enable the reader to fill in what I keep quiet. Of all the weekdays, we feared Monday the most, because it was then that they would make a circle of reeds[141] around the mizzenmast, tying our left hands to it, placing in our right hands short whips, and removing our clothing, after which they would place their daggers and pistols on our chests and force us to lash each other. Throughout this torture, the humiliation and agony we felt doing this was matched stroke by stroke by the applause and rejoicing with which they celebrated it.

Once my comrade Juan de la Cosa became indisposed and was incapable of performing the onerous duties weighing us down. Captain Bel attributed this to what he termed "a flux or distemper,"[142] for which he said he had a very simple cure. I beg pardon of the reader for the lack of respect and decency in what I am about to relate, but the Captain's cure was nothing other than, first, to have his own excrement dissolved in water and then, second, to have it offered to Juan as a drink at knife point, an encouragement meant to indicate that refusal would accelerate the arrival of his death. But, though such an unheard-of medicine caused Juan to be disgusted and vomit repeatedly, by chance he subsequently recovered his health; from that point on it was prescribed to all of us, to the great cheers of the pirate crew, whenever we should to our great misfortune become ill.

I endured all of these things for the love I bore my life, lamenting on the many occasions when they spent the entire day drunk that I had not a larger party of men to avail myself of, who could slaughter the pirates and run away with the frigate, escaping back to Manila.[143] But in any case I could not put my trust in the men I did have, for there was only one other Spaniard, Juan de Casas, amongst them. One day when I found myself incapable of doing anything by reason of absentmindedly musing on these thoughts, an Englishman by the name of Cornelio came up to me and, having spent many words on me enjoining complete confidentiality, proceeded to sound out whether I had enough courage to help him with my men in a mutiny. Fearing a trap, I was loath to answer but did so cautiously,[144] at which point he assured me that several of his mates, whose names he provided, were already with him on this venture, which news convinced me to say he could count on me when it came time, but not without first making a pact with him for those measures that I believed would ensure my own security.

Far from being entrapment, I maintain that Cornelio's plans were sincerely stated, and indeed I think not a few of his messmates were applauding his efforts; but in the long run, and for motives I was never party to, he desisted from carrying them out. I became persuaded in the end, however, that it was he who intimated to Captain Bel that my men and I were planning to kill him, because from that moment on they began to live with greater vigilance, training two loaded ordnance pieces on the fo'c'sle, our place on the ship,[145] as well as proceeding cautiously in all of their actions. These precautions did not fail to worry me greatly and, upon asking Master Gunner Nicpat, my patron[146] aboard, the cause thereof, he answered nothing but that we should all look to ourselves when sleeping. Cursing the day I ever listened to Cornelio, I prepared myself as best I could for death. That same night, they tied me roughly to the mizzenmast and began to torment me so that I would confess the strategies with which I was disposing to seize the ship. I denied all of this with as much conviction as I could muster, but I attribute it to the Master Gunner's persuasions that they eventually stopped tormenting me; after this he approached me and assured me that I would not be in danger if I confided in him. I revealed to him everything I knew, and he then untied me and led me to the Captain's cabin.

Kneeling before Captain Bel, I narrated all the plans that Cornelio had proposed, the news of which caused him great terror and prompted him to demand that I swear to the truth of the matter as related while at the same time he threatened me with punishments for not having told him beforehand. The Captain's charges of treason and sedition reduced me to begging him in tearful supplications for mercy, to which Master Gunner Nicpat added his humble entreaties;[147] together, our requests absolved me of the charges, but the Captain made it a condition of sparing me that I promise to keep the entire matter secret on pain of death. Not long afterward, they laid hands on Cornelio and his mates and sentenced them for their mutinous plans to such a violent whipping that I doubt not the memory of it will stay with them for the rest of their lives; they were warned to stay away from me and my men on pain of the same punishments— and even worse. I saw proof of the wide-reaching benefits of this lashing in the actions of one of the "patients" treated in this way, whose name was Enrique: he immediately took his share of their prizes, in silver, gold, and diamonds and, perhaps suspecting that this sentence might be imposed on him again, jumped ship on the island of San Lorenzo.[148] All of Captain Bel's attempts to recover him failed.

A deduction[149] that one might draw from these facts—and indeed it is inevitable—is that in cruelty and abominations these pirates could compete with any of the men whose names appear at the top of the roster for excelling in the exercise of this particular profession, but I suspect that the evil of their manner in treating us was increased by the presence of a *Spaniard* in their company, a native of *Seville* whose name was *Miguel*. No intolerable task[150] given to us, no occasion for mistreatment or hunger enforced on us, no danger to life sent our way ever came without his having had a hand in planning and executing it. He gloried in how these acts boldly pronounced to the world his godlessness, his abandonment of his native Catholic faith, and his commitment to living a pirate and dying a heretic. It pained me most—and my company as well—when he would join the Englishmen in praying and reading from their books on their feast days, which were every Sunday in the calendar and Christmas. May God grant him the enlightenment he needs to correct his life and merit the Lord's forgiveness for all the iniquities of his actions.[151]

CHAPTER 5

Alonso Ramirez and his companions sail with no clear knowledge of their
initial location or of their ultimate destination; their struggles[152] and
anxieties until the moment their boat ran aground are described

Enough of these laborious miseries, for merely as written words they are too
much to bear; let us go on to other, different labors.[153] Neither I nor any of my
companions knew where we were or what the outcome of our voyage might be,
for I could not understand the Dutch waggoner and did not have a chart which,
amidst the great confusion which afflicted us, might serve a practical purpose,
since none of us had any experience of the place where we now found ourselves.
Pondering all of this, and mindful of the warning the pirates had given that they
would kill us if they captured us a second time, I stood out to sea westward.[154]
After six days of keeping a steady course, we sighted dry land which seemed to
belong to the mainland, given its breadth and height, and so I set the helm west-
northwest and on the following day, about dawn, came upon three islands of
little consequence. Accompanied by Juan de Casas, I took a small canoe[155] which
was aboard the frigate and set out for one of them, where we found scrub fowl[156]
and booby birds,[157] many of which we captured and took back to the ship to cure
for food.

We coasted close to land for ten days and discovered another island[158] at six in
the morning which appeared to be quite large. At that very moment we caught
sight of a large fleet of men-of-war, up to twenty vessels, it seemed, of various
rates, and setting course toward us they hoisted English colors and hailed my
ship by firing off one of their cannons. I began to doubt I could round the island in time, and considering how they might not believe my story if they came

aboard and saw so many English articles on my frigate, I reached the conclusion that they would presume I had killed her owners and taken possession of her and was now sailing those seas as a fugitive. A storm was then drawing near at the time, so I took it to be sent by God for my escape and had the topsails unfurled, commanded all sails be set and trimmed—something that none of the English warships dared do in those conditions—and took over steering personally; I finally managed to escape, setting the helm on a north course and making way for the rest of the day and that night without any change in direction.

The next day I veered westward to my original course and on the following day brought her head about to the east, where I reached an island.[159] As we came near it, a canoe approached us, manned by six men intent on examining us; but as soon as they knew we were Spanish and we realized they were English, a cold sweat coursed through our bodies, and we determined to die first of hunger among the waves rather than expose ourselves to suffer any more of their impious acts. They said to us that if we wanted to trade with them we would find that they had brown sugar, tobacco, and other good articles for commerce. I responded that this was indeed what we intended on doing but that it was too late for us to find a good anchorage and that we were going to have to heave to and ride the waves for the night and come into port on the following day. Accepting our pretext, they departed: I, without delay, set the helm to the east and headed out into the open sea.

Ignorant of these parts and persuaded we would find only Englishmen wherever we landed, my companions and I became inconsolable, all the more so upon seeing how our victuals were being quickly depleted and how we would have been absolutely without water had it not been for the occasional showers from which we collected water. I ran east, as mentioned above, and then northeast by east for three days, veering course northwest afterward, and keeping the helm steady for six straight days I came to a tall, wide island. Upon reaching it, I began heading in to explore it along a point that stretches out east into the sea when a launch with seven men made its way out from the island in our direction. Once they knew from me that I was a Spaniard seeking water and wood and some rations, they told me that the said island was called Guadalupe[160] and was settled by the French, whose Governor would grant me leave without any reservations to take on whatever provisions were necessary, and if I wanted to I could engage in commerce, as often Spaniards did who arrived on that island.[161] I answered that I did want to anchor there but that I did not know how, lacking a chart or pilot to guide me, and requested they inform me what part of the world we now found ourselves in; but hearing this question caused them to become violently alarmed, and they began to insist I tell them from whence I had sailed and where I was bound for. I immediately regretted ever having asked them for our bearings and without proffering a reply to their queries bade them farewell.

Let not the gentle reader be astounded at our ignorance concerning these islands, for having left my homeland[162] at an early age I never knew which islands lay near it or any of their names (nor did I ever take any pains to gather this information later in life); there was even less reason to expect Juan de Casas to be familiar with these islands, being a native of Puebla in the mediterranean[163] part of New Spain; the origin of the rest of my companions in Oriental India argued even more strongly against their having any applicable knowledge, since they do not need information about these seas in those parts. Notwithstanding all this, I presumed with confidence that we were now upon some part of America.[164]

Before setting sail away from that island, though, I proposed to my companions the following: that it seemed to me impossible now to go on as before, for we could no longer tolerate continuous travails which sapped our strength and brought us hunger. Finding ourselves as we did at that point with almost no food, and given that the French were Catholic, we should come to anchor, I said, and ride fast by their island as they had offered, putting our trust in their mercy, in the sure knowledge that the narrative of our misfortunes would constrain them to Christian charity and compel them to become our protectors. My companions, however, were greatly opposed to my reasoning and rejected it vehemently and, addressing themselves to the color of their skin and the fact that they were not Spaniards,[165] argued that they would be made slaves upon the instant and pledged it would pain them less to be sent headlong into the ocean by my hands than to place themselves into those of foreigners and endure their mistreatment.

So as not to plunge them further into grief, feeling less my own disconsolate state of mind than theirs, I steered away northward all day and on the following bore off north-northeast, at the end of which course in three days' time I sighted an island.[166] Rounding it on its south side, I sailed between it and another island[167] to the larboard, and after two days sailing northwest and west-northwest I found myself surrounded by islets set between two larger islands.[168] I expended great care in the navigation of an exit from this place, made difficult by the heavy seas and the high winds; but running west with only the foresail set for three days, I discovered a great island, tall and mountainous.[169] Unfortunately, at dawn our frigate stood six leagues leeward and to the south of this island, and, though I altered course northwest and set the ship a-yawing,[170] the weather never allowed me to reach it. We spent more or less another three days without succeeding in gaining this island, but I sighted two small islands to the southwest,[171] whereupon I brought the tiller round in their direction. But after one uneventful day's sail during which we could not make land, we cut our losses and headed northwest again. On the second day's leg of this course I discovered and approached a large island,[172] on which I saw, as much as our distance from it allowed, a harbor[173] with a few beached canoes[174] and many larger vessels moored within it.

Just then I caught sight of two ketches[175] with English colors making their way seaward in order to intercept and inspect my frigate, so I took in my sails, laid my ship by the lee, and awaited their arrival. However, this action, or perhaps some other motive of theirs, caused them not to dare to draw too near me; and thereafter they retired to their port. Thereupon I set sail again on the same course as I had before, but to round a headland on our bow I put the helm round to the south and standing off quite a way to sea came about west and west-northwest until in the course of two and a half days' voyage I reached an island five or six leagues in length but very flat,[176] from which a ketch flying an English flag came out to see me. I hove to and again furled my sails, but the ketch gained the weather gauge on us and reconnoitered behind our stern, then slowly proceeded to draw away toward the island. I hailed her by firing blank shot, but she paid us no attention. You may attribute my lack of determination in not landing on this island or entering the port on the previous occasion to the pitiful petitions and tears of my companions, who, the instant they saw anything having to do with Englishmen, lost their resolve and began to shake ceaselessly like victims of mercurial poisoning.[177]

I began to feel sickened by my own indecisiveness and vowed never again to acquiesce to their pleas. Considering that we ate nothing but what we managed to fish out of the ocean and relied on water provisions amounting to but a small barrel and two earthen jars, I concluded to head for land directly and come to an anchor, no matter whether the inhabitants were English or otherwise. To this end I steered west and west-southwest, the eighth day of which course at eight in the morning marked the beginning of the end of our pointless, aimless voyage—for it was at that point that suddenly and before I knew it I saw rocks along a very extensive sandbank dead ahead,[178] the sight of which gave me a fright that I concealed as best I could from the rest of the crew. Coming about somehow on this lee shore and sailing alongside it for a while, I finally managed to cross through a break in the reef,[179] despite which accomplishment there was no prospect of land until five o'clock in the afternoon. Seeing how dangerously near it we had come—for it was extremely low-lying land and we had not been able to foresee it though it was extensive—I sent a man to the top before night fell to keep an eye out for any more shallows we might have to guard ourselves from and kept us tacking for the rest of the day until we came to an anchor just after sunset in four fathoms of water on a rocky bottom. We put out one kedge anchor because we had no other but played it out with a piece of hemp cable ten fathoms long spliced to[180] a sixty-fathom length of hawser made from reeds, the very same rope we had fashioned long before in Puliubi; having considered this anchor—it was more a four-fluke grappling hook than a proper anchor[181]—I came to the conclusion that it was too light and rather more suitable for a barge than for a ship, so I shoed a piece of ordnance onto it and hitched it up with a fifty-fathom *guamutil* cable.[182] As night darkened the wind began to freshen and then stiffened into a strong steady gale, which just after five in the morning, and no doubt because we were riding on a rocky bottom, caused the cables to snap.

Sensing the ship was lost, I clapped on as much cloth as her yards would bear in the hope that I might steer clear of a point of land I saw lay ahead, but the current came on so furious and powerful that it allowed us neither the time nor the place to close-haul the ship away from the lee shore, and she began more and more to fall off, not answering to the helm and drifting leeward until in the end we ran aground on some rocks[183] on the very same point of land. As the sea stormed about us, our ship struck so horribly against the rocks that I sensed my companions were defeated, and even I, who had so recently looked forward anxiously to touching land anywhere, felt at a loss about what to do next, for we had no ship's boat to launch that would survive these waters. The waves crashed continuously, not only over the rocks round the point we had run aground on but also dreadfully on a coastline farther away which we could just make out, and with every roaring wave that heaved the ship with it onto the rocks came the horrible image of the abyss opening wide and swallowing us up whole. Knowing full well at that moment that indecision meant extreme peril, I began spouting feverish prayers of contrition in the hope that the sacrifice I was about to make of my life for the lives of my poor companions would merit God's mercy; I tied a thin line around my middle for them to pay out and threw myself into the ocean. God granting me His pity, I struggled onto shore and tied the line there. Turning around, I succeeded in using the rope as a lifeline for those who did not know how to swim, for it convinced them that the crossing was not as difficult as the image which fear had put in their mind's eye, at the end of which just past the middle of the afternoon they were all safe, though not before two almost drowned.

CHAPTER 6

The trials of thirst, hunger, illness, and death that hounded them on this coast;
unexpectedly they come upon Catholic people and come to realize
that they are on mainland Yucatan in North America

The rocky expanse we had alighted on at the end of this point of land was some
two hundred paces long. But it was surrounded on all sides by the sea, and its waters from time to time would violently wash over it, lashing the rocky headland
from stem to stern and beating down on us with great strength. There was not
a tree on it, nor anything that might furnish us with protection against a wind
which blew vehemently and wildly about us, so, despairing and persuaded that
we would never leave this place, we each one begged God repeatedly and made
Him promises and thus spent the night. The wind did not abate but continued
howling for three days until it finally died down and the seas following it began
to calm as well. However, the morning after [our shipwreck] we realized how
close the mainland lay to us, so we crossed over to it,[184] a matter of a hundred
paces or so from our rocky landing, the water being nowhere deeper than our
waists. We were all deadly thirsty, but there was no fresh water to be had anywhere we looked. After pondering over this dilemma for a while I decided not to
think about the risks but rather only the convenience and relief of those miserable souls and go aboard our vessel again. I commended myself with all my heart
to Our Most Holy Mary of Guadalupe, jumped in the sea, and swam up to the
ship, from which I returned with an axe to cut wood and the necessaries for making fire. I made a second trip afterward, shoving a small barrel of water along on
the way back, which miraculously made it onto the beach without breaking. Not

daring to make a third crossing to the ship that day, we all quenched our burning thirst, after which I instructed the strongest amongst our party to cut down some of the palm trees that were strewn about the place so that we might eat the palm hearts. A fire having then been lit, we bedded down for the night.

The next morning we found puddles of fresh water, though somewhat brackish, in between the palm trees. While our companions celebrated making this find, Juan de Casas and I went over to the ship, from which we extracted the flat-bottomed canoe[185] we kept there and, with the constant threat of high seas and strong winds, took down the foretopsail, the two foresails, the mainsail, and a few other pieces and brought them all out onto the beach. Additionally we took from the hold guns, powder and shot, and whatever else appeared to us as a necessary protection against any occurrence.

Having rough-built a cabin which covered all our heads in comfort, we did not know in which direction to start walking to look for people, so I chose at random a southerly route. Juan de Casas accompanied me as we walked for about four leagues that day before coming upon four wild pigs, which we promptly killed; but thinking it unpardonable to let so much meat go to waste in our collective necessity, we loaded them up and carried them back to the camp for our comrades to have a share in. Consequently, the next morning we had to redo the previous day's walk, eventually reaching a saltwater river, the width and depth of whose exit into the sea was such that it put an end to our progress, but not before we discovered several very old run-down shelters made from straw that persuaded us we would come upon people soon. However, four days of effort made it clear to us that it was impossible to continue across the river, and we made our way back to the camp in dour spirits.

Upon our return, I realized that my companions' afflictions were worse than mine, for the puddles they relied on for water were dwindling, and I found that all of their bodies were swelling, as if they were suffering from dropsy.[186] Two days later our provision of water ran out; and though we were driven ceaselessly by our need to search for more for five days, the bitterness of what we did find exceeded even the seawater's. By the night of the fifth day we all lay prostrate on the ground. We asked—more by our expressions than with words, for we could not articulate any—our Most Holy Virgin of Guadalupe, since she is an eternal spring of hope for those devoted to her, to look down on us compassionately as death's agonies began to pain us and to come to our aid as her children, pledging that if our lives were to receive such a boon we would always keep her in our memories in gratitude. You, my beloved Mother and Lady, know that this is a true narrative of what happened. Before this prayer was done, a storm brewing to the southwest came upon us and delivered a rain so intense that it filled our bodies with cold numbness, but in like measure it filled our canoe and our cups and every receptacle we owned full to overflowing and thus saved our lives.

Our location was desolate and waterless, and moreover morbidly unhealthy, and although I could get my companions to agree with me on this, their fear of dying if they took to their feet and walked was even greater, so I was at a loss as to how I might convince them to leave this place. But God designed it so that the mosquitoes, who also haunted this spot, accomplished with their annoyance what I had not been capable of with all of my entreaties; undoubtedly it was these mosquitoes who with their constant pricking had mostly caused the swelling on their bodies. In all we spent thirty days here eating nothing but *chachalaca* birds,[187] hearts of palm, and some shellfish. When it finally came time to leave, and so as not to leave any diligence undone, I crossed over once again to our ship, still afloat and with seams not yet fully breached, and proceeded to load all the ordnance I could with powder and ball and shot it twice.

My purpose amounted to calculating that, if there were people inland, they might wonder what caused such explosions and come to our camp and thus with their arrival put an end to our great suffering.[188] In this hope I continued shooting throughout that night and for an entire day thereafter, but on the second day's night a ten-pound ball-and-powder cartridge I was carrying exploded in my hand by accident, burning it, some of my thigh, part of my chest, and my entire face, stripping the hair from my head. I was cured with a white unguent found in the medicine chest that the Master Gunner had left me aboard ship.[189] I then gave my companions as much encouragement as I could, though in point of fact at that moment I needed it more than they did, and we finally set off.[190]

We left the frigate, though in hindsight I wish we could have carried her off, even, if need be, on our very backs, for reasons which I will explain shortly; as I say, we abandoned the frigate that the pirates had given us freely as recompense for all the work my men and I had done for them. She was—or I should say she is, for she may still be there—sixty-two feet along the keel,[191] triple-planked,[192] all her masts and yardarms of the most excellent pine to be had, and her entire design of a lovely cut, so much so that with a fresh wind she would easily do eighty leagues in a day's run.[193] We left nine iron pieces of artillery aboard her and on the beach, with more than two thousand four-, six-, and ten-pound shot, all lead, as well as at least a hundred hundredweights of this metal, fifty bars of tin,[194] fifteen hundred pounds of iron, eighty bars of Japanese copper, a great quantity of

China, seven elephant tusks, three barrels of powder, forty musket barrels, ten matchlocks,[195] a medicine chest, and numerous surgeon's instruments.

Well provisioned with powder and munitions, though lacking in everything else, we set off walking along the same shoreline in a northern direction, each man carrying his own musket. However, we advanced only slowly given the weak and extenuated conditions of my companions and took two days to reach a freshwater creek, red in color, less than four leagues from our starting point. In considering this slow rate of progress, I concluded that the only destination we would ever attain would be death itself, and that very speedily, which thought obliged me to propose to the company a remedy, in the gentle terms which my affection for them dictated I use. Pointing out to them that water would not now be a problem for them and that the many birds which we saw attending this place would sustain them, I asked them to accept that I, in company with Juan de Casas, would proceed onward until we should find some population, from whence I committed myself to return to them with refreshment and lead them out of their misery.

In response to this suggestion, they raised their voices in pitiable cries and spilled countless tears, which state evoked in me a corresponding flood of them from the bottom of my heart. Hanging onto me, they desperately beseeched me with the utmost love and gentleness not to abandon them. They asked me to bless them, as the father to them that I was, in the last few mouthfuls of food they had, arguing that, nature being what it is, the strongest of them would probably not survive for more than four days; if I conceded, they would gladly accept my leaving them in search of a rest which misfortune and ruin denied them in such foreign climes. Their tears convinced me to carry out their requests. Six days passed without their state improving until they realized that I too was beginning to swell up and that my death would accelerate theirs. Consequently fearing mine more than their own, they finally agreed with me and I managed to get them back to traveling slowly, bit by bit.

Juan de Casas and I went ahead to scout out the route for the rest to follow, with Francisco de la Cruz, the *sangley*, bringing up the rear. He was of all of us the most ill and had been since the whipping that the English had given him before our arrival in Caponiz, suffering a thousand maladies, the last of which now took his life in the form of two spots on his chest that swelled up and another in the middle of his back, which ailments reached all the way to his brain. A league or so farther ahead we stopped, although it was after nine o'clock in the evening before we all finally came together, because each one advanced at his own pace according his strength, but Francisco de la Cruz did not arrive. We spent the night waiting for him. However, before dawn broke, I ordered Juan de Casas to continue with the rest while I returned along our path in search of Francisco. I found him about half a league behind us, still in his senses but almost at his last breath. Thoroughly distraught and overwhelmed by tears, I tried to gather my wits about me, and though my feelings dimmed my reason I spoke words of comfort to him, as much as I could manage, to ensure that he would be able to die in conformity with the will of God and mindful of His grace. Just before noon his spirit passed away. It took two hours before I overcame my emotions and managed to dig him a deep grave in the sand; with prayers to Divine Majesty that his soul be at rest, I buried him. After raising a cross on the spot made from two rough pieces of wood, I returned to my men.

I found them camped about a league farther along from where I had left them, with Antonio Gonzalez, the other *sangley*, now also near death. Having no relief to offer him or medicine with which to strengthen him, I began consoling him as best I could. Through either sadness or exhaustion I fell asleep; but, awakened shortly thereafter by my worrying, I realized he had died. On the following day, the whole company gave him burial. Making of both their deaths a lesson for us all, I urged them to get up and walk again no matter how slowly, persuading them that it was the only way we could save our lives. We managed something like three leagues that day, and on the following three days' journey we advanced roughly fifteen more, a happy occurrence since our perspiring heavily as we walked seemed to cure us of our swellings and give us strength. We now found ourselves upon a saltwater river which was not too broad but very deep, in addition to which a large, tangled mangrove swamp kept us from reaching the river's open water for an entire day. Once there, we sounded the bottom but could not find a ford anywhere and so had to cut down palm trees to bridge the river, which feat was accomplished, though I was suffering from a fever at the time.

On the second day after the river crossing, Juan de Casas and I were at the head of the group when a misshapen bear crossed our path. I wounded it with my musket, but it nevertheless lunged for me. Though I tried to protect myself with the gun barrel, I was as weak as it was strong; had it not been for my companion coming up just then to help me, I would certainly have been killed. We left the bear lying there and continued on. Five days after this event we arrived at a rocky point of land.[196] I did not believe I could survive crossing it, because the fever had sapped all of my energies, unlike my companions, whose health had improved dramatically to such a degree that they were now in fact perfectly sound. We made camp while they headed inland[197] up into the hills looking for food, and I retired to a makeshift tent they had built for me by hanging a blanket we had brought on the side of a rock. My slave Pedro guarded over me. My distressed mind then began to conjure up wild imaginations, the most bothersome of which was that we were undoubtedly upon the coast of Florida in America and would lose our lives at the bloody hands of its inhabitants, who were well known to be extremely cruel.

At that very moment my boy[198] interrupted these rambling thoughts with a great yell, screaming that he saw people coming at us along the coastline and that they traveled naked. Greatly afraid, I got up and, picking up my musket, left the tent and clambered up behind the rock which had sheltered us. I saw two naked men approaching us, carrying small bundles on their backs and making gestures as if they were looking intently for something. I was happy to see that they carried no weapons, and, since they were within gunshot, I got up and advanced toward them. They were incomparably more upset by the sight of me than I was by the sight of them and fell to their knees as soon as they saw me, raising their hands in supplication and crying out for quarter in Castilian. I threw my gun away then and ran up to embrace them; they answered my questions, telling me that they were Catholics and were looking for amber along those beaches in the company of their master, who was traveling behind them, a man by the name of Juan Gonzalez who was a resident of the town of Tejosuco.[199] They also said that their name for this coast we were on was Bacalal[200] and that it lay in the province of Yucatan.

We followed this happy information, so very felicitous in contrast to the vehemence of my recent depression when considering us lost amongst barbarians, with immediate and repeated thanks to God and His Most Holy Mother. When we shot off our guns three times—the return sign agreed upon with our companions—they came running back without delay and joined us in our celebrations. We could see, however, that the Yucatecans were not completely satisfied with us, suspicious that we might belong to one of the many companies of English or French pirates who frequent that coast, but they opened up their backpacks and gave us some food to eat, to which gesture we responded by handing them a couple of our guns, not in trade but merely to dislodge the fear which we saw in their eyes. They nevertheless would not take them. Shortly thereafter their master saw us; he had been walking at a leisurely pace behind his Indians, but on the shock of seeing us it was clear that he meant to return as quickly as possible to hide in the deepest part of the forest, where it would be not be easy to find him. We kept one of his Indians as a surety with us but begged and persuaded the other to go and assure his master of our peaceful intentions.

We observed the Indian and his master conversing at length until the latter finally approached us, but by his words and demeanor it was clear that he was afraid and wary. Consequently I spoke with him in peaceful, friendly terms and gave him a brief account of my great hardships,[201] while handing him all of our weapons to lessen his sense of fear. In the end I convinced him to stay with us that night by urging that we would go with him wherever he would take us in the morning. Our conversation then extended to many subjects, but he said to us that we should thank God for his mercy, because if his Indians had discovered us first from far away, instead of the other way round, they would have taken us for pirates and fled into the deepest part of the forest, averring that given our lack of a boat we would never have gotten out of this solitary, uninhabited place.

CHAPTER 7

They travel to Tejosuco and from there to Valladolid, where they experience
trouble; they reach Merida, but Alonso Ramirez returns to Valladolid,
where the troubles increase; the reason he came to Mexico and
what resulted from his trip there

It is commonly acknowledged that a joy that comes too suddenly can kill us with
its violence, and in a similar way my fever was ended just as suddenly by the joy I
felt at this latest turn of events, whose magnitude the reader may well appreciate.
My men and I completely cured, we all struck out from that place at daybreak;
after walking along the beach for about a league up the shoreline of the bay, we
found a small port where they had beached the canoe that they had used to get
across. We got in and set out, but they changed course and made a stop on the
way at a small island, one of the many which dot the place, to quench the great
thirst we were all complaining of. Here we came upon a small edifice that appeared to be very ancient, composed of only four walls with a small door in the
middle of each one; in the center of the edifice, higher up, were another four
walls aligned with the bottom ones[202] (the height of the outside walls was about
eighteen feet).[203] Nearby we saw wells carved into the rock by hand, full of very
good water. After drinking our fill from them, we wondered at finding fresh
water and the kind of building just described on an island scarcely 200 paces in
circumference. We were told that this edifice as well as many other, much larger
structures to be found in this province were constructed by people who came
here many centuries before the Spaniards conquered it.[204]

  We continued on our voyage and about nine in the morning sighted a canoe
of great size. Taking them initially for English pirates, we were reassured by the

type of sail the canoe carried that they were not (for it was made from *petate*, which means the same thing as reeds).[205] Juan Gonzales, turning to me, proposed that we attack them and take them for a prize. The pretext he came up with as a justification for his suggestion was that the men in the canoe were gentile Indians from the mountains and that in taking them to the priest in his village to catechize (this was customarily done there) we would be doing him a great favor. To this reasoning he added the fact that, having only brought enough supplies for the three of them, we were now a company of nine men with many days still to travel without hope of getting new provisions to replace those we would use up in reaching civilization;[206] and this, he argued, made it not only feasible but also meritorious to take the provisions which the Indians undoubtedly were carrying.

To me his arguments seemed reasonable, and so we gave chase with all speed, using both oars and sails.[207] The fourteen people, not counting several children, who were traveling in the canoe put up a strong resistance to our attack, shooting a shower of arrows at us; however, they were terrified by the sound of our muskets going off, which, though furious and continuous, were blank shots. I had ordered my men stringently to do this because I thought it would have been an immoral act[208] to kill these poor souls, who had done us no offense, even of the smallest degree. After we boarded them, they began speaking with Juan Gonzales, who understood their language, and begged him for their freedom, in exchange for which they promised him a piece of amber that weighed two pounds and as much corn from their supply as we might want. He suggested to me that we accept their offer, but I disliked the notion that an appetite for amber should supersede our desire to bring these miserable gentiles into the fraternity of our Catholic faith;[209] after all, this had been how Juan and his men's plan first insinuated[210] itself into my mind. So I did not agree. Juan Gonzales nevertheless took the amber and stowed it away for himself; tying the two canoes together and securing the prisoners, we continued on our course until we had crossed the bay and landed after sunset on the farther side.[211]

We spent the following day grinding corn and preparing food for the six days they said it would take us to get through the uninhabited part of the route we were to traverse.[212] Setting off, we commanded the Indians to travel with our provisions well ahead of the main column. That night I tried to light a fire with my musket matchlock. Thinking it was not loaded and as a result inadvertently dropping my usual care, I let it slip from my hand and it went off, wounding me in the chest and head: caught completely by surprise, I dropped down senseless.

I did not recover from the blow until I woke up about halfway through the night when a torrential rain began to fall, so powerful that it inundated the area we were camped in, the coursing waters reaching almost to our belts. Unprepared as we were for it, we lost most of our provisions and all of our powder except for what I kept in my own flask.[213] This discomfort was added to that of having to be carried by two Indians because I could not move. Leaving us his two servants as guides, Juan Gonzales went ahead in search of some refreshment and in order to be able to give prompt notice to the Indians in the neighboring towns through which we would travel that we were not pirates, as they would inevitably think, but rather lost men who needed their help.[214]

We continued along our way, but with two Indians fewer, one man and one woman, for they had fled from us, taking advantage of the rainstorm. Suffering excessively from pangs of hunger, we eventually stumbled into a banana field. Filling our bellies with fresh bananas and cooking some more to take with us as supplies, we proceeded onward. The beneficiary of the church in Tejozuco (of whom I will have more to relate) had been informed by Juan Gonzales of our misfortunes and consequently had sent out men to set up a substantial refreshment for us along our path. Having fortified ourselves with it, the next day we arrived at a town in his parish called Tila, which is about one league from his parochial seat, and here people sent out by the priest awaited us with a sumptuous repast and chocolate[215] for our relief. We stayed in that town until horses arrived, which we mounted. Thus riding the rest of the way and surrounded by Indians who came out from their houses to see such a rare spectacle, we arrived in the town of Tejozuco around nine o'clock in the morning.

This town is not only large but delightful and beautiful. Many Spaniards attend there, including Don Melchor Pacheco, to whom the Indians are bound[216] as their *encomendero*. The parochial church, built with three naves and adorned with excellently fashioned altars, is in the care of a beneficiary priest by the name of Licenciado *Don Christoval de Muros*. I will never be able to repay sufficiently what I owe him; words fail me in praising him. He came out to greet us with fatherly affection and led us into the church to give the thanks due to Our Lord God for having brought us out of the oppressive tyranny of the English, for having saved us from the dangers of so many seas, and for having delivered us most recently from our suffering along these coasts. Once our orations were finished, he took us, accompanied by the entire town, to his home.

In the eight days that Juan de Casas and I spent with him, he set the table for us with all the food he possessed and always sent out plates of various things for the town's poor. He also assisted in like manner, abundantly, and in proportion to our own rations not only my old companions but also the gentile Indians. He distributed them, after clothing them, amongst some of their own nation whom he had already baptized in order that they be catechized. He prepared us for the confession that had been made impossible for us over such a long time and, listening to us with a patience and kindness I have never seen in anyone else, made it possible for us to receive communion on the day of Saint Catherine.[217] While these events were transpiring, he sent word to the alcaldes[218] in the city of Valladolid (within whose jurisdiction this town lies), relating to them our story. He then gave us a letter to show them as well as the guardian of the vicarage in Tixcacal, who later received us with great warmth, and we set off for the city from Tejosuco with his blessing. A sergeant sent by the alcaldes to take us to the city met us in the town of Tixcacal; having finally arrived there and been admitted into their presence, I offered them the letter. There were two alcaldes in this city, as is the case everywhere in these parts, one called Don Francisco de Zelerun,[219] a man who appeared to me not at all meddlesome and quite well intentioned, and the other Don Zepherino de Castro.

I cannot continue without relating something that happened here which was both amazing and extremely humorous.[220] I had responded to queries concerning the little black boy Pedro by clarifying that he was my slave, upon which one of the men who had interrogated me waited until we were alone and then, approaching me and throwing his arms around me, said:

"Is it possible, my old friend and beloved fellow countryman, that I'm truly seeing you again? Oh, how many occasions can I recall when I've been drowned in tears, crying as I remembered you! Who would have believed that I would ever find you in such misery? Give me a strong hug, then, for you are the second half of my soul, and give thanks to God that I am here with you."

I asked him who he was and what his name was because in no way did I recognize him.

"How can this be so?" he answered. "How can you ask that, when in your childhood you had no greater friend? Just so you'll know that I'm still the same friend I was then, let me tell you that rumors are flying that you're a spy for some corsair,[221] and as soon as the Governor of this Province finds out he'll arrest you and, without doubt, have you tortured. Now, I happen to have certain business affairs in hand that have given me an opportunity to build an intimate acquaintance with his Lordship; when I suggest anything, he carries it out immediately. Gain his favor by presenting him with this black boy as a gift. And in order to do this, it wouldn't be a bad idea if you handed him over to me first. Consider, now, how extremely dangerous the situation that I find you in really is. Keep this secret but look to yourself if you fail to follow my advice: take to heart that I can only redeem you from your troubles, dear beloved and ancient friend of mine, if my plan is carried out."

"I am not as simple as that, sir," I answered. "I recognize you for the great swindler you undoubtedly are; you could give lessons in robbery, sir, to the best of the corsairs! I will happily give my black boy away, sir, but only to someone who will present me with the 300 pieces of eight he's worth. God's speed to you, sir!"[222]

He did not have a chance to answer me, for the alcaldes' officials were calling for me and I left.

Don Francisco de Zelerun was not only an alcalde but also the city's governor,[223] and the declaration I made to him concerning my tribulations[224] led to the whole city knowing my story, including the fact that I had left much on the beach. Many thought that I would make a cheap bargain of these goods because of the extreme necessity in which I now found myself and began offering me money just for whatever had washed up on the beach[225] if I would only sell; one offered 500 pesos on the spot.[226] I wanted to accept it and return to the wreck, for the buyers were prepared not only to accompany me personally back to the site of the wreck but also to help me repair the frigate and rescue whatever was left in her hold. Unfortunately, Don Zephirino de Castro sent me notice that, on pain of serious punishment, I was not to leave the city to return to the beach, because he maintained that the vessel and all its contents belonged to the Cruzada.[227] This news left me dispirited and unsure of what to do, but I thought back on Miguel, the Sevillian, and just shrugged my shoulders.[228] It also became known publicly that I had given two gifts to Don Melchor Pacheco, the *encomendero* of Tejozuco, a *criz*[229] and a rusty rapier I had brought with me, of which he became inordinately fond. This information reached Don Zephirino, who, concluding no doubt from the story I had told about the sack of Cicudana that both *criz* and rapier must have gold-plated hilts encrusted with diamonds, ordered Don Melchor instantly to appear before the authorities on pain of the same punishments should he fail the summons. I informed the alcalde, however, that I was taking this issue to court in defense of my rights and that I was determined to have my case heard before a judge;[230] on the second day [after this incident] they sent me off to Merida.

They carried me there with as much haste as I had been in the habit of using whenever I caught sight of English ships on the seas, and, without allowing me to pay my respects at the miraculous sanctuary of Our Lady of Ytzamal, they arrived in the city, with me in tow, on December 8, 1689.[231] The resident Governor and Captain General of that Province is Don Juan Joseph de la Barcena,[232] whose hand my companions and I promptly kissed when we were presented to him.[233] I gave him an unofficial statement[234] concerning my case, after which he sent me to the residences called the Royal Apartments of San Christoval.[235] On the fifteenth, at his command, Sergeant Major Francisco Guerrero[236] took down my declaration; and on January 7, 1690, Bernardo Sabido,[237] the Royal Notary, certified[238] that since the moment of my delivery from wandering the coast completely lost I had remained in the city of Merida.[239]

The inconveniences I suffered in this city are imponderable. Every inhabitant forced me to tell my story with all the details, just as it is written down in this book, and not only once but many times over. To this effect, they would drag me—and my companions—from house to house, but without fail they would cut me off at noontime.[240] This city—and, generally speaking, the entire Province—is rich, fertile, and very economical,[241] despite which I received assistance from very few of its people, except for three: Licenciado Don Christoval de Muros, my sole benefactor; a servant of Don Melchor Pacheco who gave me a greatcoat; and His Lordship the Bishop Don Juan Cano y Sandoval,[242] who assisted me with a present of two pesos. Apart from these three people, no one else extended a helping hand to me or my companions, though they saw that we were almost without clothes and at the point of starvation. We were not even fed in the Royal Apartments of San Christoval (an honorable inn in which travelers take up residence), other than the food that the Indians who work there gave us, which amounted to nothing more than corn tortillas and beans every day. On one occasion, I suggested to the Indians that they should alter their diet from time to time, to which they responded by saying that I should be content with the free victuals, since they were giving us food with no hope of ever being repaid for it by those who had put us in that place.[243] Acknowledging to myself the truth of what they said and recognizing the obligation under which I now stood of adding their names to the short catalogue of my benefactors, I shut up.

It soon came to pass that I found myself even without the beans with which the Indians in the Royal Apartments of San Christoval had sustained me; on the very same day the notary handed me the certificate that I mentioned above, I was set at liberty, free to head out for wherever I might please. In the next step that I took I sought the support of Second Lieutenant Pedro Flores de Ureña,[244] a fellow countryman of mine who would have achieved great power had Fortune joined hands with his natural dignity and sense of honor. After providing evidence of my ownership of the black slave Pedro, in the way of affidavits from my companions[245] and a declaration from himself that he did indeed belong to me as a slave, I sold him for 300 pesos. I then applied these funds to clothing the rest of my company and giving them a bit of money to cover the costs of making their way in life without me (for they had sworn to remain my assistants for life), thus permitting them to set their helm on whatever course their spirits might call them to in the future.

Don Zephirino de Castro, meanwhile, continued with the investigation that he had set in motion with the idea of impounding what was left on the beach and aboard my frigate, applying the frivolous pretext of the laws governing Cruzadas to justify his claim over all that shipwrecked property which I deemed was legally mine under the provisions of the Bull In Coena Domini.[246] He then made plans to open up a road through the wilderness to the beach where lay the wreck and its cargo, judging that mule teams might be able to accomplish a task which Indian shoulders might not easily carry out. However, Don Christoval de Muros, the beneficiary [of the church in Tijosuco], opposed his plans strongly, arguing that such a road would facilitate the entry of privateers and pirates inland;[247] for they are always cruising along the coastline there and effectively the magistrate would be building them a completely undefended walking route to all the villages in Don Christoval's parish, which they could then easily pillage and plunder.[248] The confirmed notice of all of this which I received[249] took me back to Valladolid, from whence I wanted to proceed to the beach to witness with my own eyes the iniquity of what was being done to me and my companions by people who were, as Spaniards and Catholics, in fact obliged to come to my aid and assistance with their own wealth. Coming to the town of Tila, I was stopped by Antonio Zapata, a Second Lieutenant,[250] who did not permit me to proceed further and told me he was under orders from Don Zepherino de Castro to warn me that if I did so I would be declared a traitor to the King.

With the encouragement and support of Don Christoval de Muros, I was persuaded to return to Merida, along the way spending Holy Week in the sanctuary at Ytzamal. I arrived in the city on the Wednesday after Easter. The Governor then declared after I filed my petition that he had received orders from His Excellency the Viceroy of New Spain that I was to go to him without delay. The Governor ignored my responses to this order and did not even allow me to prepare myself for the voyage. I left Merida on Sunday, April 2. On Friday, April 7, I arrived in Campeche. On Thursday, April 13, I boarded a ketch,[251] commanded by Captain Peña,[252] which left port that day. On Sunday, the sixteenth,

I jumped ashore at Vera-Cruz, where the Royal officials came to my aid with twenty pesos. Finally, I set out from that city on the twenty-fourth of that same month and arrived in Mexico on April 4 [May 4].[253]

On the following Friday I was able to kiss the hand of His Excellency, whose affability toward me corresponded to an aristocratic character. At first mourning for the hardships[254] I had undergone and then celebrating my freedom[255] with expressions of joy and congratulations, he proceeded to listen attentively to everything that has befallen me in my voyage around the world,[256] which now is preserved in writing but which I then related to His Excellency in the form of a brief summary. He then commanded that I visit Don Carlos de Siguenza y Gongora, the King's cosmographer and professor of mathematics in the Academy of Mexico and principal chaplain of the Amor de Dios Royal Hospital in this city of Mexico (all high-sounding titles that benefit him only in small measure and which he undertakes more for the sake of his reputation than for his convenience). In this His Excellency might have been motivated by the affection he feels for this man, or perhaps by the hope that I would entertain the ailing Don Carlos in his current suffering and bring him out of it with the news of the many details of my past suffering. The latter felt compassion for the hardships I had endured and fashioned this account of them[257] and, in addition, through his intercession and requests on my behalf—and in my presence—convinced His Excellency the Viceroy to issue three decrees: that I be provided financial assistance by Don Sebastian de Guzman y Cordova, the Royal Treasuries' Bursar and Chief Financial and Accounting Officer,[258] which command this official diligently carried out; that I be assigned temporarily to the Windward Fleet until I settle on a more permanent post;[259] and an order to the Governor of Yucatan commanding that he ensure that whatever the officials had embargoed or secured of my ship's property, whether found on the beach or lying in the wreck's hold, be turned over entirely to myself or any agent of mine without delay, pretext, or rejoinders. Don Carlos arranged that I be accompanied down to Vera-Cruz by Don Juan Enriquez Barroto, Captain of Artillery in the Royal Windward Fleet and a young man of consummate skill in hydrography, who is also very knowledgeable in the mathematical sciences, as a result of which accomplishments he was an intimate friend and guest in the professor's house at the time. Don Carlos then helped me outfit myself for my forthcoming trip as much as his accounts allowed but, in the end, never would permit me to repay him for all the pains he took on my behalf.

Notes

CHAPTER ONE

1. I use "American" in the original seventeenth-century Spanish sense of "Spanish American." Only six men accompanied Ramírez all the way to Yucatan:
"Juan de Casas, a Spaniard born in Puebla de los Angeles in New Spain [Mex-
ico]; Juan Pinto and Marcos de la Cruz, the former a Pangasinan Indian and
the latter a Pampanpango Indian [Philippine Islanders from the main Spanish
island, Luzon]; Francisco de la Cruz and Antonio Gonzalez, *sangleyes* [Chi-
nese immigrants on Luzon]; Juan Diaz, a Malabar Indian; and Pedro, a black
boy from Mozambique who was my slave" (*Misfortunes*, Chapter 4).

2. Bazarte Cerdán, "La primera novela mexicana."

3. For brief discussions of this wide-ranging literary and historiographical debate, see the introductions by Vindel, Vallés Formosa, Rodilla, and Lucrecio
Pérez Blanco in their editions of *Infortunios de Alonso Ramírez*; especially important are Anderson Imbert, *Historia de la literatura hispanoamericana*, 95; Vidargas, introduction, in *San Juan de Ulúa y Carlos de Sigüenza y Góngora*, 5–6;
and Irizarry, "Introducción," in *Infortunios de Alonso Ramírez*, 11–13, 65.

4. Cummins and Soons, eds., *Los infortunios de Alonso Ramírez* (cf. Sigüenza y
Góngora, *Seis obras*); and Lorente Medina, *La prosa de Sigüenza y Góngora*. A
few scholars follow Lorente Medina, taking Ramírez's existence for granted
but not delving into the evidence: e.g., Mayer González, *Dos americanos*, 92.

5. I published a report of my 2006 discovery of the first documentary proof for a
historical Ramírez in 2007: "La mentira histórica de un pirata caribeño."

6. Galve arrived in San Juan de Ulúa on September 18, 1688, but did not officially take the reins of power until October 11 in Tlaxcala, arriving in Mexico City a week later; his first report to the king was sent the following March. AHNSN, Osuna 54, 40, 12, 5 and 13.

7. In his letters and reports Galve invariably called all of the Yucatan "Campeche," unlike most of his contemporaries in the colonial administration.

8. AHNSN, Osuna 55, 11, 2.

9. AHNSN, Osuna 55, 61.

10. Nadelmann, "Global Prohibition Regimes," 524; cf. Cruz Barney, *El combate a la piratería en Indias, 1555–1700*, 28–36. Spain's critical role in the formation of international law dates back to the famous Salamanca school of natural law (Vitoria) and the mid-sixteenth-century debates concerning the just conquest of the Americas studied by Lewis Hanke; but as the most interested party in the creation of settler societies in the Indies, the Habsburg monarchy also led the way in antipiracy and privateering legislation from the 1590s onward. It pushed for the establishment of legal international systems to recognize settlement and exploration.

11. Banks, *Chasing Empire across the Sea*, 184–216.

12. Alden, *The Making of an Enterprise*, 229.

13. Gracián, *El criticón*, 13.

14. For an important recent discussion of this, see Cañizares-Esguerra, "New World, New Stars."

15. Storrs, *The Resilience of the Spanish Monarchy*, 232–234; Goodman, *Spanish Naval Power*, 254–261 (in contrast to Stradling, "Chapter 4, Years of Defeat 1656–78," and "Chapter 5, Pathology of a Power System, 1678–1700," in *Europe and the Decline of Spain*; and Lynch, *The Hispanic World in Crisis and Change*, 171). Storrs's interpretation is congruent with evidence adduced by other scholars, such as Artola, *La hacienda*, 216–221; and Sánchez Belén, *La política fiscal*, xi, 309; even Kamen, *Spain in the Later Seventeenth Century*, 103–105, 239, was impressed by the financial reforms of the 1680s and 1690s. Beginning in the 1660s, American treasure shipments, for some the barometer of imperial success, rose after earlier low points in the 1640s, reaching 87 million pesos in the five years from 1670 to 1674. Lynch, *The Hispanic World in Crisis and Change*, 282–283, citing the study of nonofficial European gazette reports by Morineau, *Incroyables gazettes et fabuleux métaux*.

16. Sanjay Subrahmanyam's recent discussion of Portuguese and Spanish imperial "connected histories" ("Holding the World in Balance") underplays the significance of their maritime structure.

17. Burkholder and Chandler, *From Impotence to Authority*, 11, 15–36; Lynch, *The Hispanic World in Crisis and Change*, 287–298; Crosby, *Ecological Imperialism*, 2–3.

18. Yun Casalilla, *La gestión del poder*, 206–219; cf. Sánchez Belén, *La política fiscal*, 83–84, 96; Yun Casalilla, "Old Regime Aristocracies," 10; Manuela Cristina García Bernal, "La élite mercantil de Campeche, 1590–1625," Angel Sanz-Tapia, "Criollos compradores de cargos públicos," and Carmen Paula Palomo Sousa, "Los corregidores de Zacatecas: Una élite de poder (1700–1786)," in Navarro García and García Bernal, eds., *Elites urbanas en Hispanoamérica*; Elliott, *Empires of the Atlantic World*, 3–16, 219–251.

19. These geopolitical groupings would correspond roughly to merchants licensed to trade in Cadiz and Seville in Spain (Andalusia); in Lima and Panama (Peru); in Veracruz and Acapulco, Mexico (New Spain); and in Cartagena, Colombia (New Granada).

20. García Bernal and Ruiz Rivera, *Cargadores a Indias*, 131–141, 160–178, 195–197.

21. Montemayor, *Discurso político, histórico, jurídico*, 123 (quotation); AGI, Escribanía 230B, fols. 172r–173v; AGI, México 363, 4, 32; García Bernal, *La sociedad en Yucatán*, 18; Alsedo y Herrera, *Piraterías y agresiones*, 136, 147, 152; Chatelain, *The Defense of Spanish Florida*, 59–80; *The Building of Castillo de San Marcos*, 1–3, 7, 22–26; Manacy, *The History of Castillo de San Marcos*, 12–20.

22. *CSP*, vol. 8, entry 83, 25; cf. entries 83 vi, 29, and 83 v. Dampier's confusion at discovering self-ascriptively "Spanish Indians" in Latin America (that is, loyal to the Spanish crown) points to the difference between Spaniards' more flexibly political and cultural definitions of "Spanishness" and his own, more firmly somatic (that is, racial) definitions (*NV*, 84, 188). A similar discovery was made by the Pennsylvania passengers of the *Reformation*, a brigantine shipwrecked in Florida in 1696, who were immediately delivered by the local Indians to authorities in Spanish St. Augustine. Dickinson, *God's Protecting Providence*.

23. AHNSN, Osuna 54, 12, 1, fols. 4–9.

24. "Alboroto y motín de los indios de México," in Sigüenza y Góngora, *Seis obras*, 113 (cf. 120–133).

25. "Este corral se alquila para gallos de la tierra y gallinas de Castilla." Robles, *Diario*, vol. 1, 257; cf. Rubio Mañé, *Introducción al estudio de los virreyes*, vol. 2, 52.

26. Cañeque, *The King's Living Image*; Herzog, *Defining Nations*; Cañizares-Esguerra, *How to Write the History of the New World*. For an excellent example of the demographic ties linking transatlantic Hispanic societies, see Altman, *Transatlantic Ties in the Spanish Empire: Brihuega, Spain, and Puebla, Mexico*.

CHAPTER TWO

1. For the Irish-Spanish admiral, Don Arturo O'Bruin, see López Lázaro, "Labor Disputes, Ethnic Quarrels, and Early Modern Piracy." Lorencillo, the ex–Spanish naval officer turned pirate, is discussed below.

2. Scandal attached itself to his appointment. His second wife, Elvira María Ossorio de Toledo, seems to have been amorously involved with Galve's brother, Infantado, and saw the posting as a forced exile. Dodge and Hendricks, *Two Hearts, One Soul: The Correspondence of the Condesa de Galve*. We do not know if Galve suspected Elvira of anything other than the type of institutionalized flirtation (*galanteo de corte*) which had characterized Madrid's court life for decades; nevertheless, Galve's appointment did coincide with King Carlos II's outlawing of *galanteos*. AHNSN, Osuna 54, 31. A copy of the death certificate issued by Antonio Felipe de Mora, including a *memorial* by Elvira, can be found in AHPM, Mora registry, March 12, 1697. I have found no instance in which Galve and his brother allude to this issue in any of their correspondence. Hanke, *Guía de las fuentes*, vol. 1, 173; Rubio Mañé, *Introducción al estudio de los virreyes*, vol. 1, 295–296; *DIPCA*, vol. 1, 38; on the debate concerning long vice-regal terms in office, see Cañeque, *The King's Living Image*, 242; two decades later, Francisco de Seijas y Lobera (*Gobierno militar y político*, 308), a disgraced Mexican official with an axe to grind against Galve, gossiped to Louis XIV's court that Infantado had simply bought the office for his brother.

3. AHNSN, Osuna 225, 6; Salazar y Castro, *Historia genealógica de la Casa de Silva*, vol. 2, 212; for the Galve-Infantado family, see Arteaga y Falguera, *La Casa del Infantado*; Gutiérrez Coronel, *Historia genealógica de la Casa de Mendoza*; Dodge and Hendricks, eds., *Two Hearts, One Soul*; Fernández de Béthencourt, *Historia genealógica y heráldica*; and Vilar y Pascual, *Diccionario histórico, genealógico y heráldico*. The house of Infantado controlled over eight hundred towns and villages and nominated more than five hundred officials for public office in Spain alone. Kamen, *Spain in the Later Seventeenth Century*, 232–239; Count of Pötting, *Diario*, vol. 1, 349; *DIPCA*, vol. 1, 31 and 34 (cf. Maura Gamazo, *Vida y reinado de Carlos II*, 197; and Peña Izquierdo, *La crisis sucesoria*, vol. 2, 210ff.). While the rumor that Gregorio died owing nothing to anyone, unlike any other Spanish grandee of his time, was an exaggeration (he was still paying off some *censos* or consignatory mortgages), he no doubt stood at the apex of his class. Yun Casalilla, "From Political and Social Management to Economic Management?" 88.

4. Their correspondence contains many instances in which Infantado was clearly acting as Galve's private conduit to the king, as an effective counter to influential ministers who might disagree with the brothers' policies. AHNSN, Osuna 54, 11, 28, 29, 35, 46, 56, 58, 61, and Osuna 55, 4.

5. Robles, *Diario de los sucesos notables*, vol. 2, 178–179 (quotation); Sánchez Belén, *La política fiscal*, xiv, 160–200; Cárceles de Gea, *Reforma y fraude fiscal*, 117–120; Maura Gamazo, *Vida y reinado de Carlos II*, 542. The Vélez-Veitia partnership marked the height of reformist naval and colonial policy under the last Habsburg ruler of the Spanish crown. Like Veitia Linaje, Vélez also wrote

a long text detailing his program for financial reform: *Norte de la contratación de las Indias Occidentales* (1672). Maura Gamazo, *Vida y reinado de Carlos II*, 417–450; Kamen, *Spain in the Later Seventeenth Century*, 373.

6. AHNSN, Osuna 54, 5. We should resist romanticizing Galve's populism: he was firmly against the frequent and popular colonial practice of selling government posts to men from "the mechanical professions." Osuna 54, 12. Some of these measures Galve instituted in his own administration in New Spain, such as the strict auditing of financiers and accountants working for the crown; however, he confessed just one year after arriving in Mexico and conducting a budget study that there was simply not enough money to meet the king's obligations in the New World *and* supply Madrid with all the funds it wanted for European expenses. AHNSN, Osuna 54, 39, 44, 55 and 56. Infantado shared his brother's fascination with France, inspired by his official visit to Paris in 1679 to organize the Spanish king's first marriage. Villar, *Lettres*, 155, 307. A portrait of Infantado in fancy French court dress survives, contrasting noticeably with the austere dress of his Prado portrait (see the illustrations at the end of the Introductory Study). Arteaga y Falguera, *La Casa del Infantado*, Fig. 14, facing p. 140.

7. AHNSN, Osuna 54, 40. When interrogated, the crew members confessed that they had been cruising off Campeche and Laguna de Términos, but they defended themselves from the accusation that they were pirates by stating that they had merely been cutting "logwood" there, the famous bark of the tropical tree *Haematoxylon campechianum*, from which red and purple dyes were manufactured, in itself an illegal activity. They were arrested, but I have not yet found the record of their trial.

8. Lorencillo's biography is poorly known (e.g., Mota, *Piratas en el Caribe*, 31; Kinkor, "Black Men under the Black Flag," 200; and Kemp and Lloyd, *Brethren of the Coast*, 73). He acquired the title of "Sieur de Graff" when he entered the French navy and afterward served in Pierre Le Moyne d'Iberville's expedition to Louisiana. Lorencillo died in Mobile, an "honored citizen," in May 1704. Juárez Moreno, *Piratas y corsarios*, 37–39. Even less is known of Grammont: some reported that he disappeared at sea in the Bermuda Triangle in 1686, but French sources identify him as still active in 1687. Urdaneta, *Marco y retrato de Granmont*, 28–29; AN, Série coloniale C8A 4–1687, fol. 302; André, *Gramont*.

9. Juárez Moreno, *Piratas y corsarios*, 214, 226 (quotation); Mota, *Piratas en el Caribe*, 311. Holding towns and cities for ransom was common practice during war; during the siege of Bruges, Louis XIV's general, Louis de Crevant, the Maréchal d'Humières, burnt to the ground any nearby towns that refused to pay "exorbitant contributions." Letters, Louis XIV to Maréchal d'Humières, Versailles, October 24 and November 1, 1683, in *Oeuvres de Louis XIV*, vol. 4, 263–273.

10. AHNSN, Osuna 54, 51.

11. Haring, *The Buccaneers in the West Indies*, 267–268.

12. AHNSN, Osuna 55, 11 (emphasis added). In the same letter Galve praised the stalwart resistance to such incursions by islanders like the "bellicose" Puerto Ricans and noted the remarkable escape of several pirate captives, all of which he used to convince the king that the monarchy should allot more resources to supporting his American vassals' struggles against foreign aggressors. These comments coincided with the specific details of Ramírez's account, which he sent on to Infantado shortly thereafter.

13. Haring, *The Buccaneers in the West Indies*, 253.

14. Crouse, *The French Struggle for the West Indies*, 146.

15. Robles, *Diario de los sucesos notables*, vol. 1, xi, and vol. 2, 181–182. Robles was one of the executors of Don Carlos de Sigüenza y Góngora's will.

16. AGI, Filipinas 12, 1, 45; cf. AGI, Filipinas 331, 8, fols. 270–271. Having been expelled from China by the Manchus, Koxinga in turn threw the Dutch out of Formosa and then sent an ultimatum to the governor of the Spanish Philippine Islands to submit immediately. AGI, Filipinas 330, 6, fol. 198v, Fipilinas 43, 39, and Filipinas 43, 49; Koxinga's Chinese-Japanese ancestry contributed to the celebration of his naval exploits in the early eighteenth-century puppet play *Kokusenya Kassen* by Chikamatsu Monzaemon. Keene, *The Battles of Coxinga*, 44–75; Purcell, *The Chinese in Southeast Asia*, 521–524 (cf. ICS, 77n45); Costa, *Readings in Philippine History*, 53–68, 342, 483–484, 582–583; Barrantes, *Guerras piráticas contra mindanaos y joloanos*; Montero y Vidal, *Historia de la piratería malayo-mahometana*, vol. 1, 155–254.

17. Antonio García-Abásolo, "La difícil convivencia entre españoles y chinos en Filipinas," in Navarro García and García Bernal, eds., *Elites urbanas en Hispanoamérica*, 494 (quotation); Seijas y Lobera, *Gobierno militar y político*, 301.

18. AHNSN, Osuna 55, 12.

19. AGI, Filipinas 12, 1, 45, Filipinas 18, fol. 22, and Filipinas 331, 8, fols. 270v-271v ("infesting our coasts"), and Filipinas 13, 1, 9, fols. 1–14; RAH, 9/2668, 26, 65, 125, 130 ("present state of affairs"); AGS, Ultramar 562, 2, fols. 15–21; AGN, Marina, vol. 1, 11, fols. 98ff.; and Robles, *Diario de los sucesos notables*, vol. 2, 174; a few of these reports are reproduced in Lévesque, *History of Micronesia*, vol. 9, 63, 110.

20. Moreyra y Paz-Soldán and Céspedes del Castillo, *Virreinato peruano*, vol. 1, 88; official reports on the English pirates who entered via Panama can be found in AGI, Panama, 96 and 168.

21. Lynum, *William Hack*, 3–15; Williams, *The Great South Sea*, 76–132; cf. Spate, *The Spanish Lake*; and Chatelain, *The Defense of Spanish Florida*. Concurrently, a European pirate invasion was taking place in the Indian Ocean, with

Madagascar becoming a base for the exchange of stolen goods with reputable merchants from New England and Europe. Judice Biker, *Collecção de tratados*, vol. 3, 170; Deschamps, *Les pirates à Madagascar*; and Rediker, *Between the Devil and the Deep Blue Sea*, 56–58, 257. According to a prominent Portuguese merchant, galleons crossing the Indian Ocean traveled with their cannons stored in their holds until the second half of the 1600s. Boxer, *Francisco Vieira de Figueiredo*, 16–17, 51–53.

22. See the correspondence of Don Pedro de Ronquillo (1630–1691), ambassador in London from 1681 until his death: Maura Gamazo, ed., *Correspondencia entre dos embajadores*; Alsedo y Herrera, *Piraterías y agresiones*; Sáiz Cidoncha, *Historia de la piratería*, 162–207; Galvin, *Patterns of Pillage*; Castillero Calvo, *La ruta transístmica*; and *AE*, particularly vols. 5 and 6.

23. Flynn and Giráldez, "Born with a 'Silver Spoon': The Origin of World Trade in 1571," in *Metals and Monies*, 259.

24. AHNSN, Osuna 54, 59, 2, and Osuna 55, 42; AGS, Estado 4135; AGI, Escribanía 230B, 5, fols. 15v-18r; for the massive fortifications built by Galve's administration, see the studies in *Puertos y fortificaciones en América y Filipinas*, 65–68, 147–224; Gutiérrez, *Las fortificaciones de Iberoamérica*; *Fortificaciones del Caribe*; Chatelain, *The Defense of Spanish Florida*, 40–80; *The Building of Castillo de San Marcos*; and Manacy, *The History of Castillo de San Marcos*; for the Veracruz works, see AGI, Patronato 243, 6. Similar efforts by Peru's viceroy almost bankrupted the Lima Audiencia. Moreyra y Paz-Soldán and Céspedes del Castillo, *Virreinato peruano*, vol. 1 (1689–1694), 13, 17, 84–296; for English and French reports of Spanish corsairs, see *CSP*, vol. 7, entry 1,705 (p. 529) and vol. 8, entry 515 (p. 168); and AN, Série coloniale C8A, fol. 330, and Série coloniale C8A 5, fols. 22–37; cf. Sáiz Cidoncha, *Historia de la piratería*, 298–299. A general royal command authorizing colonial officials to use privateers on their own authority was not issued until 1728. AHN, Códices 761, fol. 275, 67.

25. *Ou-Mun*, 42.

26. Sáiz Cidoncha, *Historia de la piratería*, 142, gives the details of the 1624 attack on San Salvador (Bahía). Don Fadrique was named viceroy of New Spain in 1672 but declined. Rubio Mañé, *Introducción al estudio de los virreyes*, vol. 1, 260.

27. *CDMFN*, vol. 11, 70–73.

28. Sigüenza y Góngora, *Trofeo de la justicia española en el castigo de la alevosía francesa*. Tortuga had been invaded by Spanish forces three times before, but every evacuation led immediately to reoccupation by Spain's enemies. When a Spanish garrison was withdrawn on June 26, 1655, for example, in order to reinforce the Spanish guerrillas resisting English invaders on Jamaica, the Spanish governor wrote that "a bark full of Frenchmen watched it leave from one

side of the harbor as they entered it from the other." Sáiz Cidoncha, *Historia de la piratería*, 230; cf. AGI, Escribanía 230B, 5, fol. 72r.

29. AGI, Escribania 230B, 5, fol. 55v. Dampier noted in *NV*, 75, that the highly effective defensive measures taken on land and sea by officials from Peru to California forced his company to give up raiding.

30. AGS, Estado 3963, Consultas, June 3, 1687, and November 16, 1689; see López Lázaro, "Pirates of the Caribbean," 13n21; cf. Seed, *Ceremonies of Possession*.

31. Haring, *The Buccaneers in the West Indies*, 255.

32. AGS, Estado 3965, Consultas, March 7 and September 30, 1689, and Letter, Ronquillo to King, December 5, 1689. One trigger for Spanish distrust was article 14 in the Anglo-Dutch Naval Treaty of April 1689; see López Lázaro, "Labor Disputes, Ethnic Quarrels, and Early Modern Piracy."

33. See Schmidt, "The Idea and Slogan of 'Perfidious Albion.'"

34. Alsedo y Herrera (writing ca. 1740), *Piraterías y agresiones*, 113, 122–123 ("the projects of emulation") (Alsedo y Herrera had extensive American administrative experience as president of the Audiencia in Quito and then in Panama). *DIPCA*, vol. 1, 8; Haring, *The Buccaneers in the West Indies*, 28, 33–34 ("rifle, plunder and bring home").

35. Barrionuevo, *Avisos*, vol. 1, 87.

36. RAH 9/2668, 122 (Old Legajo 2, 122) has a complicated history which has misled historians, including Cummins and Soons, who failed to pursue this clue (ICS, 78–79n70). Emma Helen Blair and James Alexander Robertson partially translated this bundle of documents as "Events in Filipinas, 1686–1688," in *The Philippine Islands*, vol. 39, 131–148; but they relied on the transcripts made by a Spanish antiquarian, Don Ventura del Arco, and joined it to RAH 9/2669 (at some unidentified point the bundle "Jesuitas" 9/2668 was constructed from odds and ends from originals written on rice paper and copies on regular paper). This creates the false impression that 9/2668 and 9/2669 are a continuous "diary" of events, thus compromising the original composition's historical significance. Ventura del Arco's transcripts were bought by the American collector and Western history buff Edward E. Ayer and ended up in Chicago's Newberry Library, where Horacio de la Costa also consulted them for *The Jesuits in the Philippines*. Rodrigue Lévesque complemented the Ventura del Arco–Blair/Robertson materials with related excerpts from some Manila Jesuit letters which survive solely in a 1923 catalogue from the bookseller Maggs Brothers of London (mostly to their patroness, the Duchess of Aveiro), but he cut out the key part of the RAH report in *History of Micronesia*, vol. 9, 61–64. On the nature of the Asian Jesuits' reports, see Arcilla, *Jesuit Missionary Letters*; Zubillaga and Hanisch, *Guía manual de los documentos históricos de la Compañía de Jesús*; and Carreira-Afonso, *Jesuit Letters and Indian History*.

37. RAH 9/2668, 125 (old Legajo 2, 125) and RAH 9/2668, 128; cf. AHNSN, Osuna 54, 7, and Osuna 55, 16, 5. The Jesuits exacerbated the conflict by repeatedly refusing "to recognize the competence of the judge on the grounds of notorious partiality"; the Audiencia, "after two years of litigation, decided against them" on February 23, 1688. Costa, *The Jesuits in the Philippines*, 494-500.

38. According to the Real Academia Española's *Diccionario de la lengua castellana*, a *caván* was a Philippine islands measurement equaling one Spanish *fanega*, four *celemines*, and two *cuartillos* or one *gant*, roughly equivalent to seventy-five liters. Three thousand *caváns* would be 6,187.5 bushels. The large *balandra* (a *balandro* was a small sloop) could thus hold at least eight thousand cubic feet of cargo.

39. RAH 9/2668, 122 (Old Legajo 2, 122), "Diario de novedades de Filipinas desde Junio de 86 hasta el de 87."

40. AGI, Filipinas 341, 8, fols. 55–56, Filipinas 331, 8, 54–55, Filipinas 44, 22, and Filipinas 33, 2, 68 and 145. Spanish quartermasters not only made crews obey commands but also took care of the loading of supplies. Rico de Mata, *Tratado de galafatería*, 41. For the movement of Manila ships, see Lévesque, *History of Micronesia*, vol. 20, 591.

41. Pangasinan is consistently shown as a city on contemporary maps. Quirino, *Philippine Cartography*, 39, 62, 69, 82, 85, 86.

42. Preston and Preston, *A Pirate of Exquisite Mind*; Gill, *The Devil's Mariner*.

43. Dampier may have had help back home in England between 1691, when he began transforming his logbook into manuscript form (one survives: "William Dampier's Second Voyage into the South Seas with Captain Cook," BL, Sloane MS 3236, hereafter cited as DNV), and 1697, when the book was published. Clennell Wilkinson, *Dampier*, 149; John Masefield, "Introduction," in *Dampier's Voyages* (1906), vol. 1, 14; Sir Albert Gray, "Introduction," in *NV*, xliv-xlv. Dampier relates that he gave Edward Barlow, mate aboard Captain Poole's *Rainbow of London*, a copy of his journal near Vietnam in 1689 (*NV*, 339), but Barlow did not mention it in his journal (*Barlow's Journal*, vol. 2, 397–398). One of Captain Swan's pilots, Michael Shillito, surrendered to Spanish authorities in Manila five logbooks (*derroteros*), covering the voyage from London to Mindanao. AGI, Filipinas 12, 1, 60, 3.

44. *NV*, 193, 257–258, 297, 318; cf. Lussan, Raveneau de Lussan, 70–71.

45. *NV*, 246 (despite Dampier's reference to "ships" on 259). This is confirmed in the testimonies of pirates from the *Cygnet*, who surrendered to Spanish officials in Manila. AGI, Filipinas 12, 1, 60, 3, fols. 6–143.

46. Dampier's draft is entitled "William Dampier's Second Voyage into the South Seas with Captain Cook" (DNV, fol. 203). Internal evidence strongly suggests that our surviving copy of this draft was written by someone else following

dictation (perhaps Dampier's). For instance, phrases are crossed out and immediately amended in a way indicating conversation (for example, at fol. 207: "We came in here [Pulo Condore] the 13th day of March; ~~by the 20th day of April I say March~~ and by the 20th day of April we were ready to sail again"). After the January 1687 mutiny which divided Captain Swan's crew into two groups, Dampier describes the command structure of the *Cygnet* as follows: John Read "of Jamaica," captain; Josiah Teat, master; Henry Moore, "company's quartermaster"; and David Shaham, "captain's quartermaster" (DNV, fol. 199). To my knowledge no historian has commented on the existence of two concurrent types of quartermaster aboard a seventeenth-century English ship.

47. This is an uncharacteristic nautical error, probably typographical in origin: they were clearly on the southwestern end of Luzon. Having just described how they were anchored off the northwestern end "of the Island Mindora [*sic*]" between February 19 and 22, Dampier would not have miscalculated his ship's position on the following day as being over 250 miles to the southeast. The route from Mindoro Island to Mariveles is 50 miles straight across open water to the north. Besides this, Dampier tells us flat out that they took "these two Vessels within seven or eight leagues [about twenty-one to twenty-four miles] of Manila," which of necessity places them just southwest of Manila, according to his own map printed in the 1697 edition of his account.

48. DNV, fol. 203.

49. *NV*, 260.

50. Cummins and Soons hesitated to link Dampier with Ramírez (ICS, 79*n*70 and *n*82).

51. Rudyard Kipling, *Just So Stories* (New York: Doubleday, Page and Company, 1907), 83.

52. "New Style" refers to the English adoption of a January 1 date for New Year's. Several date conversion guides are available, both published and online. Remarkably enough, many of these are defective, including Cheney, *A Handbook of Dates:* the table on 172–173, which corresponds to 1687, New Style, gives February 22, 1687, as a Saturday. Given the nature of his text, it is easy to confirm that Dampier kept his journal in the New Style, dating the beginning of the year from January 1, not from March 25. Using John Evelyn's references to weekdays in the 1955 edition of his *Diary* (with New Style dates), particularly entries for September 19 (525) and October 18 (527), 1686, and March 16, 1687 (543, note *b*), we can calculate that February 22 was a Tuesday (Evelyn, *The Diary*, vol. 4, 525–543). We can confirm this retrogressively by using the dates in the diary of Samuel Pepys, such as April 18, 1669, which was a "Lords [*sic*] day [Sunday]" (*The Shorter Pepys*, 1009).

53. Although Cummins and Soons correctly understood in 1984 that the "disparity

in dates" was "not a real one," they discounted the possibility that Ramírez lied, accepting his story that "Bautista and Carvalho" were traveling at some remove from him (ICS, 79n82 and n88). William Bryant also failed to make the connection in his edition of Ramírez's account (Sigüenza y Góngora, *Seis obras*, 43n42). Antonio Lorente Medina came closest to stating the historical basis of Ramírez's narrative in *La prosa de Sigüenza y Góngora*, 163–183.

54. DNV. The two printed editions of Dampier's journal (by Gray and Masefield) give the same date: Wednesday, February 23, 1687. Gray's edition was based on the seventh edition of *A New Voyage* in 1729, while Masefield's reproduced the sixth edition of 1717, titled *Dampier's Voyages.*

55. *NV*, 199; see the discussion of this in Cheney, *A Handbook of Dates*, 17.

56. The Spanish had withdrawn from Mindanao in 1663. Montero y Vidal, *Historia de la piratería malayo-mahometana*, 248–249.

57. *NV*, 255–256.

58. Ibid., 255.

59. Ibid., 256.

60. December 31 was simply officially eliminated from the calendar. Molina, *The Philippines through the Centuries*, vol. 1, 260.

61. "Discurso sobre la razón por que viniendo de las Yslas Philipinas a Macam en la Yndia se encuentra un dia adelantado," in *CDMFN*, vol. 18, 211–212.

62. Cummins and Soons identify "Mariveles" with the "island of Corregidor" (ICS, 78n68).

63. AGI, Filipinas 12, 1, 60, 2. For more on the *Aránzazu*, see Lévesque, *History of Micronesia*, vol. 20, 591, vol. 8, 606, 610, 623–638, vol. 9, 79–92. The crew rosters show that the frigate was normally run by fifteen to twenty-five men, but the names of the November 1686 crew prove that Ferrer's contingent replaced them sometime thereafter.

64. "Enco" (a forty-six-year-old "non-Christian Chinese [*sangley*] sailor" from Amoy) and "Chingco" (a twenty-seven-year-old mixed-race *sangley* sailor from Cochinchina resident in Batavia) were both pilots (*timoneles*) aboard a small frigate from Java bound for Japan with varied cargo, including silks, taken by the *Cygnet* near Canton in the summer of 1687. Mateo Francisco's testimony delivered in Manila in 1688 corroborates Enco and Chingco's story. AGI, Filipinas 12, 1, 60, 4.

65. AGI, Filipinas 12, 1, 60, 4.

66. *NV*, 256–260.

67. The following reconstruction combines the testimony of all thirteen eyewitnesses plus the report filed by the soldier Bartolomé Prieto y Córdoba, who interviewed some of the fifty-two released captives from Capones Island. AGI, Filipinas 12, 1, 60, 2 and 4. Discrepancies are noted.

68. AGI, Filipinas, 12, 1, 60, 2, fol. 1.
69. AGI, Filipinas, 12, 1, 60, 2, fols. 2–4 and 9–10. Bartolomé Luis's memory of the limited firepower of the crew defeated in the afternoon/evening parallels Ramírez's, but the similarity is not exact: Ramírez listed "four pikes" and "two muskets" as their weapons; Bartolomé Luis "four *pinsotes*, six muskets, and one shotgun." We do not know if the *Aránzazu* carried or used cannons, but it would be surprising if it did not. The stern of many smaller ships often did not carry heavy guns, making Mateo Francisco's testimony that the pirogue "se travesó" (kept itself athwart the ship) significant because it explains why a navy frigate was incapable of sinking a relatively smaller vessel such as a pirogue (this was not the only occasion on which the odds favored a larger crew on a smaller vessel).
70. AGI, Filipinas, 12, 1, 60, 2, fol. 16. Miguel Flores was the only witness who said that the battle began after sunset.
71. AGI, Filipinas 12, 1, 60, 4, fol. 24.
72. AGI, Filipinas 12, 1, 60, 2, fols. 5 and 14, and Filipinas 12, 1, 60, 4, fol. 2.
73. Again, the unreliable Flores differed from the rest in his testimony, stating that he had heard one of "our sailors" calculate that the pirates headed off on a west-southwest course. AGI, Filipinas 12, 1, 60, 2, fol. 14.
74. *NV*, 260.
75. There was no strict correspondence between English and Spanish terminology for navy and merchantmen crew ranks in the early modern period, but rough approximations can be made. Generally, a *despensero* (steward) ranked below a *guardián* (roughly equivalent to a quartermaster's mate or assistant), but not all ships had a *guardián*. Pérez-Mallaína, *Los hombres del océano*, 84–102 (English translation: *Spain's Men of the Sea*, 75–98), gives the ranks on a sixteenth-century fleet as pages (*pajes* or cabin boys), apprentices (*grumetes*), sailors, gunners and professional men (*artilleros y oficiales*), typically carpenter, caulker, scribe, barber-surgeon, and chaplain; next up the ladder of authority came the commanding officers: the steward (*despensero*), the quartermaster (*contramaestre*) and his mate (*guardián*), the pilot, the master (sometimes the ship's owner), and finally the captain. The navy also had constables (*alguaciles*), government overseers (*veedores*: inspectors, purveyors, accountants, and treasurers), army officer ranks up to captain general, and, at the top, admirals. A 1706 document lists the twenty-one-year career of one sailor as follows: cabin boy, apprentice, sailor, artilleryman, *guardián*, constable of the water (*alguazil del agua*), *contramaestre*, and finally captain. *CDMFN*, vol. 11, 193.
76. *NV*, 201–211; several eyewitness accounts of these events, including Fr. Kuklein's, survive in Spanish archives. They were written by Jesuit missionaries, Guam officials, and *Santa Rosa* officers and were transcribed by Lévesque in

History of Micronesia, vol. 8, 548–553, 620–638, vol. 9, 19–20, 48–70, 109–117, 152–161, and vol. 13, 100. Fr. Kuklein was kept aboard for nine days to guarantee Spanish compliance with pirate demands. The English pirate deserters' testimony which I discovered in AGI, Filipinas 12, 1, 60, 3, fols. 1–143, provides more evidence corroborating these events.

77. AHNSN, Osuna, 54, 7 and 10; Lévesque, *History of Micronesia*, vol. 9, 59–60, 175–183, vol. 10, 398, and vol. 20, 591. Robles's error of calling the ship the *Santa Rosa* reflects how the new galleon essentially replaced the older one (*Diario de los sucesos notables*, vol. 2, 174–178).

78. Robles, *Diario de los sucesos notables*, vol. 2, 179–180. Jaramillo became one of Galve and Infantado's preferred go-betweens (AHNSN, Osuna 54, 50).

79. "The seizure of a merchant ship," writes Marcus Rediker, "was followed by a moment of great confrontational drama. The pirate captain or quartermaster asked the seamen of the captured vessel who amongst them would serve under the death's head and black colors, and frequently several stepped forward" (*Between the Devil and the Deep Blue Sea*, 260).

80. Irizarry, "Introducción," in *Infortunios*, 11–84.

81. *NV*, 55.

82. E.g., *CDMFN*, vol. 11, 193, 200, 335–340; Lantéry, *Un comerciante saboyano*, 295, 313; and Seijas y Lobera, *Gobierno militar y político*, 471, 522, 525; cf. AN, Série coloniale C8A 4, fol. 414; Corrente Domingues, *Os navios do Mar Oceano*, 451–458; and Torres Ramírez, *La Armada de Barlovento*, 304. Contemporary French *contremaître* and Portuguese *contramestre* are linguistically both analogous to the Spanish and therefore do not solve the riddle of Ramírez's odd hybrid word; only the Dutch word *kwartiermeester* is similar to English. Bruijn, Gaastra, and Schöffer, *Dutch-Asiatic Shipping*, vol. 1, 210. In fact, I have been unable to find any occurence of *cuartomaestre* or *cuartamaestre* in any Spanish books or archives of the time, except for one doubtful nineteenth-century transcription. *CDMFN*, vol. 11, 194.

83. *NV*, 65, 83, 96. During the Cape Horn incidents, Dampier was aboard Captain Cook's ship. Cook died in the summer of 1684 near Cape Blanco, Costa Rica. Quartermaster Edward Davis was made captain in his stead. Dampier joined Captain Swan's crew a year later, when Davis headed back to Peru and Swan turned north toward Acapulco. Ibid., 157.

84. *NV*, 252. Ramírez's count of 140 crew members roughly matches the calculations of Brouwer and Dampier, but only if we subtract the number of deserters and add an equal number of prisoners, slaves, or Mindanayan recruits.

85. AGI, Filipinas 12, 1, 60, 3, fols. 6–143. The Irish prisoner believed that two Sevillians named Miguel were aboard, but William "Bans" only remembered one non-Indian, nonmestizo, nonblack, non-English subject, "whose caste

he did not know." Uriarte was either one of the "two Mulattos" captured near Salagua (Manzanillo) on December 1, 1685, or, more likely, the livestock driver taken at Mazatlan in late January 1686 or the Spaniard taken near Tepic ("Santa Pecaque"/Santiago Ixcuintla) on February 18. *NV*, 177–192, 252. This cruel "Miguel" must be distinguished from the equally cruel "*Michael* a *Mindanayan*" mentioned by Dampier: ibid., 345. For San José de Copal, see Montes González, "Reflejos de una ambición novohispana," 159. Miguel is not the only recorded Spanish convert to anti-Spanish piracy: *AE*, vol. 5, 180, records the curious case of Diego Grillo, a Havana creole who terrorized Caribbean waters until he was captured and executed in the early 1670s; Grillo apparently specialized in killing all European-born Spaniards.

86. Lévesque, *History of Micronesia*, vol. 9, 186; nevertheless, Cushner argues that shipyards in Cavite and elsewhere in this period were suffering from labor shortages, "the perennial problem in the process of shipbuilding," particularly after the revolt among the Pampango forced-labor woodcutters in 1660 (*Spain in the Philippines*, 117–126).

CHAPTER THREE

1. AHNSN, Osuna 54, 59, 3, and Osuna 55, 10.
2. Clayton, *Los astilleros de Guayaquil colonial*, 79.
3. AHNSN, Osuna 51, 59, 1–2, Osuna 54, 47, Osuna 55, 7, 2, and Osuna 53, 3 and 6; Stanhope, *Spain under Charles II*, 11; Chatelain, *The Defense of Spanish Florida*, 159n11. French officials in Europe as well as the Americas were dealing with an equally critical financial shortfall. AN, Série coloniale C8A 4, fols. 423–427; Peter, *Le Port et l'Arsenal de Toulon sous Louis XIV*, 209–235.
4. AHNSN, Osuna 55, 43, 1.
5. Vélez, head of the Council of the Indies, sent a letter to the viceroy on March 22, 1691, essentially accusing him of insubordination for privileging American initiatives over European ones; Galve accused Madrid of ignoring American realities, a "capricious willfulness." Letter, Viceroy to Council of the Indies, May 15, 1693, AGI, México, 617; cf. Leonard, *Spanish Approach to Pensacola*, 54, 116–117, 123–131, 194.
6. Even so, 500 pesos was equivalent at least to ten years' salary for a seaman, over a year's salary for a naval commander, and half a year's salary for a governor. Phillips, *Six Galleons for the King of Spain*, 238–239; García Bernal, *La sociedad en Yucatán*, 76: for legal versus illegal Caribbean markets, see Zahedieh, "The Merchants of Port Royal, Jamaica, and the Spanish Contraband Trade," 582.
7. Sinnapah Arasaratnam, "The Dutch East India Company and Its Coromandel Trade, 1700–1740," in Prakash, ed., *European Commercial Expansion in Early Modern Asia*, 148.

8. Viraphol, *Tribute and Profit*, 51–59; Berthold Laufer, "The Relations of the Chinese to the Philippine Islands," and C. R. Boxer, "Plata es Sangre: Sidelights on the Drain of Spanish-American Silver in the Far East, 1550–1700," in Flynn et al., eds., *European Entry into the Pacific*, 55–85, 172–181; Bentley Duncan, "Navigation between Portugal and Asia in the Sixteenth and Seventeenth Century," in Prakash, ed., *European Commercial Expansion in Early Modern Asia*, 2; Risso, *Merchants and Faith*, 46, 53.

9. *RRSFC*, vol. 5, 158; *Ou-Mun*, 139.

10. ANAM, Sous-série B7 60, Letter, Lagny to Monsieur de la Touche, October 19, 1689, fols. 274v–275v (quotation). The Dutch were the only Europeans at the time allowed to trade with Japan. Leur, *Indonesian Trade and Society*, 160–161; cf. *RRSFC*, vol. 2, 50–51, 157, 240; Costa, *The Jesuits in the Philippines*, 122; Hall, *Maritime Trade and State Development in Early Southeast Asia*, 244; M. T. Paske-Smith, "The Japanese Trade and Residence in the Philippines: Before and during the Spanish Occupation," in Flynn et al., eds., *European Entry into the Pacific*, 163; and Breazeale, "Thai Maritime Trade," in *From Japan to Arabia*, 35.

11. Quoted in Hutchinson, *Adventurers in Siam in the Seventeenth Century*, 113–114.

12. Coolhaas, *Generale Missiven*, vol. 5, 169; *RRSFC*, vol. 2, 39–43, 130–135; D. K. Bassett, "British 'Country' Trade and Local Trade Networks in the Thai and Malay States, c. 1680–1770," in Prakash, ed., *European Commercial Expansion in Early Modern Asia*, 275–276; Adrian B. Lapian, "Power Politics in Southeast Asian Waters," in Breazeale, ed., *From Japan to Arabia*, 143, Hutchinson, *Adventurers in Siam*, 115.

13. Viraphol, *Tribute and Profit*, 20–21 (quotation); Teixeira, *Portugal na Tailândia*, 44.

14. *Ou-Mun*, 205.

15. Luis Filipe F. R. Thomaz, "The Portuguese in the Seas of the Archipelago during the Sixteenth Century," in Prakash, ed., *European Commercial Expansion in Early Modern Asia*, 33; Reid, *Southeast Asia in the Age of Commerce*, 116; Hall and Whitmore, "Southeast Asian Trade and the Isthmian Struggle, 1000–1200," in Hall and Whitmore, eds., *Explorations in Early Southeast Asian History*, 322; *Ou-Mun*, 205.

16. *RRSFC*, vol. 1, 5, 93, and vol. 3, 117–244; Coolhaas, *Generale Missiven*, vol. 5, 157; Glamann, *Dutch-Asiatic Trade*, 178; Viraphol, *Tribute and Profit*, 7.

17. Reid, *Southeast Asia in the Age of Commerce*, 118 (quotation); Om Prakash, "Trade in a Culturally Hostile Environment: Europeans in the Japan Trade, 1550–1700," Sanjay Subrahmanyam, "The Coromandel Malacca Trade in the Sixteenth Century: A Study in Its Evolving," and Arasaratnam, "The Dutch East India Company and Its Coromandel Trade," in Prakash, ed., *European*

Commercial Expansion in Early Modern Asia, 125, 44–45, 146; Kristof Glamann, "The Dutch East India Company's Trade in Japanese Copper, 1645–1736," in Flynn and Giráldez, eds., *Metals and Monies*, 104; Viraphol, *Tribute and Profit*, 16, 28–62; Glamann, *Dutch-Asiatic Trade*, 113.

18. Gervaise, *The Natural and Political History of the Kingdom of Siam*, 232 (quotation); Glamann, *Dutch-Asiatic Trade*, 178; Nagazumi Yoko, "Ayutthaya and Japan: Embassies and Trade in the Seventeenth Century," in Breazeale, ed., *From Japan to Arabia*, 102; compare *Ou-Mun*, 140.

19. Hutchinson, *Adventurers in Siam*, 2, 54; Breazeale, "Thai Maritime Trade and the Ministry Responsible," in *From Japan to Arabia*, 29.

20. Forbin, *The Siamese Memoirs*, 99.

21. *RRSFC*, vol. 4, 37, 30 (quotations), and vol. 8, 198–199, 220–222.

22. *RRSFC*, vol. 4, 50, 148 ("that notorious, ungrateful, naughty man"); Coolhaas, *Generale Missiven*, vol. 5, 123–124; Forbin, *The Siamese Memoirs*, 181 (quotations); on the French position, see also Hutchinson, *1688 Revolution in Siam*, 46. On Phaulkon, see Hutchinson, *Adventurers in Siam*; Cruyse, *Louis XIV et le Siam*; Sioris, *Phaulkon, the Greek First Counsellor at the Court of Siam*.

23. *RRSFC*, vol. 4, 37 ("all the English"), 54, 60–61, 89, 97, 100 ("hanging some"), 102–105, 132–134, 149; Hutchinson, *Adventurers in Siam*, 131–213; Wood, *A History of Siam*, 207–213; Jumsai, *History of Anglo-Thai Relations*, 17–27. This was the same Captain Weldten and *Curtana*, carrying Dampier, which Barlow met in 1689 off Vietnam.

24. *RRSFC*, vol. 4, 142–146.

25. AHNSN, Osuna 55, 16, 5.

26. *RRSFC*, vol. 4, 183–200.

27. Coolhaas, *Generale Missiven*, 156–157.

28. Barlow, *Barlow's Journal*, vol. 2, 393; cf. *RRSFC*, vol. 4, 64; Hutchinson, *Adventurers in Siam*, 145; Anderson, *English Intercourse with Siam*, 335–349; Mukherjee, *The Rise and Fall of the East India Company*, 79; Wood, *A History of Siam*, 199; and Smithies, *A Resounding Failure*, 57–61. Dampier later served aboard Weldten's ship in 1688 (*NV*, 338). For the machinations of Weldten and White, see Collis, *Siamese White*.

29. KA VOC 1320, Letter, Joannes Camphuys (Gouv.-Gen.) et al. to Heren XVII, Batavia, December 23, 1687, reproduced in Coolhaas, *Generale Missiven*, vol. 5, 123–125; AHNSN, Osuna 55, 16, 5; cf. Smithies, "Madame Constance's Jewels."

30. On Dampier and Mindanao, see Quiason, *English "Country Trade" with the Philippines*, 112–138.

31. *NV*, 228, 252–255, 337.

32. AGI, Filipinas, 12, 1, 60, 3, fols. 14 and 16.

33. *NV*, 337.

34. KA VOC, 1320, Letter, Joannes Camphuys (Governor-General) et al. to Heren XVII, Batavia, December 23, 1687, fols. 73v-74v: Brouwer arrived on Mindanao on November 5. Coolhaas, *Generale Missiven*, vol. 5, 110; AGI, Filipinas 12, 1, 60, 3, 6–143.

35. *NV*, 298.

36. In summer winds are from the southwest; in winter they settle back into the regular trade wind pattern, blowing out of the northeast and dictating a schedule for Siamese fleets to China, Japan, and Manila. *Ou-Mun*, 83, confirmed by Dampier, "A Discourse of Winds, Breezes, Storms, Tides, and Currents," in *Dampier's Voyages* (1906), vol. 2, 229–321; cf. Viraphol, *Tribute and Profit*, 35–41; and *RRSFC*, vol. 2, 51, 55, 105.

37. *Ou-Mun*, 70.

38. One frigate arrived on July 29 and the other on August 2. Le Blanc, *The History of Siam, 1688*, 16, 84, 111–112.

39. DNV, fol. 207. "Ships coming and going to and from China and Japan," wrote the East India factor of Chusan in 1700, "pass by in sight thereof . . . so that in respect of it's [*sic*] situation 'tis far better than this or any other part of China to settle upon in respect of all the Coasts of India, because it will be an intercepting Port to and from China and Japan, both which Countries will doubtless go no farther than Pullo-Condore for Trade, if they find a plentiful market of buying and selling there." *RRSFC*, vol. 5, 160; cf. Wilbur, *The East India Company*, 224; Quiason, *English "Country Trade" with the Philippines*, 36, 54*n*18; and Teixeira, *Os militares em Macau*, 71.

40. AGI, Filipinas 12, 1, 60, 4, *NV*, 270–274.

41. For this context, see Hutchinson, *Adventurers in Siam*, 89; Smithies, *A Siamese Embassy Lost in Africa*, 64–65.

42. DNV, fol. 207.

43. Two copies of Ambrose Cowley's journal describing Eaton's voyage survive, BL, Sloane MS 54 and 1050. For the split between Eaton and Cowley, see Sloane 1050, fols. 67ff. The quotation is from Hacke's transcription of the printed Cowley journal reproduced in Kerr, *A General History and Collection of Voyages*, vol. 10, 233. See also *NV*, 54–76, 83–106; and Williams, *The Great South Sea*, 93–98.

44. The *Good Hope*'s voyage can be reconstructed from the two archival copies of the declaration of Dr. Henry Watson, George Robinson, and Francis Cooke in IO 5582–5583; cf. BL IOR H/36, fol. 321. Charles Hill's transcription of these in "Episodes of Piracy in Eastern Seas" contains a few mistakes. In 1984 Cummins apparently failed to consult the primary documents, unfortunately relying on Hill, and consequently fell victim to the most important of these errors.

Hill carelessly transcribed the first words of both IO 5582 and 5583, "April 30th 1687," as the date of the testimony of Hopkins instead of what it clearly was: the day on which the *Good Hope* arrived in Bengal. This misled Cummins into believing that "a disparity in dating destroys the hypothesis" linking Mackintosh to Ramírez in "*Infortunios de Alonso Ramírez*: A Just History of Fact?" 301–302. For the date of the veering of the monsoon, see DNV, fol. 207.

45. IO 5582–5583. Only Mackintosh and Beard were apparently caught and hanged at Guinea, sometime after 1687 and before 1690 (5582 was received in London on July 29, 1690).

46. Ramírez begins the paragraph by listing his two principal allies aboard, "Nicpat" the "Master Gunner" (without naming his captain) and "Dick" (specifying "Captain Bel" as his captain) but finishes with Captain Donkin coming to his aid at a critical moment in his release when many of the crew wanted to cut the Spanish captives' throats. I take the inconsistent reference to the two captains' names at this tightly composed and tense point in Ramírez's story as a conflation of the two British captains. Perhaps this was involuntary: Bel appears consistently as the cruel "captain," Donkin as the lenient one, so it made narrative sense to distance the rebellious Nicpat and Dick from Bel instead of Donkin (but also see below for a discussion of his two "releases").

47. The first name is spelled "Dunkin" in IO 5582–5583.

48. DNV, fol. 203.

49. Perhaps even three if he spent time aboard the *Cygnet*.

50. IO 5582–5583. It is perhaps significant to recall here that Ramírez was the son of a ship's carpenter and was probably experienced in the same shipboard work as Cornelius.

51. Several of the Spanish eyewitnesses testified that the *Cygnet* sailed to Siam with the intent of capturing a specific ship but failed to do so because it ran aground on the sandbars at the entrance to the river leading up to Ayutthaya (Bangkok). AGI, Filipinas 12, 1, 60, 4, fol. 3.

52. Ramírez: one sampan, one ship belonging to the king of Siam, and two Portuguese ships; Dampier (draft: DNV, fols. 203–209): one junk attacked unsuccessfully; one small vessel ("small junk"), one large junk, one bark; Dampier (printed book: *NV*, 265–274): three barks, two small vessels, and one junk (he only implies that any of these six vessels were taken as prizes); *Good Hope* eyewitnesses (IO 5582–5583): one ship, one prow, two junks, all attacked but none taken.

53. It would be too speculative to argue without further archival evidence that the *Aránzazu* was Ramírez's shipwrecked frigate. The only indication of this possiblity is Ramírez's admission in Chapter 3 that the pirates attacking Sukadana had more large ships (*embarcaciones mayores*) than just the *Good Hope*:

perhaps Ferrer cruised with Mackintosh all the way to Madagascar or beyond.

54. The king of Siam lost several of the European ships in his service to privateers or pirates in 1687, including the *Revenge, Kiddaree, Mary, Resolution* (taken at Mergui during the massacre of July 14), and a Portuguese vessel named the *Santa Rosa*, commanded by Don José de Heredia; but the details of these captures do not allow us to link them specifically to Ramírez's events off Pulo Ubi. *RRSFC*, vol. 4, 192; Hutchinson, *Adventurers in Siam*, 137.

55. AHM, Leal Senado 531, fols. 5v-6, February 23, 1686; *Ou-Mun*, 128–136, 169; Letters, Manuel Pires de Moura to Fr. Soares, January 28, 1721, and Fr. Soares to Sennado, June 30, 1721, *AM*, vol. 1, 155–156 ("time of our greatest vexations"); Teixeira, *Portugal na Tailândia*, 141 ("605 *cates*")–148. The Qing did not forgive Macao for supplying the retreating Ming dynasty forces with heavy artillery between 1621 and 1644. Teixeira, *Os militares em Macau*, 135, 197–269.

56. AHM, Leal Senado 37, fol. 64, Leal Senado 319, fols. 103, 115, and 120–138, Leal Senado 331, fols. 80–81 and 90, Leal Senado 531, fols. 29v-30.

57. For this embassy, see Smithies, *A Siamese Embassy Lost in Africa.*

58. Colomba, *Resumo da história de Macau*, 33–43.

59. Seabra, *A embaixada au Sião de Pero Vaz de Siqueira*; Smithies and na Pombejra, "Instructions Given to the Siamese Envoys Sent to Portugal, 1684," 125.

60. Burnay, "Notes chronologiques sur les missions jésuites du Siam au XVIIe siècle," 193–194; Teixeira, *Macau e a sua diocese*, 169–204. The *padroado* conflict originated in disputes over secular versus religious control of missions but spread as Jesuits, Franciscans, and others faced off against the Congregation of the Faith. Assento, viceroy in Council, Panelim, February 25, 1684 (not 1694 as printed in the 1875 published transcript), reproduced in *Archio Portuguez-Oriental*, vol. 6, 1298; ANAM, Sous-série B7 58, Letter, Lagny to Des Granges, consul in Lisbon, September 25, 1686, fol. 268; Forbin, *The Siamese Memoirs*, 171; Teixeira, *Portugal na Tailândia*, 295, 320–321, 383–386. Phaulkon seems to have preferred to use Portuguese soldiers and missionaries as emissaries and spies, if we believe the suspicions of Fr. Claude Céberet, who was in Siam in 1687–1688. Jacq-Hergoualc'h, ed., *Etude historique et critique*, 70, 114.

61. RAH 9/2668, 125 (old Legajo 2, 125), Letter, Luis Pimentel, S.J., to Procurador General, December 20, 1687; Teixeira, *Portugal na Tailândia*, 296 ("greedy merchants"), 304–313, 431 ("Kantoor"/"trading post").

62. In later years Fr. Soares took over Maldonado's role as mediator between Siam and foreign powers. AHM, Leal Senado 319, fols. 120–125v.

63. Maldonado died in Cambodia in 1699. Teixeira, *Portugal na Tailândia*, 41, 69–70, 385; Fr. Pierre Joseph d'Orléans, S.J., *Histoire de M. Constance*, 19–21, 92; Fr. Claude Céberet, S.J., in Jacq-Hergoualc'h, ed., *Etude historique et critique*, 114; Père Guy Tachard, *Second voyage*, 137.

64. Dorsey, "Going to School with Savages," 399.
65. Quoted by Teixeira, *Portugal na Tailândia*, 435–439. Galve had heard about all this as well as the "revolution in Siam" which had toppled Phaulkon and destroyed French ambitions by February 1690. AHNSN, Osuna 55, 16, 2–4.
66. The Chinese fleet in 1688, for example, arrived on February 8, bringing live silkworms, which one Franciscan hoped would soon provide a direct supply for "all of America and Europe." AHNSN, Osuna 55, 16, 3. Given that everyone in southeast Asia knew about the triangle trade and its schedule, Dampier's comment that the pirates chose Pulo Condore because they "might lie snug for a while" there, far from "any great Place of Commerce," sounds misleading (*NV*, 264).
67. Maldonado was back in the Siamese capital on June 23, 1687, because on that day he expedited the marriage certificate of a "sieur Coche," an employee of the French trading company established in Ayutthaya. Burnay, "Notes chronologiques sur les missions jésuites du Siam," 193. Teixeira, learning of the parallel between Ramírez's account and 1680s Portuguese-Siamese diplomacy from Edgar Knowlton (late of the University of Hawaii), believed that it was the 1684 Pero Vaz de Siqueira mission which Ramírez encountered (*Portugal na Tailândia*, 152).
68. Teixeira, *Portugal na Tailândia*, 41; AHM, Leal Senado 531, fol. 7.
69. *Ou-Mun*, 139.
70. The city council and merchants' organization were still arguing over these Siamese payments in early 1687. AHM, Leal Senado 531, fols. 13–14.
71. AHM, Leal Senado 531, fols. 14–17. The two Siamese vessels set sail for home on September 1, 1687; Teixeira based his reconstruction of these elusive details in *Portugal na Tailândia* (42, 340) on the *Mémoire* of Claude de Bèze (1657–1695) and on the Tokyo Bunko, a Portuguese archival collection from Macao sold to Japan in 1917 by the Australian George Ernest Morrison, former political advisor to the People's Republic of China.
72. This conflated Phaulkon, who was born Greek but was Italian by education and Venetian by citizenship until he took up English and then Siamese service, with Siam's mercantile agent and governor in Mergui, Samuel White and Richard Burnaby. White and Burnaby, in connivance with Elihu Yale (then governor of Madras and future founder of Yale University), were responsible for the Mergui massacre, as noted above. Bèze, *1688 Revolution in Siam*, 47n1 and n2; Wilbur, *The East India Company*, 235.
73. Hutchinson, *Adventurers in Siam*, 103, 113, 117; cf. Smithies, *A Siamese Embassy Lost in Africa*, 64.
74. Forbin, *The Siamese Memoirs*, 85–87. "Portuguese-Creolian . . . is the name they give to those born in the Indies" (quoted in Smithies, *Mission Made Impossible*, 83, 229).

75. Shortly thereafter Phaulkon grew jealous of Forbin's increasing influence with the king and conspired against him, releasing all the Portuguese prisoners and recalling those who had been banished. Forbin, *The Siamese Memoirs*, 85–87 (adapted with minor alterations from the excellent translation by Michael Smithies); cf. Orléans, *Histoire de M. Constance*, 37–38; cf. AHNSN, Osuna 55, 16, 5.

76. AHNSN, Osuna 55, 16, 2–5.

77. Cruz Barney, *El combate a la piratería en Indias*; Ritchie, *Captain Kidd and the War against the Pirates*; Hebb, *Piracy and the English Government*, 272; Bennett, "Cary Helyar, Merchant and Planter of Seventeenth-Century Jamaica," 59; Earle, *The Wreck of the Almiranta*, 103–110.

78. James Brand, who knew Dampier personally from cruises together, once said to his novice shipmates aboard the *Roebuck* (which Dampier commanded from 1699 to 1701) that "they would find Captain Dampier another sort of man when he came on the other side of the equatorial line." Gill, *The Devil's Mariner*, 267. Ramírez clearly did not share Dampier's naturalist aspirations on *this* side of the equatorial line, as evidenced in the many geographical, botanical, and zoological interruptions to the flow of the pirating account in *A New Voyage*.

79. 1694 House of Commons resolution quoted in Mukherjee, *The Rise and Fall of the East India Company*, 84 ("right of all Englishmen"); *RRSFC*, vol. 4, 112, 137–138, 144–146; Wood, *A History of Siam*, 219; Hutchinson, *Adventurers in Siam*, 165; Ritchie, *Captain Kidd and the War against the Pirates*, 135–136; Howell, *Complete Collection of State Trials*, vol. 13, 456 ("the barbarous Nations"); Baer, "'Captain John Avery' and the Anatomy of a Mutiny," 17 ("battlefield between supporters and opponents"); Baer, "William Dampier at the Crossroads"; Gill, *The Devil's Mariner*, 6, 247, 262–266; *The Truest and Largest Account of the Late Earthquake in Jamaica*, 20 ("great Day of Tryal"); cf. Barnard, *Ashton's Memorial*. Dampier survived the maelstrom. By the time Dampier had dinner with the famous Samuel Pepys and John Evelyn on August 6, 1698, his dubious past had been forgiven by the English elite. Gray, "Introduction," in *NV*, xliv; cf. ibid., xxii, xxxv; Cordingly, *Under the Black Flag*, 85; and Preston and Preston, *A Pirate of Exquisite Mind*, 1. The patronage of Sir Hans Sloane, founder of the British Museum as well as secretary and then president of the Royal Society, helped in Dampier's transformation. Wilkinson, *Dampier*, 4, 150.

80. López Lázaro, "Pirates of the Caribbean."

81. IO 5582–5583.

82. Indirect evidence of the Sukadana sack might come from the subsequent Borneo retaliatory attacks on two ships at the port of Banjarmasin, the English-captained Dutch ship *De Fortuyn* on July 15, 1687, and the English ship *St. Catherine* on August 9, 1687. Coolhaas, *Generale Missiven*, vol. 5, 185. On Sukadana's economic importance, especially in terms of diamond exports, see

Beeckman, *A Voyage to and from the Island of Borneo*, 45, 89–90; Coolhaas, *Generale Missiven*, vol. 5, 124–125; *RRSFC*, vol. 2, 154; Reid, *Southeast Asia in the Age of Commerce*, 170; María Lourdes Díaz-Trechuelo, "Eighteenth-Century Philippine Economy: Commerce," in Flynn et al., eds., *European Entry into the Pacific*, 255; Irwin, *Nineteenth-Century Borneo*, 5.

83. BL, Sloane MS 1050, fols. 61–96; this alliance is confirmed by Spanish evidence: AGI, Filipinas 3, 57.

84. Such long-distance coordination may seem improbable, but it was a common buccaneering and pirate strategy. Dampier himself related several examples of how the original Franco-English buccaneering fleet of ten ships he had belonged to split up and rejoined several times off the Pacific Coast of the Americas in 1685, often with clear schedules for meeting up at particular places.

85. BL IOR E/3/48, 5690, "Captain William Friki, his Misfortunes." For more on Deerrow, see NA C9/123/33. East India Company officials estimated by the mid-1690s that pirates had created "45 settlements on St. Mary's island": "There is no safety among the company's sailors, soldiers or English servants, the alluring gain of piracy too often prevailing upon them to join with the pirates." BL IOR H/36, fol. 329; for Dampier's accounts of the voyages of Knight and the *Cygnet*, after he jumped ship at the Nicobar islands, see *NV*, 300, 338–342.

86. Ovington, *A Voyage to Suratt*, 102-103; cf. Barlow, *Barlow's Journal*, vol. 2, 403; from Dampier's evidence, Captain Read of *Cygnet* fame "and five or six more" were apparently aboard it on their way to pirate retirement (*NV*, 341).

87. Perhaps Ramírez's occasional conversations with their crews at St. Augustine explain why he confused the routes of the *Cygnet* and *Nicholas* across the Pacific and through the Philippine Islands; compare Chapter 3 of *Misfortunes* with Cowley's journal (BL, Sloane 1050, fols. 3–67) and Spanish eyewitness testimony (AGI, Filipinas 12, 1, 60, 5, fol. 5).

88. BL IOR E/3/48 5690; not during Dampier's first stay in Sumatra in June 1688 or his third in 1690 (*NV*, 336–338).

89. This is based on my re-creation of the dates for Ramírez's Caribbean course, estimating back in time from the dates he gives for his stay in Yucatan: see Map 3.2; for Hewetson's movements, see *APCE*, vol. 2, entries 282 (p. 128), 291 (p. 130), 294 (p. 131); and *CSP*, vol. 8, entries 312 (p. 112), 348 (p. 123), 548 (p. 175), 771 (p. 219), 789 (pp. 226–234); Spencer, *A True and Faithful Relation of the Proceedings of the Forces of Their Majesties*; Ritchie, *Captain Kidd and the War against the Pirates*, 30; Crouse, *The French Struggle for the West Indies*, 159. There is a much slimmer possibility that Ramírez saw the French fleet of Admiral Jean Du Casse. For the admiral's movements, see AN, Série coloniale C14 66–73, C8A 34, 116–122, 258–261, and 371–372, C68A 410; Guérin, *Histoire maritime de France*, vol. 3, 463–464; Gasser, "De la mer des Antilles à l'océan Indien," 1;

Granier, *Marins de France au combat*, 142–151; and Du Casse, *L'Amiral du Casse*. Ramírez narrowly missed bumping into the not-yet-notorious Captain William Kidd as he sailed by St. Kitts. *CSP*, vol. 8, entry 345 (p. 122).

90. Given the relative unimportance of a stray small frigate during a state of war and Governor Hinselin's hit-and-miss reporting style, it is not surprising that the correspondence between the French Caribbean officials makes no reference to the brief encounter. AN, Séries coloniales C68A and C8A.

91. Nadelmann, "Global Prohibition Regimes," 485.

92. Bernecker, *Contrabando, ilegalidad y corrupción*, 48; see also Feliciano Ramos, *El contrabando inglés en el Caribe y el golfo de México*.

93. AHNSN, Osuna 55, 15, 2, and Osuna 54, 59, 3.

94. *NV*, 303, 287, 160; cf. *NV*, 58, 127, 128, 277; and Haring, *The Buccaneers in the West Indies*, 237n3.

95. AGI, Escribanía 230B, 5, 68–71, 88–90; AHNSN, Osuna 55, 53, 2, 6 and 7, Osuna 55, 67, Osuna 56, 13, and Osuna 55, 15, 2; Torres Ramírez, *La Armada de Barlovento*, 303–308; Vidargas, *San Juan de Ulúa y Carlos de Sigüenza y Góngora*, 10–11; Zapatero, "Las 'llaves' fortificadas de la América Hispana," 134; Rodríguez del Valle, *El Castillo de San Felipe del Golfo Dulce*; Arroyo, "El Reconocimiento de la península de Yucatán realizado por el ingeniero militar Juan de Dios González"; and Moncada Maya, "En torno a la defensa de la península de Yucatán durante el siglo XVIII"; Zahedieh, "The Merchants of Port Royal," 582–586 (quotations).

96. Perhaps Juan López is one of the merchants by that name mentioned in AGI, Contratación 5435, 3, 86, Contratación 5441, 2, 63, Contratación 5438, 56, Contratación 5442, 56, Contratación 5442, 142, Contratación 5448, 121, Contratación 5452, 53, or Contratación 5454, 3, 94.

97. Ramírez's relative is not the Don Luis Ramírez Guerra who traveled repeatedly between Seville and New Spain from 1678 to 1683 (AGI, Contratación 5442, 54, Contratación 5540A, 1, fol. 296v, Pasajeros, 13, 1277, and Contratación 5445, 15, Pasajeros, 13, 1870) but rather the very prominent Oaxacan nobleman Don Luis Ramírez de Aguilar, who was named *regidor* (town councillor) on March 9, 1677. AGI, México 195, 15; a record of his service and merits in Indiferente 132, 49, notes that by 1689 he had held several important posts, including *regidor* in Teutitlán and Macuysuchil. In the 1690s Don Luis would even take on the descendants of Hernán Cortés in a legal battle. AGI, Escribanía 181B and 959.

98. Cuicateca and Mixe were linguistically defined subgroups of the Mixteca and Mayan language groups; "Chontal," however, simply meant "foreigner" in Nahuatl and in colonial times referred to a diverse set of peoples inhabiting the regions of the Tehuantepec isthmus, the Chiapas mountains, and areas south into

Central America; likewise, colonial usage applied "Soconusco" to a large area from the marshy lowlands on the Coatzacoalcos River in Veracruz southeast into the Guatemalan highlands. Scholes and Royes, *The Maya Chontal Indians of Acalan-Tixchel*, 164–165, 326; Garibay K., *Diccionario Porrúa de historia, biografía y geografía de México*, s.v. "Soconusco." Ramírez's "master" López died in the city of "Talistaca."

99. Lantéry, *Un comerciante saboyano*, 264.

100. In 1688 Tijosuco had a declared *encomienda* population of 1,800 Indians. García Bernal, *Población y encomienda bajo los Austrias*, 124. For the Pacheco-Poblete connection, see AGI, Indiferente, 194. The *encomienda* survived until 1785 in the Yucatan, unlike other areas in New Spain. The top oligarchic provincial family, the Pachecos, dominated the strongest *encomienda* region, Valladolid. García Bernal, *Desarrollo agrario en el Yucatán colonial*, 35, 43, 93, 257. Of the top twenty-four families in Yucatan in the late 1600s, half intermarried with the Pachecos, due to their importance. García Bernal, *La sociedad en Yucatán*, 90–101. For Melchor Pacheco and his family, see AGI, México 242A, 31, Indiferente 450, A 5, fols. 255v–256, Indiferente 451 A 8, fols. 159–160, México 242B, 61, México 244, 6, 1, Indiferente 120, 50, and Indiferente 455, A 25, fols. 133–35, Escribanía 306A, México 244, 10, fol. 123 (April 3, 1660); López de Cogolludo, *Historia de la provincia de Yucathán*, 165–169, 223; Rubio Mañé, *Introducción al estudio de los virreyes*, vol. 2, 100–110; Scholes and Roys, *The Maya Chontal Indians*, 164; and Dumond, *The Machete and the Cross*, 14.

101. Ceferino de Castro y Belasco's titles of *regidor* and *fiel ejecutor* were both confirmed on April 21, 1689. AGI, México 198, 50.

102. López de Cogolludo, *Historia de la Provincia de Yucathán*, 223.

103. Duuren, *The Kris*, 14, 16, 22, 26, 50, 59–61, 79, 81.

104. AGN, *Real cédula*, November 14, 1690. Only officers on board pirate vessels were executed under Spanish law until 1690; all other crew members were sentenced to galley service (hard labor). After 1690, however, anyone in a pirate crew who had participated in actual physical violence or property damage could be executed. Cruz Barney, *El combate a la piratería*, 36, 59–60.

105. AGI, Contratación 5539, 3, fols. 119–122 (in the registry, Pasajeros, 12, 1276, November 14, 1657).

106. The diagram summarizes the main points of the Spanish Law of Prizes in the second half of the seventeenth century according to the 1633 *Ordenanzas del buen govierno de la Armada*; Montemayor, *Discurso político, histórico, jurídico*; Escalona, *Gazofilacium*; Abreu y Bertodano, *Tratado jurídico-político*. The "questions" on the diagram do not correspond to any systematic form of original preestablished questions or Romano-canonical legal *quaestiones*; they merely help to summarize issues discussed in the various sources.

107. Montemayor, *Discurso político, histórico, jurídico*, fols. 3, 24, 29, 93. Montemayor agreed with Robert Bellarmine's innovative 1624 argument that soldiers looting during a war which was not conducted in a proper manner to redress the wrongs listed in the declaration of war (question 8) were guilty of sin but not of theft or robbery. Ibid., fols. 18–21. Galve admired Montemayor's legal work. AHNSN, Osuna 54, 56.

108. Article 397, *Ordenanzas del buen govierno de la armada*; Montemayor, *Discurso político, histórico, jurídico*, 25, 51, 72–74. *Derecho de postliminio* remained highly controversial into the nineteenth century: e.g., Bello, *Principios de derecho internacional*, 194.

109. Seijas y Lobera, *Gobierno militar y político*, 387, and introduction by Pérez-Mallaína Bueno, 94; Torres Ramírez, *La Armada de Barlovento*, 287–288 (quotations); Lantéry, *Un comerciante saboyano*, 285.

110. The medieval jurist Bartolus of Sassoferrato allowed 100 miles; Jean Bodin in the sixteenth century, 60 miles; Hugo Grotius, almost none. Grotius, *Commentary on the Law of Prize and Booty*, 239. Seventeenth-century practice increasingly held to the cannon-shot rule, which averaged out to 3 miles. Scott, "Introduction," in Bynkershoek, *De Dominio Maris Dissertatio*, 16–21, 364–401; Nys, *Etudes de droit international*, 260–272; for an important case study, see Ittersum, "*Mare liberum* in the West Indies?"

111. For example, ANAM, Sous-série B7 62, fol. 75 and Sous-série B7 63, fol. 75. The *Ordenanzas del buen govierno de la armada del mar océano* of January 24, 1633, were still in effect in the second half of the century. Torres Ramírez, *La Armada de Barlovento*, 287, 303. "It hath been usual for many Years past," wrote Dampier, "for the Governour of *P. Guavres* [Port au Prince] to send blank Commissions to Sea by many of his Captains, with Orders to dispose of them to whom they saw convenient," to create a "Sanctuary and Asylum" for "all People of desperate Fortunes" while "increasing their own Wealth" (*NV*, 136).

112. Abreu y Bertodano, *Tratado jurídico-político*, 149, 189–220, citing the 1718 *Ordenanza*, which on these points did not deviate from the 1624 royal *cédula*, Roman law (*Institutes*), royal statutes (*Recopilaciones*), continental common law, and Spanish juridical literature (especially Gregorio López); see also Grotius, *Commentary on the Law of Prize and Booty*, 97, 325–326; Wilkins, *Captain Kidd and His Skeleton Island*, 191; and, for a typical French Caribbean case, Gasser's discussion of the September 27, 1689, decision by governor-general Charles de Courbon, Count of Blénac, in "De la mer des Antilles à l'océan Indien."

113. Escalona, *Gazofilacium*, 209–211; Abreu y Bertodano, *Tratado jurídico-político*, 16–30, 105. By the early 1700s nine documents were required (in ascending order of importance): a license to sail (*pasaporte*), the ship's registration (*letras del mar*), a logbook, a health certificate, proof of manufacture or purchase, a

cargo and passenger registry (*libro de sobordo*), the freight and/or voyage contract (*contrato de fletamento* or *carta-partida*), a receipt for cargo (*conocimiento* in the Atlantic and *póliza* in the Mediterranean), and an account of cargo value (*factura*).

114. Ladero Quesada, *Fiscalidad y poder real en Castilla*, 59, 207; Cárceles de Gea, *Fraude y desobediencia fiscal*, 169–197; Goñi Gaztambide, *Historia de la bula de la cruzada en España*, 630 (quotation). The copies of the papal bull printed for 1690 had arrived in New Spain on October 25, 1689 (Robles, *Diario de los sucesos notables*, vol. 2, 190–192) and had been published with "an accompanying sermon by Fr. Francisco Florencia, S.J.," on Sunday, November 27. AGI, Mexico 1102, 42, 2, fol. 48; cf. Stanhope, *Spain under Charles II*, 35.

115. Flores, *Iconografía colonial*, 27, 73–74, 108, 111; Escalante Colombres, *Descripción de las honras fúnebres*.

116. Alsedo y Herrera, *Piraterías y agresiones*, 204; cf. Villars, *Lettres*, 250. Ramírez and his companions would also have to make good on any *votos* (devotional promises) to the Virgin out of the funds distributed to them from the frigate and its cargo if it was found to be a fair prize. Montemayor, *Discurso político, histórico, jurídico*, 110.

117. The tribunal was created in 1573 not in 1605, as Sánchez Bella implies in *La organización financiera de las Indias*, 120. Alsedo y Herrera, *Piraterías y agresiones*, 204; Escalona, *Gazofilacium*, 209–210, 213.

118. Grotius, *Commentary on the Law of Prize and Booty*, 113–114, following Bartolus, Bellarmine, and Sylvester; Martín de Azpilcueta Navarro, cited in Alloza, *Flores summarum*, 404 (quotation); Earle, *The Wreck of the Almiranta*, 122. Spanish law contrasted with northern European traditions, which granted salvagers greater rights, though scholars reject the romanticizations of past writers like Jenkin in *Cornish Seafarers*.

119. Quoted by Selden, *Of the Dominion, or Ownership, of the Sea*, 105; see also Montemayor, *Discurso político, histórico, jurídico*, 25.

120. Herbermann et al., eds., *The Catholic Encyclopedia*, vol. 7, s.v. "In coena domini" ("in spite of the opposition" and "confessors were often ordered"); Earle, *The Wreck of the Almiranta*, 84 ("gold, silver" and "excommunication"); Abreu y Bertodano, *Tratado jurídico-político*, 210–211 ("any private person"); Lantéry, *Un comerciante saboyano*, 325. One bishop even used *In Coena Domini* in 1690 to excommunicate the entire Supreme Court of the Philippine Islands. Blair and Robertson, *The Philippine Islands*, vol. 40 (*1690–1691*), 24; Costa, *The Jesuits in the Philippines*, 499.

121. AGI, México 363, 4, 32, 11 (April 4, 1689); Galve's many letters on the subject of pirates in Yucatan are reflected in government policies. For example, AGI,

Escribanía 230B, 5, *Real cédula*, Madrid, December 20, 1692, fols. 64-67.

122. Murillo Velarde, *Geographia histórica de las islas Philipinas*, vol. 8, 74-75.

123. Montemayor, *Discurso político, histórico, jurídico*, 63.

124. Ibid., xx.

125. Holland and Portugal did so in 1692. ANAM, B14, Latin text of treaty agreement.

126. AGI, Escribanía 230 B, King to Galve, December 30, 1694, fols. 586–587v; cf. Pérez-Mallaína Bueno, "Introducción," in Seijas y Lobera, *Gobierno militar y político*, 77n101.

127. Escalona, *Gazofilacium*, 222; cf. 273–291. Escalona's legal treatise summed up his extensive experience as a lawyer, judge, and customs inspector. Popescu, *Studies in the History of Latin American Economic Thought*, 104.

128. AGS, DGT Inventario 24, 172.

129. Montemayor, *Discurso político, histórico, jurídico*, 34.

130. Ibid., 110, citing Escalona, *Gazophilacium*, and the 1633 *Ordenanzas del buen govierno de la armada del mar océano*.

131. Benton, "Making Order Out of Trouble," 373.

132. Lantéry, *Un comerciante saboyano*, 274.

133. Cf. Aizpurúa, *Curazao y la costa de Caracas*; Perusset, *Contrabando y sociedad en el Río de la Plata colonial*. As Walther L. Bernecker has pointed out, it is anachronistic to apply a twentieth-century definition of such accommodationism as "corruption": "Jurisprudence did not yet formally consider bribery a punishable offense" (*Contrabando, ilegalidad y corrupción*, 99).

CHAPTER FOUR

1. Poussou, "Journaux et récits de voyage."

2. This motto accompanies the image of a ship in Joseph Furttenbach, *Architectura navalis* (Vim: Jo. Saurn, 1629), reproduced in Pérez-Mallaína, *Los hombres del océano*, facing p. 76 (English version: Pérez-Mallaína, *Spain's Men of the Sea*, 64).

3. García Bernal, *Desarrollo agrario en el Yucatán colonial*, 64, commenting on the Xukú *estancia* case, ca. 1728.

4. Escalona, *Gazofilacium*, 209-211; AGI, Escribanía 231A, 16; cf. García Bernal and Ruiz Rivera, *Cargadores a Indias*, 210–212.

5. AGI, Escribanía 230B, 5, *Real cédula*, Madrid, December 30, 1693, fols. 92-93.

6. Gutiérrez Lorenzo, *De la corte de Castilla al virreinato*, 44.

7. It would be surprising if he turned out to be sergeant major Don Antonio Ramírez, a nobleman who killed one of Admiral Don Antonio de Astina's officers in a duel shortly after the Windward Fleet entered San Juan, Puerto Rico,

in 1691. AGI, Escribanía 230B, fol. 150. Torres Ramírez, *La Armada de Barlovento*, 322, records Don Antonio's continuing service in 1692 as a *capitán de mar* (sea captain), which fits what we know of Ramírez's experience and qualifications, but it is unlikely that we are dealing with the same man.

8. Barroto had an illustrious career, punctuated by his excellent map of the completion of the Morro fortifications in Havana. AGI, MP Santo Domingo, 104. More documents testifying to Ramírez's appointment will doubtless be found in due time among the numerous bundles of materials concerning the fleet in 1690-1691 (AGI, Indiferente 2516, "Ordenes, despachos y disposiciones," Indiferente 2550 and 2551, "Decretos, cartas, y consultas"). Gentlemen were often allowed to board ships without an express military commission for command or without a *plaza sencilla* (regular military posting) within a particular corps. Several royal orders were issued in the course of the century, attempting to limit such practices (e.g., *CDMFN*, vol. 11, 51).

9. Junta de Guerra response to General Jacinto López Gijón, October 31, 1690, AGI, Indiferente General 2550; Torres Ramírez, *La Armada de Barlovento*, 324.

10. AGI, Indiferente 2516, 5; Galve was told that all future financial decisions had to pass through the king's councils, particularly the Finance Committee (Patronato 243, 6).

11. Seijas y Lobera, *Gobierno militar y político*, 512-514.

12. Kamen, *Spain in the Later Seventeenth Century*, 25.

13. Tomás y Valiente, *Los validos en la monarquía española del siglo XVII*; cf. the collection of studies updating Tomás y Valiente's work: Escudero, *Los validos*.

14. The Duke of Infantado's status as a *valido* has not yet received the attention that it merits.

15. Stradling, *Europe and the Decline of Spain*, 185.

16. This type of factional infighting was famously decried by Alexander Stanhope: "This court is most miserably distracted with factions, who mind nothing but the ruining each other" (*Spain under Charles II*, 72).

17. Burkholder and Chandler, *From Impotence to Authority*.

18. AGI, Escribanía 230B, *Real cédula*, Madrid, July 13, 1693.

THE TRANSLATION

1. The Royal Chancillery of Mexico is more usually referred to as the Audiencia of Mexico.

2. The phrase *acogerme al sagrado de V. Exa.* specifically referred to the legal protection from immediate prosecution that those accused of serious crimes gained by entering a church.

3. *Libra astronómica y philosóphica* contains Sigüenza's famous dispute with Eusebio Kino over the scientific, natural, and religious interpretation of the 1680 comet. Leonard, *Don Carlos de Sigüenza y Góngora*, 58–73.

4. *trabajos.*

5. The fascinating Spanish term *piedad* encompasses the meaning of the two etymologically related English words "pity" and "piety."

6. *à los desvalidos en nombre de quien me dio el asunto para escrivirla*; note that Sigüenza y Góngora believed that Galve's charity extended to Ramírez's companions as well.

7. This Puerto Rican poet (1630–1708) is not well known according to Cummins and Soons, except for his introductory poems attached to other authors' works (ICS, 75n6 and n7). When Ayerra Santa María lived in the conventual house of El Amor de Dios, he and Sigüenza were neighbors. Sigüenza wrote an encomiastic history of Ayerra's convent entitled *Paraíso occidental.*

8. *Aeneid* 1, 203: "Even this will someday be a joyous memory" (ICS, 75n8).

9. "May your life have its own Roman Homer," an adaptation of "the Gallo-Roman poet Decimus Magnus Ausonius" (AD 310–393/394), as Cummins and Soons note (ICS, 75n9).

10. "Oh that someone might grant my speeches to have been written down! Oh that someone might allow them to have been graven with iron pen in a book or at all events sculpted in stone!" This quotation from the Book of Hours pertaining to the Mass for the Dead was idiosyncratically paraphrased by Ayerra Santa María from *Job* 19:23–24 (ICS, 75n13): *Quis mihi tribuat ut scribantur sermones mei! Quis mihi det ut exarentur in libro stil ferreo et plumbi lammina vel certe sculpantur in scilice!*

11. "Hard though it may be, hold up; for the rock face should not be covered in silence, but should be exhibited as an example to others." Identified by Cummins and Soons as *Biblia sacra, cum Glossa ordinaria, primum quidem a Strabo Fuldensi collecta* (Paris, 1590), vol. 3, 210 (ICS, 75n16).

12. *patria.*

13. Cummins and Soons point out but do not analyze the use of the Arawak/Carib name of the island; nor do they suggest that it may be indicative of Ramírez's regionalism (ICS, 76n19).

14. *corsantes.*

15. Geographical terms are translated as follows to avoid confusion: "las Indias" is given in English as "the Indies" and "India" as "East Indies," in preference to "Indies" and "India," because seventeenth-century usage in Spanish dictated that the entire south and southeast Asian area be referred to as India.

16. "Puerto Rico" literally means "Rich Port."

17. Although Ramírez's birthright included some sort of noble status, it apparently

did not contain any of the typical "service" sheet of recommendations (service which garnered the crown's patronage).

18. Perhaps Ramírez's father was Don Alonso de Villanueva Segarra, who was a captain appointed sergeant major of the presidio in San Juan, Puerto Rico, on October 3, 1651. This raises the tantalizing possibility that the Captain Juan "del Corcho" mentioned below is the same as Juan López, "a pilot," suspected in a corruption and smuggling case in the 1650s along with Villanueva Segarra and one of the island's judges. AGI, Escribanía 1190 and Contratación 5430, 2, 2, Escribanía 123A, Residencias, Puerto Rico, 1659, fols. 22–24, 62, 146, 209–212. Estelle Irizarry made the possible connection between the sergeant major and Alonso Ramírez, though she argued—incorrectly in my mind—that Alonso was trying to conceal his *marrano* or crypto-Jewish status (*Infortunios* [1990], 37–41). Irizarry relied on a letter that Villanueva Segarra sent to the king in 1657 found and cited by López Cantos, *Historia de Puerto Rico*, 330.

19. This piece of internal evidence implies two things: if Ramírez gave these autobiographical details truthfully, then the use of the present tense connoted that his mother—as far as he knew—was still alive in 1690. Ramírez took his mother's last name, a practice which was common in early modern Spanish-speaking societies, as Cummins and Soons note: "Arzánz de Orsúa y Vela, the historian of Potosí, used five different names" (ICS, 76n22).

20. *hurtarle el cuerpo a mi misma Patra*; along with his previous comments on corsairs and Puerto Rican poverty, Ramírez ironically points here to the central theme of his narrative: piracy (thieving).

21. *Urqueta* is the diminutive of *urca*, a small flat-bottomed, wide-buttocked ship. These were pioneered by the Dutch, whose fly-boats (either lateen or square-rigged) were used in coastal navigation and were occasionally attached to the navy. An *urqueta* weighed in at less than the typical 300 tons of an *urca*. Kemp, *The Oxford Companion to Ships*, s.v. "urca" and "fly-boat."

22. We have no record of any coastal pilot named Juan del Corcho. Perhaps "Corcho" is a pun: "to travel like a cork floating in water [*andar como el corcho sobre el agua*]" proverbially indicated someone who was lazy, mischievous, and shameless. Real Academia Española, *Diccionario*, s.v. "corcho."

23. The reference to the age of thirteen is not an indication of legal status as a minor. That age was twelve for girls and fourteen for boys, contrary to the Pérez Blanco edition (1988), 75–76. Cabin boys or "pages" were the youngest and lowest members of a crew and typically entered service when less than ten years old. For the son of a *carpintero de ribera* (ship carpenter) to enter service as a page was a lowering of social status, because carpenters were among the more skilled and higher-paid maritime workers. Ramírez was starting as a generic "ship's page" of the lowest status, like runaways and orphans without the

protection of shipmates, family, or friends. Pérez-Mallaína, *Spain's Men of the Sea*, 23–62, 75–78.

24. *las islas de Barlovento*; in Spanish usage, these Windward Islands included the large Caribbean islands and not just the smaller Antilles to the east, as in English usage.

25. San Juan de Ulúa lies opposite the much larger city of Veracruz, the mainland town founded by Cortés in 1519.

26. A carpenter could never seriously expect to become rich or to be offered the opportunity of wealth.

27. *resolucion indiscreta.*

28. In common parlance "Mexico" at the time referred almost exclusively to the city.

29. Without a record of service or merit (*servicios y méritos*), Ramírez hoped to live off the magnanimity of others or to find employment that would provide "conveniences" and riches, chimerical ambitions to which piracy served as a short cut.

30. Cristóbal de Medina Vargas Machuca was an ambitious master builder in Mexico in the 1670 and 1680s. He was made *maestro mayor de obras* in the city on March 8, 1680, and designed Mexico City's Santa Fe aqueduct in 1688. AGI, Mexico 196, 16, Escribanía 179A, and MP 81, "Diseño de los arcos y atagea [*sic*] por donde viene el agua de Santa Fé a la ciudad de México, Cristóbal de Medina, autor."

31. The equivalent of 80 sea leagues is roughly 240 to 280 miles. Like other European measurements of the time, Spanish terrestrial and nautical leagues varied from almost 6,500 meters down to a typical 5,500 meters (about 3.5 miles), but sailors often rounded the nautical league down to 3 miles; seventeenth-century evidence even suggests occasional use of a "short league" of 3,894 meters (2.4 miles), Rojas Sandoval, "Nautical Charts and Measurement Systems," 96.

32. This is convoluted syntax: I have taken the *sensibilísimos* and *por* of *despegos sensibilísimos por no esperados* in a less common construction to mean that Ramírez was sensitive to the indifference of his putative relatives and unprepared for them, as opposed to making this indifference "sensible." Don Luis Ramírez de Aguilar was concerned for his own reputation at that time: he was filing for a knighthood, which he would finally receive in the Order of Santiago on March 16, 1689, along with the post of alcalde of Cuycatlán and Papalo. AGI, Indiferente 132, 49, 1.

33. *Grana* was a common name for the cochineal bug that thrives on several species of *Opuntia* cactus in many parts of Mexico. It was a lucrative business: the extract from the insects produced cochineal, the common red and purple dye of the early modern period and one of Mexico's principal exports. Yucatan

produced two key raw materials used for dyes: *palo de tinte negro* from the tree *Haematoxylon campechianum*, also known as *palo de Campeche*, and *añil*. Contreras Sánchez, "Los circuitos comerciales del palo de tinte," 171–174; García Bernal, *Desarrollo agrario en el Yucatán colonial*, 45. Cummins and Soons note that *grana* (cochineal) was "the staple product" of Oaxaca (ICS, 11).

34. The term *sabandija* in early modern Spanish referred to lice or any noxious small creature or animal such as an insect or reptile that annoys humans, according to Real Academia Espanõla, *Diccionario de la lengua castellana*, s.v. "sabandija."

35. The town of Santiago de Chiapas is the capital of the region.

36. Modern Oaxaca.

37. San Francisco de Telixtlahuaca is west of Oaxaca (ICS, 76n38).

38. Take note that Ramírez implies that the heirs gave him nothing, since he was without reales, the common coinage of the time.

39. Internal chronology places Ramírez's return to Mexico City sometime after one year spent in Mexico City plus an indeterminate time in Puebla, Oaxaca, and then briefly again in Puebla, making it thus no earlier than 1676 or 1677 and probably slightly later.

40. Doctor Juan Millán de Poblete (d. 1680), a well-known personality in Mexico City, belonged to a distinguished dynasty of churchmen. AGI, Filipinas 348, 5, fols. 123–124, Filipinas 23, 8, 26. Juan's brother, Miguel de Poblete, was archbishop of Manila from 1653 to 1667 and published popular religious books. AGI, Filipinas 9, 2, 34, and Filipinas 86, 54; Costa, *The Jesuits in the Philippines*, 426, 489; Flores, *Iconografía colonial*, 141, 167–168; cf. ICS, 76n40. Through his marriage Ramírez became a nephew-in-law of the archbishop, although I have been unable to clarify whether Doña María de Poblete was Juan's sister or sister-in-law.

41. Ramírez may not have revealed the entire truth of his self-imposed exile to Sigüenza. In 1684 Miguel Ortiz de Covarrubias filed a request from Manila with the Mexican authorities to be transferred from the Philippine capital to fill Poblete's vacant post in the Mexican cathedral. He justified his request by stating that "the death of his relative Juan de Poblete, former dean in Mexico," had left his three sisters, whom Poblete had supported "as their near relative," without anyone to care for them. The request was denied due to the tarnished reputation of Ortiz de Covarrubias. The Dominican Fr. Andrés González reported in 1674 that Ortiz de Covarrubias was only of "mediocre capacity," lived unmarried with a local woman in Manila, and was rumored to have fathered a bastard child. This suggests that Ramírez sought the help of Ortiz de Covarrubias, a relative by marriage, in Manila after his job with Estevan Gutiérrez turned out to be a flop. AGI, Filipinas 86, 54.

42. The convict chain gang sentenced to exile in the Philippines left from Mexico City that year on March 8; "the ship itself, the *Santa Rosa*, sailed on March 28," as Cummins and Soons note, arriving in Manila on July 23 (ICS, 77n42). For Nieto's and Coello's well-documented careers, as well as the *Santa Rosa*'s movements, see AGI, Filipinas 23, 8, 23, Filipinas 331, 7, fols. 240-241, Filipinas 24, 2, 11, Filipinas 331, 7, fols. 400 (August 21, 1682) and 422, Filipinas 56, 5, Filipinas 349, 6, fols. 167–169, Filipinas 15, 1, 7, Filipinas 332, 10, fols. 142–144, Filipinas 13, 1, 9, 5, Filipinas 24, 2, 11, and Filipinas 13, 1, 9, fols. 1–14; RAH 9/2668, doc. 122; Costa, *The Jesuits in the Philippines*, 493, 498; Díaz, *Conquistas de las Islas Filipinas*, vol. 4, chapters 5, 13, and 14; and Lévesque, *History of Micronesia*, vol. 9, 27, 61, 111, 126, 399, 433–440, 539, and vol. 20, 391–394, 591–592.

43. *este puerto* refers here to Acapulco, not El Cavite.

44. *Lesnordeste y Leste.*

45. Guam.

46. *Brazas* are equivalent to fathoms. I prefer to use "fathom" rather than the older "brace."

47. Galván.

48. Cf. ICS, 35.

49. Chinese.

50. The term "colony" is unusual in seventeenth-century Spanish usage, which preferred other expressions, such as "kingdom [*reino*]," much as English usage at the time preferred "plantation"; see the discussion of this in Chapter 1 of the Introductory Study, notably Elliott's comparison of English and Spanish imperial discourses in *Empires of the Atlantic World*, 3–16.

51. Trade between Manila and India uncharacteristically flourished in the 1670s and 1680s. Quiason, *English "Country Trade" with the Philippines*, 34–61.

52. "Madrastapatan" is undoubtedly "Madraspatam," the Indian name for Madras. The English Fort St. George, built beside Madraspatam in 1640, was commonly known as Madras by the eighteenth century. It had suffered in the Anglo-Dutch wars of the decades before the 1680s. Ramírez may have confused the name of Madras with that of Masulipatam to the north, an "important textile factory" and preferred shopping spot for the Dutch East India Company (VOC). Parthesius, *Dutch Ships in Tropical Waters*, 5, 58.

53. Like other Spaniards in the East Indies who were influenced by Portuguese pronunciation, Ramírez here calls the apostle "Santo Tomé," not "San Tomás" or "Santo Tomás," the correct Spanish forms of his name. Jacques de Coutre did the same in his 1640 journal (*Vida*, 49–83). Note also that Sigüenza does not say "Santo Tomé" when referring to the apostle (nor have I found references to "São Tomé" anywhere in his writings); for example, see "Theatro de virtudes políticas," in *Obras históricas*, 261.

54. In contrast to Spanish American ones? This extremely short sentence has a somewhat curt, cynical tone.

55. Siamese.

56. Emigration from the Bugis states of southwestern parts of the Celebes Islands was caused by the Dutch capture of Macassar in 1667. Reid, *Southeast Asia in the Age of Commerce*, 47, 93–170, 204–234; S. Arasaratnam, "Dutch Policy in the Malay Peninsula," in Prakash, ed., *European Commercial Expansion*, 181; Ibn Ahmad, *The Precious Gift*, 2.

57. Several things indicate that Ramírez may have been a weapons merchant in Asia between 1682 and 1687. His knowledge of the kris, a distinctive southeast Asian weapon, is attested by his reference to quite specific elements of kris culture (see the discussion of the gift symbolism of krisses in Chapter 3 of the Introductory Study and his mention of a special oil used to darken kris handles, "landaian," analyzed in note 88 below). In this revealing section, the telling climax to Ramírez's description of Batavia's preeminence in Asian trade is that "excellent weapons are produced there for anyone who might care to purchase them." Perhaps he acquired this mercantile expertise through working with Bugis crews, then in the process of taking over southeast Asia's coastal shipping by fitting "into the interstices in European trade" aboard ships much like the sampan on which Ramírez was probably taken prisoner in 1687. Ammarell, *Bugis Navigation*, 19. Rivalry with the Dutch over control of the East-West trade network connecting the Singapore straits area with the spice islands to the east (especially the Moluccas with their nutmeg and mace) culminated in the Dutch conquest of Macassar, in south Celebes Island (modern Sulawesi), in 1669. This victory limited Macassar trade, but Bugis groups fought on both the Dutch and Macassar sides and subsequently exploited new opportunities. Pelras, *The Bugis*, 48, 138-145, 250. The first Bugis mass emigration took place as a result of these wars in the 1660s, according to the most reliable accounts, as "thousands" fled Sulawesi, settling in Singapore, Thailand, and Malaysia as well as neighboring islands like Borneo and Sumatra, where "some turned to piracy"; most "established themselves as seafaring traders and mercenaries to local kings." Ammarell, *Bugis Navigation*, 18. Ramírez's geographical summary of his five years as a merchant in Asian waters includes the classic Bugis navigational network from Malacca through Singapore and Batavia to Macao, though we know they also visited Manila. Ramírez evinced a clear animosity toward the Dutch and distinguished "Macassars" from "Bugis," which also suggests an association with—or at least a deep knowledge of—the contemporary Bugis seafaring diaspora. This deduction is reinforced by Ramírez's specific kris knowledge, which ties him rather closely to the way in which the Bugis dominated not just the export of the rare nickeliferous iron necessary for the manufacture of the finest krisses but trade in them across the region; the word

"landaian" for the kris hilt, furthermore, seems to derive from the characteristic slant or angle of Buginese kris handles. In addition, in analyzing Ramírez's contacts with Buginese and Malay merchants it is important to recall that he used the Malay term for kris, transliterated into Castilian as *criz*, and not the Philippine term *kalis*. Duuren, *The Kris*, 9, 26, 39, 59, 61, 79–83.

58. Macao. Sigüenza's spelling of "Macau" as "Macan" may reflect Ramírez's Portuguese-influenced pronunciation. Alternately, the typesetter may just have inverted the final *u*.

59. Gabriel y Arriola's name is variously spelled in Spanish documents as "Cruzelagui," "Curuzeleagui," or "Curuzeláegui."

60. O. H. K. Spate, in his study of Spanish Pacific exploration, defines it in these terms: "the Spanish *fregata* . . . often meant not a fairly large warship but a small or medium-sized coastal trader or felibote, often built in American yards for coasting in the first place but capable in emergency of making trans-Atlantic passages" (*The Spanish Lake*, 20). Cf. William Baker, *Colonial Vessels*, 151.

61. As discussed in Chapter 2 of the Introductory Study, neither the Pangasinan *champán* taken in the morning nor the Spanish frigate taken in the afternoon was attacked by more than one pirate ship, the *Cygnet*. Nevertheless, one eyewitness, the sailor Bartolomé Luis from the *Aránzazu*, agreed with Ramírez that two pirogues attacked the frigate. The rest of our eyewitnesses (twelve men plus Dampier) said that only one pirogue was involved in the afternoon attack.

62. For this moment of "the Distribution of Justice," see Chapter 2 in the Introductory Study.

63. Capones Island: see Map 2.1 (Approaches to Manila Bay).

64. This presumably refers to the following morning.

65. *capitana.*

66. *dueño.*

67. Stink bombs?

68. Argentina's Estrecho de le Maire lies between the easternmost tip of Tierra del Fuego Island and States Island (Isla de los Estados) and connects the Atlantic to the Pacific; cf. ICS, 79n76.

69. *champanes.*

70. The term *sangley* was used in the Philippines for a Chinese resident of the islands, so *sangley mestizo* probably refers to an inhabitant of mixed Spanish-Chinese ancestry.

71. *trabucazo.*

72. "Indian" in early modern Spanish parlance referred to Native Americans, Polynesians, Micronesians, and East Asians; thus Ramírez is stating that his quartermaster was an East Indian from the Philippine Islands.

73. This intentional misrepresentation of the facts demonstrates Ramírez's continuing pride in being able to fool his listeners, given the story just told about fooling the pirates. See Dampier's testimony regarding the *Cygnet*'s movements from February 21 to 23 quoted in Chapter 2 of the Introductory Study.

74. Cambodia. "Pulicondon" is Dampier's "Pulo Condore," the modern Vietnamese Con Dao.

75. This is a difficult passage. I posit that ship slang in the Indies might have used the phrase *dar lado a sus navíos* as a synonym for *dar carena*, to careen or clean the undersides. This meaning for *dar lado* is in keeping visually with the definition for careening, "the operation in older days of heaving a ship down *on one side* in order to expose *the other* for the purposes of cleaning the bottom of weeds and barnacles" (Kemp, *The Oxford Companion to Ships*, s.v. "careen"; emphasis added). This possible interpretation is assured by the later mention that the pirates traded for tar, which was used in waterproofing the hull. Leal y Leal's *Diccionario naval* (s.v. "dar la quilla") also registers the phrase *dar la quilla* (to expose or roll over the keel) as a synonym for *carenar* (to careen). Here he disagrees with Suárez Gil's *Diccionario técnico marítimo*, which only gives "to heel or list" as the meaning for *dar la quilla*.

76. Cf. Barlow, *Barlow's Journal*, vol. 2, 394–397.

77. *capitana*.

78. I am tempted to translate the text's vague *aguardiente* as "rum," the increasingly common nautical drink in the late 1600s, though sweet wines dominated in long-distance voyages. The Real Academia Española's *Diccionario de la lengua castellana* gives the following description (s.v. "aguardiente"): "Aguardiente: That which by artifice is made from wine, from its dregs, from wheat, or from other substances. It is called *fire-water* because it is clear like water and because it burns if flung on fire."

79. Pulo Ubi.

80. In Caribbean usage *ñame* could refer either to "true yams" of African origin (*Dioscorea* sp.) or to the sweet potato of the Americas (*Ipomoea batatas*).

81. *Bejuco verde* refers to "a species of reed which is very thin and flexible, but whose sting is venomous," according to the Real Academia Real Española's *Diccionario de la lengua castellana* (s.v. "bejuco verde"). In more modern use it corresponds to the English "reed," "rattan," or "liana."

82. Macao.

83. *cantidad de oro en piezas de filigrana*.

84. *lugar-teniente* (lieutenant).

85. The awkward redundancy in the phrase *para comerciar y vender* masks the dual nature of mercantile activity, barter and sale.

86. Either the archipelago off Chantaburi, Thailand, known today as Ko Chang,

Ko Mak, and Ko Kut or, more probably, the Anambas Archipelago, whose largest island is called Pulau Tarempa by modern Indonesians but used to be known as Siantan Island. Ibn Ahmad, *The Precious Gift*, 22–28, 46–51, 82–87, 324–337; Loubère, *A New Historical Relation*, 7 and map opposite 2; Kaempfer, *The History of Japan*, 81; Catz, *The Travels of Mendes Pinto*, 589n10; Père Bouvet, *Voiage de Siam*, frontispiece.

87. Dampier also noted that krisses were characteristic of Malays (*NV*, 271).

88. Given the context in which Ramírez mentions *lantia* (the capture of a Malay vessel carrying men armed with krisses), it is logical to conclude that "the oil which is used for *lantia*" (*azeyte . . . para la lantia*) can only refer to the Malay name for a kris hilt, *landaian*, especially krisses with large handles. Wilkinson, *A Malay-English Dictionary*, s.v. "landaian"; cf. Klinkert, *Nieuw Maleisch-Nederlandsch Zakwoordenboek*, s.v. "landai" and "keris"; Hairul, *Kamus Lengkap*, s.v. "landai, landaian"; and Wilkinson, *A Malay-English Dictionary*, s.v. "lendayan"; *landaian* was the name for the hilt in the language of polite or elite Javanese and Balinese society: Jasper and Pirgadie, *De Inlandsche Kunstnijverheid in Nederlandsch Indië*, vol. 5, 196, 203, 227. Specialists note that "to create special colour effects, the hilts in particular were often artificially darkened." Duuren, *The Kris*, 41. It is likely that this was the purpose of the oil mentioned by Ramírez. Evidence shows that coconut oil and sandalwood oil were both traditionally used. Hill, "The Keris and Other Malay Weapons," 4; Frey, *The Kris*, 87.

89. Clearly the Tambelan archipelago, lying at 1° 0' N 107° 30' E.

90. Borneo.

91. Modern Sukadana, Borneo.

92. This may reflect Ramírez's imprecise information concerning the letter which the English merchant Thomas Bowrey sent to Mindanao from Sumatra via Borneo according to Dampier (*NV*, 252, 338); see the discussion in Chapter 3 of the Introductory Study.

93. So far I have been unable to document this attack on Sukadana using either European or native Malay/Borneo published sources. Ibn Ahmad's *The Precious Gift* does not mention it, but that is to be expected given his summary treatment of seventeenth-century history; I have not been able to consult Ibn Ahmad's main source for west Borneo history, *Hikayat Opu Daeng Menambun* (a manuscript copy can be found in the Leiden library, number 1754). Dutch sources in all likelihood contain some information, though I have not been able to track it down.

94. Probably the quite small isle of Batudinging, just west of Belitung Island in the Gaspar Strait separating the archipelago from Bangka and Sumatra to the west (3° 0' S 107° 40' W).

95. Pulo Tioman, Malaysia (2° 50' N and 104° 15' E).

96. Bengal; this would seem to indicate that the pirate ship veered course from north, east, or south to the west to gain the Singapore straits.

97. This is probably not a reference to African Muslims but rather to Muslims from Bengal, as opposed to Malays.

98. *Raso* or *razo* was a lustrous silk material, thicker than taffeta but lighter than velvet, produced by raising every eighth thread on the warp. Real Academia Española, *Diccionario de la lengua castellana*, s.v. "raso." I appreciate the help of Gwenyth Claughton in identifying this cloth.

99. "Elephant tusks" refers to ivory. *Sarampares* were a commonly available multicolored cotton textile, "generally a chintz," imported into southeast Asia mostly from Nellore in eastern India (Andhra Pradesh). Wilkinson, *A Malay-English Dictionary*, s.v. "selampuri." Bowrey in the 1680s called these "Salampore" fabrics "a sort of Callico" (*A Dictionary English and Malayo, Malayo and English*, s.v. "salampooree"; cf. Dam, *Beschryvinge van de Oostindische Compagnie*, vol. 2, part 2, 461; and Coolhaas, *Generale Missiven*, 50, 427, 641). It is possible that Ramírez was referring to another weapon he became familiar with in Malay waters, the three-pronged spear known as a "serampang . . . a trident weapon used by the Bugis both in war and for spearing fish." Hill, "The Keris and Other Malay Weapons," 52; cf. Winstedt, *An Unabridged Malay-English Dictionary*, s.v. "serampang."

100. Puli Aur (2° 30' N and 104° 45' E). On Dampier's map, it appears as "Pulo Oro." This is probably the combat between Dutch ships and the *Swan* mentioned by Sutton, *Lords of the East*, 80.

101. I have translated *desembocar* with the corresponding seventeenth-century English term, meaning to reach the open sea after passing through straits. Manwayring, *The Seaman's Dictionary*, s.v. "disembogue."

102. Singapore; straits of Malacca.

103. Ramírez appears to be stretching the truth here or hiding something. Dampier did not seem to think that these straits or those east of Java allowed ships to avoid the Dutch (*NV*, 239).

104. Spanish ships were often measured by keel length, though the government had issued complicated official rules for calculating tonnage based not only on keel length (*eslora*) but also on beam and hold depth in 1613 and 1618. Phillips, *Six Galleons for the King of Spain*, 60–61, 229–230. The original *treinta y tres codos de quilla* corresponds roughly to sixty-two feet (1 *codo* = .575 m; 33 *codos* = approximately 19 m: Meehan Hermanson and Trejo Rivera, "*Nuestra Señora del Juncal*: Her Story and Her Shipwreck," 78–79; cf. Meehan Hermanson, "Criterios y procedimientos para la elección de navíos insignia").

105. *Bonga* here probably refers to mace. "*Bunga* is the general Malay word for flower . . . ; *bunga* can also mean interest on one's money, i.e. the 'flowering'

of one's money." Beekman, *The Poison Tree*, 215. Thomas Bowrey, who met Dampier at Bencoolen, Java, noted that among the specific uses of the word *bunga* was "Boonga pala" for "Mace" (*A Dictionary English and Malayo, Malayo and English*, s.v. "boonga"). Cf. "buah pala," meaning the fruit of "pala" (i.e., nutmeg), which is the hard kernel of the nutmeg tree's seed; nutmeg is encased in a valuable red substance also used as a spice, which is known in English as "mace" (Wilkinson, *A Malay-English Dictionary*, s.v. "pala"). Much less probably, Ramírez's *bonga* may refer to the cowrie shells used as currency in the Indian Ocean and southeast Asia, which were sometimes called "bongies" in Dutch documents at the time (e.g., Dam, *Beschryvinge van de Oostindische Compagnie*, vol. 2, part 2, 447). A translation of *bonga* as ganja or marijuana, a frequent trade item, is very doubtful, although Eric Tagliacozzo reports that the word "bhang" was commonly used for cannabis in the Malay Straits in later centuries (*Secret Trades, Porous Borders*, 198).

106. The small number of pirates transferred matches what we know of Mackintosh's limited crew. If Ramírez's shipwrecked frigate was this one, then one cannon had been thrown overboard or lost before it ran aground (see Chapter 6 below).

107. This is an important admission: it demonstrates that some of Ramírez's crew managed to escape from the pirate ship. His nonchalant comment about successful escape raises the question of why he himself did not attempt to leave at any point in his narrative of imprisonment, a suspicious and unexplained circumstance of his condition that is heightened by his constant use of the first-person plural, including himself in describing the pirates' voyage.

108. The vagueness here is uncharacteristic; Ramírez usually knows and remembers his geography. After a careful reading of the sources, I have been unable to document any island in the Indian Ocean (Ceylon, Andaman, Nicobar, Diego García, Cocos, the Mascarenes, the Seychelles, Comoros) that would have been known at this time to be inhabited or controlled by the Portuguese other than Goa, a highly improbable identification, and those right off the coast of Africa, which surely do not correspond to this unknown and unnamed island.

109. It is remarkable that the pirates chose to set a course northwest through the extremely dangerous and frequented straits of Singapore (or Sunda for that matter). The course they set through Singapore more than doubled the distance to New Holland. In addition, the Malacca pilot they had on board would certainly have known of this easier route. See the discussion in Chapter 3 of the Introductory Study.

110. The French Caribbean word *boucanier* (curing or smoking meat) is, of course, the origin of the term "buccaneer." Exquemelin, *The Buccaneers of America*, 58.

111. At this juncture, note how Ramírez changes from the first person plural (inclusive of his men and himself) to the third person plural (exclusive of his party), thus beginning the process of distancing himself from his pirate captors.

112. *agua ardiente.* See note 78 above.

113. The Spanish *el exercicio en que andaban* is used here euphemistically and sarcastically for piracy (going on the account).

114. A typographical error: it should be six hundred instead of nine hundred.

115. If possession of weapons was a sign of membership in the pirate company, then Ramírez's confession that he possessed a kris and a rapier (in Chapter 7) when he arrived in Yucatan indicates that he was more than a mere slave aboard the ship.

116. Cummins and Soons posited identifying this "Island of Rocks" with Ascension "or possibly Sts. Peter and Paul Rocks, on the equator in mid-Atlantic" (ICS, 82n130). However, another rocky island is mentioned in Portuguese waggoners off the coast of Angola at 27° 10'. Pimentel, *Arte de navegar*, 273. Several "rocky islands" along the coast of Namibia and Angola might qualify as well. Additionally, if Ramírez's frigate was indeed the one taken in the Singapore straits near Malacca by the pirates, then perhaps he yet again told the truth about events here but lied about their context, telescoping them in terms of time and place. An island half a league from Malacca was specifically known as "Ilha da Pedra" (Rock Island) in Portuguese waggoners; Portuguese navigators continued to use it as an anchorage into the eighteenth century. Pimentel, *Arte de navegar*, 417. Ramírez narrates how he was assigned the frigate in the following paragraphs at the beginning of the next chapter (right after mentioning an "Island of Rocks" here), so it is not impossible to theorize that the division of loot and prizes happened in Asia, when the frigate was taken, and not much later in Ramírez's voyages, at the mouth of the Amazon delta, as he stated in 1690.

117. *Con brizas largas* means with steady winds blowing from abaft the beam. This would be sailing "large" according to Manwayring, *The Seaman's Dictionary*, s.v. "large": "When a Ship goes neither by a-wind, nor before the wind, but as it were, betwixt both (that is quartering) and such a wind that carries her so, we call a large-wind"; see also Kemp, *The Oxford Companion to Ships*, s.v. "points of sailing."

118. Since Captain Mackintosh's voyage seems to have ended with his hanging for piracy in Guinea, this "wide river" might have been in Africa instead of South America. However, the short, specific distances mentioned by Ramírez in Chapters 5 and 6, which put him in the Caribbean, argue against such a hypothesis.

119. *Condestable;* Pérez-Mallaína, *Los hombres del océano*, 87 (English version: *Spain's Men of the Sea*, 79).

120. The independence of quartermasters on pirate ships had no parallel in either the merchant marine or the navy of the time. Ramírez's experiences are consistent with a fairly poorly understood shipboard phenomenon of pirate life; see, for example, the principal accusation against Dampier by one of his sailors that he failed "to support the lieutenant against the insults of inferior officers," a courtesy that pirate captains would not expect anyone to offer their quartermasters except in very specific circumstances. Baer, "William Dampier at the Crossroads," 107.

121. *los de su sequito.*

122. Since Captain Mackintosh was Scottish, Ramírez's earlier implied grouping of Nicpat and Dick with Bel may indicate that he was toggling between an "English" crew and a Scottish one in his memory.

123. The speech shifts to plural at the very end, an awkward reflection, no doubt, of Ramírez recalling the rest of his fellow captive crewmates.

124. Ramírez contradicts his other statements about the frigate's valuable cargo at this point.

125. Dutch waggoners were the best charts for Asian waters, prized for their comprehensiveness; for a French example, see ANAM, Sous-série B7 60, fol. 20.

126. *Tinaja* means a jar or pot made of clay; it was more typical to carry water in casks in ships of the day.

127. The bibliography on the Virgin of Guadalupe is immense: for her status in seventeenth-century Mexico, see, for a start, Lafaye, *Quetzalcóatl and Guadalupe*; and Poole, *Our Lady of Guadalupe.*

128. This story has two significant aspects, one ironic but both equally revealing. The irony of a Protestant pirate ship implicitly protected by the image of the Virgin Mary would not have been lost on the seventeenth-century Catholic audience for this text. They would know that ships typically flew pennants from the masthead on feasts and saints' days. The second point to make is that Ramírez's admission that he was sent aloft demonstrates that he had the run of the deck during his captivity. This relative freedom on the pirate ship means that he could have escaped, as others in his party did or at least tried to do. Ramírez gives no indication in his entire narrative that he ever did so. For a discussion of the pennants, see Real Academia Española, *Diccionario de la lengua castellana*, s.v. "tope" and "grimpolas." See also the general description of onboard festivities in Phillips, *Six Galleons for the King of Spain*, 161.

129. The modern city of Puebla, Mexico.

130. The Pangasinans and Pampanpangos are native Philippine ethnic groups.

131. Someone from the Malabar area of southwestern India, the original producer of black pepper.

132. It is unclear whether Ramírez acquired the slave in Africa or Asia. Because it was illegal to enslave the native Filipinos, owners purchased their slaves from

Portuguese slave traders based in "Guinea, Mozambique, and Cape Verde," according to a letter from the Audiencia to the king on June 22, 1684. The Manila government attributed the increased use of African slaves to a 1679 royal law which emancipated native slaves, mostly Mindanao Muslims who were war captives, causing a market demand for *cafres* (blacks) "because so many slaves of other nationalities have been granted their liberty." Most of the slave owners in the 1680s were non-Spanish native Filipinos, according to this report. Costa, *Readings in Philippine History*, 77–78.

133. *trabajos.*

134. I am uncertain how to translate *saulas*, having not found this term in the regular reference works on nautical use. This might be a typographical error for *jarcias* (spars), but it is more likely that *saulas* refers to the *sagulas* (lighter ropes or lines used in hauling items such as flags). The spelling *saula* instead of *sagula* reproduces the colloquial pronunciation of this word, an indication that the author was uneducated and unaware that the term is clearly Latin, from *sagulum* (-*a*). Real Academia Española, *Diccionario de la lengua castellana*, s.v. "sagula."

135. *hazer meollar, colchar cables, saulas, y contrabrasas, hazer tambien cagetas, embergues, y mojeles*; see the explanations in Real Academia Española, *Diccionario de la lengua castellana*, s.v. "meollar," "colchar cables," "saulas," "contrabrasas," "cagetas," "embergues," "mojeles"; Kemp, *The Oxford Companion to Ships*, s.v. "braces," "rigging," "robands," "rope," "sheet"; and particularly the highly useful Manwayring, *The Seaman's Dictionary*, s.v. "Cabell, Brases, Roapes" and "Roape-Yarnes."

136. *haviendo precedido el remojarlo para hazerlo arina* [*sic*].

137. *once costales de à dos arrobas.*

138. Roughly 4.6 liters or half a peck in dry weight.

139. Dampier informs us that it was the English who learned this technique from the Spaniards, not the other way round: "In the *South-Seas*, the Spaniards do make Oakum to caulk their Ships, with the Husk of the Coco-nut, which is more serviceable than that made of Hemp, and they say it will never rot" (*NV*, 204).

140. *bejuco.*

141. *bejucos.*

142. *floxera.*

143. Ramírez may be referring to the frigate that was captured off Singapore; but if this was the *Aránzazu*, then the escape "back" to Manila would be a logical return to its home port.

144. *respondíle con gran recato.*

145. The working sailors aboard any ship traditionally slept in the fo'c'sle, as opposed to officers and passengers.

146. *patrocinador.*

147. Once again Ramírez's narrative suggests rhetorically that he belonged to the pirate company as an active crew member: "treason" and "sedition" are hardly terms for outsiders.

148. Madagascar.

149. The rare philosophical term *ilacion* (illation) used here is probably a very visible example of the impact that the highly educated Sigüenza had on the wording of the final text.

150. *trabajo.*

151. We can see in this section how the final text was intended (undoubtedly by both Ramírez and Sigüenza) to operate in the first place as moral guidance for sinners but in the second and no less important place as a rallying call for the union in empire of Spaniards *as Catholics,* whatever or wherever they might find themselves.

152. *trabajos.*

153. The word the author chose to use here, *trabajo* (roughly translatable as "work"), is a favorite one in the original text, but it is critically ambiguous: on the one hand it refers literally to the many labors that Ramírez's men supposedly performed for the pirates, but on the other it also refers to all the miseries (the punishments and tortures) meted out to them. The Real Academia Española notes that *trabajo* meant any "exercise or occupation in some affair or ministry" (*Diccionario de la lengua castellana,* s.v. "trabajo"); but "it also means difficulty, impediment, cost, or prejudice" and even "penalty, bother, torment, or unhappy event." This link between the concept of labor and the concept of punishing pain and unhappiness is not historically accidental or, more importantly for our purposes, incidental to the nature of Ramírez's account. The etymological root for *trabajo* which the eighteenth-century Real Academia Española gives is the Latin word *trebalium,* with the explanation that it originally meant "a torture chamber" (more precisely, it referred to a three-pronged torture device). The implication of the use of *trabajo* here as elsewhere in the text is that work and pain are synonymous for Ramírez, a cultural construct reinforced by its use at this juncture. It would not be lost on the seventeenth-century audience that Ramírez was a man who always tried to get out of hard work by appealing to family connections and disliked manual labor. The key is that the story of Ramírez—as revealed by textual characterizations—revolves around a counterhero who is only partly sympathetic. He does not understand the difference between work and suffering, reminding us here at the beginning of Chapter 5 of his endless search in the early chapters for patrons who would raise him above the common weal.

154. As indicated above (note 118), Ramírez's course between Africa and the Caribbean is problematized by some of the details given. Here a direction west from the mouth of the Amazon would take him upriver, not "out to sea," suggesting

yet again that the "wide river" may lie in Guinea, not South America. The time traveled, however, must then be increased from that given by Ramírez in his account.

155. *cayuco*; a flat-bottomed canoe which draws little water.

156. I tentatively identify Ramírez's *tabones* as the Tabon scrub fowl (*Megapodius cumingii*), a fairly common large, ground-dwelling bird of Australasia, though I have not been able to identify it with certainty based on seventeenth-century records. If the text refers to this bird, it is quite in keeping with the realistic nature of the narrative that Ramírez would use the name of a bird he came to know in the Philippines and southeast Asia for a similar American one.

157. *bobos*; possibly referring to brown boobies (*Sula leucogaster*), which are common Atlantic seashore inhabitants.

158. [1690 NOTE: *La Trinidad.*] This note corresponds to a note in the original 1690 printed text. We assume that these ten original footnotes are due either to the pen of Sigüenza or to that of an unidentified editor in the printing house of the heirs to the widow of Bernardo Calderón. For the purpose of clearly identifying these original notes, these ten notes are prefaced by the phrase "1690 NOTE."

159. [1690 NOTE: *El Barbado.*] *al siguiente volvi la vuelta del Oeste â proseguir mi camino, y al otro por la parte del Leste tomê una isla.*

160. Guadeloupe.

161. The context implies that this refers to Spaniards, though it does not explicitly state that these occasional visitors granted license to trade were *only* Spaniards.

162. *patria.* Note that Ramírez's native soil was Puerto Rico but that his identity as a Catholic and Spaniard did not stand in opposition to or contradict this patriotic identification with a place of birth. It was an age when multiple concentric allegiances to a native city, region, kingdom, and monarch were integral to being a loyal Catholic Spanish subject of the king. This, of course, did not contradict the "racial" or ethnic sense of imperial community which he implied earlier when admitting that Juan de Casas, the other "Spaniard" in his company, was the only helpmate whose solidarity he really trusted. See Tamar Herzog, *Defining Nations.*

163. Landlocked.

164. "America" in the sense of the Spanish American mainland.

165. *por su color y por no ser Españoles*; see note 162 above regarding *patria.*

166. [1690 NOTE: *La Barbada.*]

167. [1690 NOTE: *La Antigua.*]

168. [1690 NOTE: *San Bartolomé, San Martín.*]

169. [1690 NOTE: *La Española.*]

170. *aunque guiñé al Noroeste*; this is a somewhat odd use of the term *guiñar*.

171. [1690 NOTE: *Beata y Altobelo.*]

172. [1690 NOTE: *Xamaica.*]

173. [1690 NOTE: *Puerto Real.*]

174. *cayuelos* (a Caribbeanism).

175. *balandras.*

176. [1690 NOTE: *Caymán Grande.*]

177. *se quedaban como azogados por largo rato.* Miners working in the mercury mines of Castile or Peru could end up suffering from this disease, whose symptoms, as the Real Academia Española explained, included "a constant movement of the body, which is racked by trembling and convulsions" (*El diccionario de la lengua castellana*, s.v. "azogarse").

178. The route they followed probably took them through Banco Chinchorro, a complete circle of reefs and islands, lying just off the eastern Yucatan coast, with a landing somewhere north of Ambergris Cay.

179. *quebrada.* Linguistic usage at the time was quite ambiguous when referring to reefs, not distinguishing consistently between coral reefs and mere sandbanks with rocks interspersed. The apparently more specific term *arrecife* (not used in this text) also meant both rocks and coral reefs and occasionally even sand; Real Academia Española, *Diccionario de la lengua castellana*, s.v. "arrecife."

180. *ayastado* in the original printed text. The actual verb is *ayustar* and not *ayastar*; neither is it the *ajustar* used in the readily available 1951 paperback Spanish transcription of the text published in Argentina (Buenos Aires: Espasa-Calpe, 1951).

181. *rezon.*

182. I have been unable to locate the meaning of *guamutil*, which seems to refer to the particular material used in the construction of the hitching cable.

183. *mucaras.* I have not been able to locate this term. It is probably an Americanism and quite possibly a variant on *múcuras*, a Colombian-Venezuelan term that refers to earthen amphoras, perhaps used figuratively in this context to mean "jagged rocks"; see *El pequeño Larousse ilustrado 2001* (Barcelona: Larousse, 2000), s.v. "múcaras."

184. *pero no obstante despues de haver amanecido, reconociendo su cercania nos cambiamos a tierra firme.*

185. *cayuco.*

186. *parecian hydropicos.*

187. *chachalacas*; probably *Ortalis vetula*, the plain chachalaca, a wide-ranging bird native to the Caribbean and Gulf of Mexico areas which is in fact prolific in marshy coastal zones.

188. *trabajos.*

189. The text implies that Ramírez cured himself.
190. It is clear from the context that their efforts at making themselves heard had not resulted in any response.
191. *treinta y tres codos*; see note 104 above. This is the second time the author gives the details of this ship's construction, perhaps indicating the carelessness or speed with which the final proofs of the text were prepared.
192. *y con tres aforros.* Dampier relates that the pirates clapped on extra sheathing on their ships at Pulo Condore in April 1687 (DNV, fol. 207). Extra sheathing was occasionally applied on Spanish ships in the seventeenth century. Meehan Hermanson, "Criterios y procedimientos para la elección de navíos insignia," 81–86. "Forros" of lead sheets with an undercoating or tarred canvas were preferred for Caribbean ships. Rico de Mata, *Tratado de galafatería*, 34–36.
193. Over 240 nautical miles (see note 31 above) per run or just over 10 knots, a remarkable speed if accurate.
194. *estaño*; the same word was often used at the time to designate pewter.
195. *llaves*, presumably for the muskets.
196. *una punta de piedra*; this probably refers to a point of land stretching out to sea, not a rocky prominence inland around which they could not travel. The January 27, 1690, letter states that they had walked along the coast keeping "close to the shore" (*manteniendose con el marino de ellas*) for forty days.
197. *entraban el monte adentro*; *monte* could refer to either to hills or to any wild, uncultivated area. I have chosen the latter, given the topography of their probable location.
198. *mi muchacho.*
199. *vezino del Pueblo de Tejosuco*; Tijosuco in Quintana Roo, 20° 15' N 88° 25' W, about thirty-eight miles from Valladolid in the modern state of Yucatan. Tijosuco (Tejosuco, Texosuc, Tihosuco) was a small town between Valladolid, the main Spanish colony, and the Bahía de la Asunción, a large bay which had always offered relative shelter on the otherwise forbidding Yucatan coast. The town appears on maps until the late eighteenth century, disappearing by 1770, but remained a dense Mayan settlement until late colonial times. Patch, *Maya and Spaniard in Yucatan*, 60–61, 152, 199, 236–238. A *vigía* (watchtower) built to protect inland communities from pirate attacks (modern Vigía Grande or Chico?) was maintained on the coast in the bay where the river from Tijosuco met the sea. González probably took the party up the country road which connected the principal towns. Colonial maps indicate that the road connecting Tijosuco with the guard tower (*vigía*) followed a string of springs and watering holes spaced at roughly three-league intervals, named—in order from the bay—Xochil, Notidonat, San Xivic, Chasanchè (modern Chanchén?), Tupich (modern Tepich), and Lacetan.

200. Modern Bacalar, 18° 45' N 88° 25' W, near the Bay of Chetumal in the modern state of Quintana Roo.

201. *trabajos.*

202. The original Spanish here can be confusing: *hallamos un edificio al parecer antiquissimo compuesto de solas quatro paredes, y en el medio de cada una de ellas una pequeña puerta, y à correspondencia otra en el medio de mayor altura.* First, *otra* must refer to *cada una de ellas* and *paredes*, not *puerta.* Second, *paredes* refers not to free-standing enclosure walls but to the building's weight-bearing walls. I read *medio* as referring to the "middle" of both the building and the walls on the ground floor. The building therefore had two floors, with a second superimposed structure centered on the roof of the ground floor.

203. *[seria la de las paredes de â fuera como de tres estados]*; in this phrase *la* must refer to the *altura* (height) of the wall; *estados* is not the "stade" or "stadion" of ancient Greek measurement, which was roughly 200 yards or meters, but a much smaller construction-related measurement. The Real Academia Español's dictionary defines *estado* as "a conventional measurement equivalent to the height of an average man; it is used normally to measure the depth of wells or other deep objects. Among builders and master masons walls built of loose stone are measured in *estados*" (*Diccionario de la lengua castellana*, s.v. "estado").

204. Over the centuries the coast along which Ramírez traveled north from the shipwreck site was alternately a long connected barrier island and a jumble of islands separated by shallow inlets and mangrove swamps. At present they form a connected barrier island. In terms of identifying Ramírez's Mayan temple, we can discount the multiple buildings at Chac Mool, which are too numerous and too large to match his description. Some other candidates remain. One of the two Punta Pájaro ruins was approximately 3 meters high, with only one door on one side and an adjacent well and a smaller structure nearby, 3 meters square; the second Punta Pájaro ruin, near Punta Arenas, now destroyed, was a similar small temple with an adjacent well. North of Chac Mool was another small temple, now destroyed, which apparently did not have an adjacent well. In the swamps just west of Chac Mool stands Tupak, a rectangular edifice with a door on one wall only, 9.5 by 5.8 meters and 4 meters high, with a superimposed smaller structure on its roof which has four doors opening to the cardinal directions, 1.8 by 1.6 meters and 1.2 meters high. Finally, as a remote possibility, Cacakal, a small temple inland from Ascension Bay on the road to Tijosuco, has two superimposed levels with four doors on the lower level, one on each side. Of these, Tupak seems to fit Ramírez's geographical location and description best, though there are certain problems with his memory of the architecture itself (the height matches, since 5.2 meters roughly equals 3 *estados*, but the number of doors is correct only for the second-floor structure, not

the ground floor, which only has one opening). The next best match among the existing temples is Cacakal, but it is too far inland for the seaside location which Ramírez remembered as an island; its architecture, however, closely resembles his description of the building, including the number of doors and the superimposed structure. The destruction of two of these coastal temples in the later centuries, in any case, probably makes a definitive identification of Ramírez's temple impossible. Escalona Ramos, "Ruinas de Punta Pájaro," 540–541; Riqué Flores, "'Tupak,'" 237–246; Lothrop, *Tulum*, 160–165; Peissel, *El mundo perdido de los mayas*, 189–205; Terrones González, "Informe de los trabajos de mantenimiento mayor," 1–17; and Terrones González, "Algunas evidencias de sacrificio," 357–361.

205. *Petate* is a Nahuatlism that the Spanish adopted from the indigenous language of the Aztecs.

206. *para llegar â poblado.*

207. *à vela y remo.*

208. *impiedad.*

209. *la reduccion de aquellos miserables Gentiles al gremio de la Iglesia Catholica.* See the explanation in note 211 below.

210. Ramírez makes it clear by his choice of words that the two Indians working for Juan were in on the plan; all three had collaborated in convincing him.

211. It is likely that González was looking for fugitive Indians as well as hunting for amber, possibly working for Melchor Pacheco in Valladolid or even the priest Cristóbal de Muros; Manuela Cristina García Bernal has proven that Yucatan *encomenderos* like Pacheco were seeking to replace the Indians who were abandoning their *encomiendas* in the late 1600s for free employment on cattle ranches: the raiders combed the southlands along the uncontrolled eastern coast, exactly as Ramírez said González was doing. This activity was called *reducción*, as in Ramírez's text here. The Maya were fleeing, García Bernal believes, "from the control of the authorities in their republics and their parish priests" (*Desarrollo agrario en el Yucatán colonial*, 241; cf. López de Cogolludo, *Historia de la provincia de Yucathán*, 145–149, 441–444; and Patch, *Maya and Spaniard in Yucatan*, 25–26, 42–56). In the Valladolid region near Tihosuco the *encomendero* and the priest were Melchor Pacheco and Fr. Muros. These raids on fugitive Indians and the independent Indian communities who harbored them became particularly virulent after a royal decree explicitly authorized them in 1686, partly on the assumption that Yucatan's southeastern Indians were allying themselves with smugglers and pirates. Caso Barrera, *Caminos en la selva*, 249–291. Despite laws to the contrary, slave raiding on Indian communities beyond Spanish territory remained relatively common on the imperial periphery into the nineteenth century. Humboldt, *Ensayo político sobre el reino de la Nueva España*, 87–88.

212. *para pasar el monte.*

213. *graniel.*

214. The wording of the phrase *hombres perdidos que ibamos à su amparo* is syntactically strange, suggesting that they were going to help the Indians and not the other way around. It is surely a typographical error. Perhaps the typesetter missed a word, as in *ibamos à pedir su amparo.*

215. *Jícaras* (mugs) of chocolate, a Pre-Columbian Mesoamerican treat, were typical refreshments in the Spanish world of the seventeenth century, in Europe and Asia as well as in America.

216. *á quien acuden los indios.*

217. November 25, 1689.

218. Chief magistrates, with both judicial and executive powers.

219. There is no prima facie reason to disbelieve Ramírez's assertion that Francisco Zealerún was one of the two alcaldes, but I have only been able to discover archival evidence that he was the *depositario general* (royal treasurer or trustee of accounts) and *regidor* in Valladolid in 1690. AGI, Escribanía 308B and México 363, 4, 31.

220. *donosissimo*, a word which connotes irony as well as humor, as in the quotation from the picaresque novel *La pícara Justina* cited in the Real Academia Española's dictionary: "It is very *donoso* to see how willingly anarchic wrongdoers [*bellacos*] obey those who command them in their anarchic wrongdoing [*bellacada*]" (*Diccionario de la lengua castellana*, s.v. "donoso").

221. Seventeenth-century Spaniards did not effectively distinguish between pirates and corsairs caught illegally marauding in Spanish waters.

222. This was indeed the fair market price locally. Slaves in the Yucatan at that time were sold for roughly 300 pesos, as can be seen in the sale of a slave in 1678 for 271 pesos in a declaration by the *contador real* of Campeche. Juárez Moreno, *Piratas y corsarios*, 63.

223. *teniente*; see Chapter 3 of the Introductory Study for a discussion of this senior official.

224. *trabajos.*

225. *lo que estaba en ellas* clearly refers to the beach, as opposed to the ship's hold.

226. This certainly appears to be a large sum, but 500 pesos is a paltry offer if we recall the quantity and quality of articles listed in the previous chapter. *Pesos* is a term used for silver coins of varying worth, but usually it referred to the famous silver pieces of eight worth eight reales. In comparison, the *alférez* (literally "standard-bearer," meaning a rank equivalent to second lieutenant) of Merida at the time, Don Gaspar de Salazar y Córdoba, bought the post (a major city office) for 551 pesos. Victoria González Muñoz, "Los alferezgos mayores en Yucatán: Poder, honor y riqueza, siglo XVII," in Navarro García and García Bernal, eds., *Elites urbanas en Hispanoamérica*, 71.

227. See the discussion in Chapter 3 of the Introductory Study.
228. It is not clear to me why Miguel, the renegade Spanish pirate, came back into Ramírez's mind at this point. Perhaps the memory of worse things allowed Ramírez to calm himself by rejecting this setback as relatively minor and inconsequential; he probably was simply alluding to the vagaries of life, which had taught him not to trust those who should, as Spaniards, have been his best allies.
229. Kris.
230. *queria yo pedir de mi justicia, y que se me oyese.*
231. Dramatically enough, December 8, Purísima Concepción, was the festival day of the Virgin of Ytzamal, patroness of Yucatan. What is even more interesting is that the most famous miracle story about this Virgin involved an Indian couple from Tijosuco, the very village where Fr. Muros had cared for Ramírez. Lizana, *Devocionario de Nuestra Señora de Izamal,* 97, 102. Her image was brought from Guatemala to Ytzamal by the sixteenth-century friar Diego de Landa, the famous Franciscan missionary. Although it has been destroyed and replaced, we know that the original image of the Virgin was kept in the convent of San Antonio de Padua, whose outdoor *atrio* (walled enclosure for outdoor mass) to this day remains the largest in Mexico.
232. Juan José de la Bárcena's appointment as governor, dated September 15, 1683, is in AGI, Contratación 5790, 3, fols. 16–21; his 1687 *expediente de información* and *licencia de pasajeros* are in AGI, Contratación 5448, 4; and his 1692 *residencia* is in AGI, Escribanía 321C. See also AGI, Indiferente 2077, 351, México 363, 4, 25, and Contratación 652, 1, 8. Prior to his appointment, de la Bárcena had commanded the *Margarita,* a *patache* in the coastal waters off Cartagena, with which he captured the pirate *balandra Isabela* in 1681, captained by a "Dutch" (Danish?) buccaneer named "Jan Jansen Tacq." AGI, Escribanía 579A.
233. This was a typical gesture of loyalty and acceptance of authority.
234. *extrajudicial relacion.*
235. The bureaucratic and administrative seat of the provincial government (but see below for the way the text describes them). It is not clear from Ramírez's account whether he was effectively under arrest, though the implications are that he was. On a 1751 map of the city, the Parish of San Cristóbal, reportedly run by Franciscans, was located inside the fort, seemingly indicating that Ramírez's stay there was far from mere hospitality. AGI, MP México, 196, "Plano de la Ciudadela de Mérida de Yucathan," dated September 22, 1751.
236. Francisco Guerrero served in Cuba for three years in the 1650s in Captain Juan Cabello's company and participated "as an honored and valiant soldier" in the defense of Jamaica organized by Governor Cristóbal de Isasi Arnaldo against the English. After settling in the Yucatan, Guerrero was named captain of four

companies of Spanish infantry in Merida on April 15, 1673, and became ser-geant major and corporal of the company on December 18, 1677. By then he had also served as an *alcalde ordinario* in the city and as a judge for the Santa Hermandad. AGI, Indiferente 127, 63, and AGS, Guerra 20, fol. 121. Guerrero was *mayordomo del pósito y alhóndiga* in Merida in 1682. García Bernal, *Desa-rrollo agrario en el Yucatán colonial*, 323n27.

237. Bernardo Sabido was appointed to the post on January 27, 1674. AGI, México 194, 33.

238. *certificacó* [*sic*].

239. This means that Ramírez was arguing that he did not break the house arrest imposed on him by Don Ceferino by returning to the wreck at any point.

240. It is unclear what this means. Perhaps Ramírez was implying that they did not wish to offer him a meal. I thank my copy editor, Kathy Lewis, for suggesting this possibility.

241. *barata.* The word was probably chosen for its meaningful ambiguity, because in early modern Spanish it meant not only "cheap" or "economical" but also "malicious trickery" or "cheap swindle, fraud"; see Real Academia Española, *Diccionario de la lengua castellana*, s.v. "barata." Ramírez, or Sigüenza, was ob-viously taking a jab at Merida's inhabitants.

242. AGI, Patronato 6, 27, contains the papal bulls of Cano y Sandoval's appoint-ment, dated December 7, 1682.

243. The phrasing *quien alli nos puso* here ambiguously refers to imprisonment or, at the very least, forcible detention (see note 235 above); the "Royal Apartments" of San Cristóbal are difficult to identify, though Ramírez was probably refer-ring to the complex of the parish church and convent of San Cristóbal, which López de Cogolludo described as lying on the south side of the main Francis-can convent, Merida's second most important place of worship (*Historia de la provincia de Yucathán*, 213). In 1841 John L. Stephens described them as the most interesting and remarkable edifice in Merida, "enclosed by a high wall, with turrets forming what is now called the Castillo" (*Incidents of Travel in Yu-catan*, 48–49).

244. Possibly the *alférez* Pedro Flores mentioned in AGS, Guerra 86, fol. 10.

245. An obvious typographical error occurs in the phrase *precediendo informacion q* [the *q* has the abbreviation symbol written above it, which renders it "que"— more evidence of the speed or carelessness of publication?] *dicon los mios de pertenecerme* in the printed text, which seems to have superimposed letters on *con. Dicon* probably should read *dieron.*

246. See the discussion of these papal bulls in Chapter 3 of the Introductory Study.

247. *corsantes y piratas*, as opposed to *corsarios y piratas*; the distinctions were prob-ably not clear in the mind of either Ramírez or Sigüenza.

248. A typical defense against coastal piracy in both the Mediterranean and Atlantic Spanish domains was to move populations inland; this is one reason for the lack of coastal settlements in parts of Andalusia, a favorite target for North African corsairs, and Mexico and Central America, a preferred target for Jamaica-based pirates in the late seventeenth century.

249. Ramírez undoubtedly heard this news from the priest in Tijosuco or from Don Melchor Pacheco.

250. *alférez*; perhaps the Antonio Zapata who was named *capitán de infantería* in 1707. AGS, Guerra 7, fol. 95.

251. *balandra.*

252. Perhaps the Captain Juan Peña who operated a slave ship in the Atlantic in the 1660s and 1670s. AGI, Escribanía 958.

253. "April 4" is obviously an error: it should read "May 4."

254. *trabajos.*

255. Note how this contrasts the concepts of work and suffering subsumed under the rubric of *trabajo* with freedom (*libertad*): for a discussion of this important debate about labor in early modern Spanish and Spanish American civilization, see MacKay, *"Lazy, Improvident People"*; and my book review comments in *Journal of Modern History* 81 (2009): 454–456.

256. The change in tense here, from simple past "proceeded" to present perfect "has befallen" (I have corrected the typographical error in *he hado* to *he dado*) indicates the chronological proximity of the writing of this text to the audience with the viceroy and the immediacy of Ramírez's voice dictating to Sigüenza.

257. *compadecido de mis trabajos, no solo formô esta Relacion en que se contienen.*

258. Guzmán y Córdova was appointed Contador de la Caja Real de México in 1675 (AGI, Contratación 5790, 1, fols. 233–236) and arrived in New Spain from Seville in the same year (AGI, Contratación 5540A, 1, fol. 153, and Contratación 5440, 2, 16); AGI, Contaduría 799 (1695–1696) contains the record of the donation that Guzmán y Córdova made to help defray "the urgent needs of the crown." The Spanish administration always included two financial officers: the *tesorero* (treasurer), who was responsible for keeping the triple-locked cashbox and receiving and expending cash, and the *contador* (comptroller), who acted as an accountant and from time to time as auditor of accounts (Escalona, *Gazofilacium*, 6–7). Guzmán y Córdova was Galve's top financial officer and a friend of Sigüenza y Góngora (he supported the publication of the cosmographer's *Libra astronómica y philosóphica:* see the title-page information, reproduced in Maggs Bros., Catalogue #442, Plate XXIV, facing 217).

259. Popular rumor held that men running from the law often signed on with the fleets "to avoid the jurisdiction of ordinary judges," as the Cadiz merchant Raimundo Lantéry recalled in his memoirs (*Un comerciante saboyano*, 200), but Ramírez's viceregal patronage obviated such a necessity.

Bibliography

Abreu y Bertodano, Felix Joseph de. *Tratado jurídico-político, sobre pressas de mar.* Cadiz: Imprimería Real de Marina, 1746.

Aizpurúa, Ramón. *Curazao y la costa de Caracas: Introducción al estudio del contrabando de la provincia de Venezuela en tiempos de la Compañía Guipuzcoana, 1730–1780.* Caracas: Academia Nacional de la Historia, 1993.

Alden, Dauril. *The Making of an Enterprise: The Society of Jesus in Portugal, Its Empire, and Beyond, 1540–1750.* Stanford: Stanford University Press, 1996.

Alloza, Juan de. *Flores summarum: Sive alphabetum morale.* Mediolani: ex typographia Francisci Vigoni, 1677.

Alsedo y Herrera, Dionisio de. *Piraterías y agresiones de los ingleses y de otros pueblos de Europa en la América española desde el siglo XVI al XVIII deducidas de las obras de Dionisio de Alsedo y Herrera* (ca. 1740). Ed. by Justo Zaragoza. Madrid: M. G. Hernández, 1883.

Altman, Ida. *Transatlantic Ties in the Spanish Empire: Brihuega, Spain, and Puebla, Mexico, 1560–1620.* Stanford: Stanford University Press, 2000.

Ammarell, Gene. *Bugis Navigation.* New Haven: Yale University Press, 1999.

Anderson, John. *English Intercourse with Siam in the Seventeenth Century.* London: Kegan Paul, Trench, Trübner, 1890.

Anderson Imbert, Enrique. *Historia de la literatura hispanoamericana.* Mexico City: Fondo de Cultura Económica, 1964.

André, Jean François. *Gramont, le grand dernier chef des flibustiers.* Paris: Tiger, 1813.

Andrews, Evangeline Walker, and Charles McLean Andrews. *Jonathan Dickinson's Journal, or, God's Protecting Providence: Being a Narrative of a Journey from Port Royal in Jamaica to Philadelphia between August 23, 1696, and April 1, 1697* (1699).

New Haven: Yale University Press, 1961; Port Salerno: Florida Classics Library, 1985.

Archio Portuguez-Oriental. Nova Goa: Imprensa Nacional, 1875.

Arcilla, José S. *Jesuit Missionary Letters from Mindanao.* Quezon City: Philippine Province Archives, 1990.

Arquivos de Macau. Macao: Instituto Cultural de Macau, 1929–.

Arroyo, Mercedes. "El *Reconocimiento de la península de Yucatán* realizado por el ingeniero militar Juan de Dios González." *Biblio 3W: Revista Bibliográfica de Geografía y Ciencias Sociales* 8 (2003) [http://www.ub.es/geocrit/b3w-474.htm, accessed on May 20, 2007].

Arteaga y Falguera, Cristina. *La Casa del Infantado, cabeza de los Mendoza.* Madrid: El Duque del Infantado, 1944.

Artola, Miguel. *La hacienda del Antiguo Régimen.* Madrid: Alianza, 1982.

Baer, Joel. "'Captain John Avery' and the Anatomy of a Mutiny." *Eighteenth-Century Life* 18 (1994): 1–26.

———. "William Dampier at the Crossroads: New Light on the 'Missing Years,' 1691–1697." *International Journal of Maritime History* 8 (1996): 97–117.

Baker, William A. *Colonial Vessels: Some Seventeenth-Century Sailing Craft.* Barre, Mass.: Barre Publishing Company, 1962.

Banks, Kenneth. *Chasing Empire across the Sea: Communications and the State in the French Atlantic, 1713–1763.* Montreal and Ithaca: McGill–Queen's University Press, 2002.

Barbour, Violet. "Privateers and Pirates of the West Indies." *American Historical Review* 16 (1911): 539–566.

Barlow, Edward. "Barlow's Journal, His Life at Sea in East and West Indiamen, 1659–1703." MS JOD/4. National Maritime Museum Archive (Greenwich, UK).

———. *Barlow's Journal of His Life at Sea in King's Ships, East & West Indiamen and Other Merchantmen from 1659 to 1703.* 2 vols. London: Hurst and Blackett, 1934.

Barnard, John. *Ashton's Memorial, or, an Authentick Account of the Strange Adventures and Signal Deliverances of Mr. Philip Ashton, Who, After He Had Made His Escape from the Pirates, Liv'd Alone on a Desolate Island for about 16 Months.* London: Richard Ford and Samuel Chandler, 1726.

Barrantes, Vicente. *Guerras piráticas contra mindanaos y joloanos.* Madrid: M. G. Hernández, 1878.

Barrionuevo de Peralta, Jerónimo de. *Avisos de Jerónimo Barrionuevo de Peralta (1654–58).* Ed. by Antonio Pax y Meliá. Madrid: M. Tello, 1892–1894.

Baviera, Príncipe Adalberto de, and Gabriel Maura Gamazo. *Documentos inéditos referentes a las postrimerías de la Casa de Austria en España.* 5 vols. Madrid: Revista de Archivos, Bibliotecas y Museos, 1927.

Bazarte Cerdán, Willebaldo. "La primera novela mexicana." *Humanidades* 7 (1958): 88–107.

Beeckman, Captain Daniel. *A Voyage to and from the Island of Borneo* (1718). Facsimile edition. Folkestone, England: Barnes and Noble and Dawsons of Pall Mall, 1973.

Beekman, E. M., ed. *The Poison Tree: Selected Writings of Rumphius on the Natural History of the Indies.* Amherst: University of Massachusetts, 1981.

Bello, Andrés. *Principios de derecho internacional.* Paris: Gauthier, 1864.

Bennett, J. Harry. "Cary Helyar, Merchant and Planter of Seventeenth-Century Jamaica." *William and Mary Quarterly,* 3rd series, 21 (1964): 53–76.

Benton, Lauren. "Making Order Out of Trouble: Jurisdictional Politics in the Spanish Colonial Borderlands." *Law and Social Inquiry* 26, no. 2 (2001): 373–401.

Bernecker, Walther L. *Contrabando, ilegalidad y corrupción en el México del siglo XIX.* Mexico City: Universidad Iberoamericana, 1994.

Bèze, Claude, Père de. *1688 Revolution in Siam: The Memoir of Father de Bèze, S.J.* Ed. and trans. by E. W. Hutchinson. Hong Kong: University Press, 1968.

———. *Mémoire du Père de Bèze sur la vie de Constance Phaulkon, premier ministre du roi de Siam, Phra Narai, et sa triste fin; suivi de lettres et de documents d'archives de Constance Phaulkon.* Tokyo: Presses Salésiennes, 1947.

Blair, Emma Helen, and James Alexander Robertson. *The Philippine Islands, 1493–1898.* 54 vols. Cleveland: Arthur H. Clark, 1903–1909.

Bouvet, Père. *Voiage de Siam du Père Bouvet.* Ed. by J. C. Gatty. Leiden: E. J. Brill, 1963.

Bowrey, Thomas. *A Dictionary English and Malayo, Malayo and English.* 2 vols. London: Samuel Bridge, 1701.

Boxer, C. R. *Francisco Vieira de Figueiredo: A Portuguese Merchant-Adventurer in South East Asia, 1624–1667.* The Hague: Martinus Nijhoff, 1967.

———. *From Lisbon to Goa, 1500–1750: Studies in Portuguese Maritime Enterprise.* London: Variorum Reprints, 1984.

———. *Portuguese India in the Mid-Seventeenth Century.* Delhi: Oxford University Press, 1980.

Breazeale, Kennon, ed. *From Japan to Arabia: Ayutthaya's Maritime Relations with Asia.* Bangkok: Toyota Thailand Foundation, 1999.

Bruijn, J. R., F. S. Gaastra, and Ivo Schöffer. *Dutch-Asiatic Shipping in the 17th and 18th Centuries.* 3 vols. The Hague: Nijhoff, 1979–1987.

The Building of Castillo de San Marcos. Washington, D.C.: United States Government Printing Office, 1942.

Burkholder, Mark, and D. S. Chandler. *From Impotence to Authority: The Spanish Crown and the American Audiencias, 1687–1808.* Columbia: University of Missouri Press, 1977.

Burnay, Jean. "Notes chronologiques sur les missions jésuites du Siam au XVIIe siècle." In *Commentarii S. Francisco Xaverio Sacri, 1552–1952,* vol. 22, fasc. 43 of *Archivum Societatis Iesu,* 191–196. Rome: Institutum Historicum Societatis Iesu, 1953.

Bynkershoek, Cornelius van. *De Dominio Maris Dissertatio* (1702). Ed. by James Brown Scott. Buffalo, N.Y.: William S. Hein, 1995.

Cañeque, Alejandro. *The King's Living Image: The Culture and Politics of Viceregal Power in Colonial Mexico*. New York: Routledge, 2004.

Cañizares-Esguerra, Jorge. *How to Write the History of the New World: Histories, Epistemologies, and Identities in the Eighteenth-Century Atlantic World*. Stanford: Stanford University Press, 2001.

———. "New World, New Stars: Patriotic Astrology and the Invention of Indian and Creole Bodies in Colonial Spanish America, 1600–1650." *American Historical Review* 104 (1999): 33–68.

Cárceles de Gea, Beatriz. *Fraude y desobediencia fiscal en la Corona de Castilla, 1621–1700*. Valladolid: Junta de Castilla y León, 2000.

———. *Reforma y fraude fiscal en el reinado de Carlos II: La Sala de Millones (1658–1700)*. Madrid: Banco de España, 1995.

Carreira-Afonso, John. *Jesuit Letters and Indian History: A Study of the Nature and Development of the Jesuit Letters from India (1542–1773)*. Bombay: Indian Historical Research Institute, 1955.

Caso Barrera, Laura. *Caminos en la selva: Migración, comercio y resistencia—Mayas yucatecos e itzaes, siglos XVII–XIX*. Mexico City: El Colegio de México, 2002.

Castillero Calvo, Alfredo. *La ruta transístmica y las comunicaciones marítimas hispanas, siglos XVI a XIX*. Panama City: Comisión de Estudios Históricos del Ministerio de Obras Públicas y Urbanismo de España, 1984.

Catz, Rebecca. *The Travels of Mendes Pinto*. Chicago: University of Chicago Press, 1989.

Chapin, H. M. *Privateer Ships and Sailors: The First Century of American Colonial Shipping, 1625–1725*. Toulon: Imprimerie G. Mouton, 1926.

Chatelain, Verne. *The Defense of Spanish Florida, 1565–1763*. Washington, D.C.: Carnegie Institute of Washington, 1941.

Cheney, C. R., ed. *A Handbook of Dates for Students of British History*. Cambridge: Cambridge University Press, 2000.

Clayton, Lawrence A. *Los astilleros de Guayaquil colonial*. Guayaquil: El Archivo Histórico del Guayas, 1978.

Collis, Maurice. *Siamese White*. London: Faber and Faber, 1951.

Colomba, Eudore de. *Resumo da história de Macau*. Macao: Mandarin, 1980.

Contreras Sánchez, Alicia del C. "Los circuitos comerciales del palo de tinte (1750–1807)." In *España y Nueva España: Sus acciones transmarítimas: Memorias del I Simposio Internacional celebrado en la ciudad de México del 23 al 26 de octubre de 1990*, 171–199. Mexico City: Universidad Iberoamericana, 1991.

Coolhaas, W. Ph. *Generale Missiven van Gouverneurs-Generaal en raden aan Heren XVII der Verenigde Oostindische Compagnie*. 11 vols. The Hague: Martinus Nijhoff, 1960–1995.

Cordingly, David. *Under the Black Flag: The Romance and the Reality of Life among the Pirates.* San Diego, New York, and London: Harcourt, Brace and Company, 1995.

Corominas, Joan. *Breve diccionario etimológico de la lengua castellana.* Madrid: Gredos 1961.

Contente Domingues, Francisco. *Os navios do Mar Oceano: Teoria e empiria na arquitectura naval portuguesa dos séculos XVI e XVII.* Lisbon: Centro de História da Universidade de Lisboa, 2004.

Costa, Horacio de la, S.J. *The Jesuits in the Philippines, 1581–1768.* Cambridge, Mass.: Harvard University Press, 1961.

———. *Readings in Philippine History.* Manila, Cebu, and Makati: Bookmark, 1965.

Coutre, Jacques de. *Vida de Jaques de Coutre natural de la ciudad de Brugas* (1640). Published as *Andanzas asiáticas.* Madrid: Historia 16, 1991.

Crosby, Alfred. *Ecological Imperialism: The Biological Expansion of Europe, 900–1900.* Cambridge: Cambridge University Press, 1986.

Crouse, Nellis M. *The French Struggle for the West Indies, 1665–1713.* New York: Octagon Books, 1966.

Cruyse, Dirk van der. *Louis XIV et le Siam.* Paris: Fayard, 1991.

Cruz Barney, Oscar. *El combate a la piratería en Indias, 1555–1700.* Mexico City: Oxford University Press/Universidad Iberoamericano, 1999.

Cummins, James. *"Infortunios de Alonso Ramírez:* A Just History of Fact?" *Bulletin of Hispanic Studies* 61 (1984): 295–303.

Cummins, James, and Alan Soons, eds. *Los infortunios de Alonso Ramírez.* London: Tamesis, 1984.

Cushner, Nicholas P., S.J. *Spain in the Philippines from Conquest to Revolution.* Quezon City: Institute of Philippine Culture, Ateneo de Manila University; Rutland, Vt., and Tokyo: Charles E. Tuttle, 1971.

Dam, Pieter van. *Beschryvinge van de Oostindische Compagnie.* 4 vols. The Hague: Martinus Nijhoff, 1932.

Dampier, William. *Dampier's Voyages: Consisting of a New Voyage round the World, a Supplement to the Voyage round the World, Two Voyages to Campeachy, a Discourse of Winds, a Voyage to New Holland, and a Vindication, in Answer to the Chimerical Relation of William Funnell* [half-title: *The Voyages of Captain William Dampier*]. London: E. Grant Richards, 1717.

———. *Dampier's Voyages, Consisting of a New Voyage round the World, a Supplement to the Voyage round the World.* Ed. by John Masefield. 2 vols. London: E. Grant Richards, 1906.

———. *A New Voyage round the World.* Introduction by Sir Albert Gray and new introduction by Percy G. Adams. London: Argonaut Press, 1927; reprint, New York: Dover, 1968.

———. "William Dampier's Second Voyage in the South Seas." Sloane MS 3236. British Library, London.

Defoe, Daniel. *The King of the Pirates: Being an Account of the Famous Enterprises of Captain Avery with Lives of Other Pirates and Robbers.* Garden City, N.Y.: Doubleday, Doran, and Company, n.d.

Deschamps, Hubert. *Les pirates à Madagascar aux XVIIe et XVIIIe siècles.* Paris: Editions Berger-Levrault, 1949.

Díaz, Casimiro. *Conquistas de las Islas Filipinas* (1718). Valladolid: L. N. de Gaviria, 1890.

Dickinson, Jonathan. *God's Protecting Providence . . . Evidenced in the Remarkable Deliverance of Diverse Persons from the Devouring Waves of the Sea, amongst Which They Suffered Shipwreck* (1699). Ed. by Evangeline Walker Andrews and Charles McLean Andrews. Porta Salerno: Florida Classics Library, 1985.

Dodge, Meredith D., and Rick Hendricks, eds. *Two Hearts, One Soul: The Correspondence of the Condesa de Galve, 1688–96.* Albuquerque: University of New Mexico Press, 1993.

Dorsey, Peter A. "Going to School with Savages: Authorship and Authority among the Jesuits of New France." *William and Mary Quarterly* 55 (1998): 399.

Du Casse, R. *L'Amiral du Casse, Chevalier de la Toison d'Or (1646–1715).* Paris: Berger-Leurault, 1876.

Dumond, Don E. *The Machete and the Cross: Campesino Rebellion in Yucatan.* Lincoln and London: University of Nebraska Press, 1997.

Dunn, W. E. "Spanish and French Rivalry in the Gulf Region of the United States, 1678–1702." *University of Texas Bulletin* 1705 (January 1927): 40.

Duuren, David van. *The Kris: An Earthly Approach to a Cosmic Symbol.* Amsterdam: Koninklijk Instutuut voor de Tropen, Pictures Publishers, 1998.

Earle, Peter. *The Wreck of the Almiranta: Sir William Phips and the Hispaniola Treasure.* London: Macmillan, 1979.

East India Company. *The Lawes or Standing Orders of the East India Company.* [London]: n.p. 1621; facsimile, Farnborough, England: Gregg International Publishers, 1968.

Elliott, John H. *Empires of the Atlantic World: Britain and Spain in America, 1492–1830.* New Haven: Yale University Press, 2006.

Escalante Colombres, Manuel. *Descripción de las honras fúnebres que la Real Universidad de México consagró a su Doctor y Catedrático, el Ilmo. Sr. Don Juan Cano Sandoval, obispo de Yucatán.* Mexico City: Guillena Carrascoso, 1695.

Escalona, Gaspar de. *Gazofilacium regium perubicum* [*Gazofilacio real del Perú*] (1647). Translated by León M. Loza. La Paz, Bolivia: Editorial del Estado, 1941.

Escalona Ramos, Alberto. "Ruinas de Punta Pájaro o Nohku, Quintana Roo." *Boletín de la Sociedad Mexicana de Geografía y Estadística* 61 (1956): 540–541, 594.

Escudero, José Antonio, ed. *Los validos*. Madrid: Editorial Dykinson, 2004.

Evelyn, John. *The Diary of John Evelyn*. Ed. by E. S. de Beer. 6 vols. Oxford: At the Clarendon Press, 1955.

Exquemelin, Alexandre-Olivier [Esquemeling, John]. *The Buccaneers of America*. Ed. by William Swan Stallybrass. London: Printed for William Crooke, 1684; facsimile edition, Williamstown, Mass.: Corner House Publishers, 1976.

———. *The Buccaneers of America*. Trans. by Alexis Brown. Introduction by Jack Beeching. Mineola, N.Y.: Dover, 2000 (reprint of Harmondsworth, England: Penguin, 1969).

———. *Histoire des aventuriers flibustiers*. Ed. by Réal Ouellet and Patrick Villiers. Paris: Université de Paris Sorbonne, 2005.

Feliciano Ramos, Héctor R. *El contrabando inglés en el Caribe y el golfo de México (1748–1778)*. Seville: Diputación Provincial, 1990.

Fernández de Béthencourt, Francisco. *Historia genealógica y heráldica de la monarquía española, casa real y grandes de España*. Madrid: E. Teodoro, 1912.

Fernández de Navarrete, Martín. *Colección de documentos y manuscritos compilados por Fernández de Navarrete*. Nendeln, Liechtenstein: Kraus-Thomson Organization/Museo Naval Madrid, 1971.

Fernández Duro, Cesáreo. *Armada española desde la unión de los reinos de Castilla y de Aragón*. 9 vols. Madrid: Est. Tipográfico "Sucesores de Rivadeneyra," 1895–1903; facsimile edition, Madrid: Museo Naval, 1973.

Flores, Romero. *Iconografía colonial: Retratos de personajes notables en la Historia Colonial de México, existentes en el Museo Nacional, con notas colegidas de diversos autores y ordenadas por el Jefe del Departamento de Historia de la misma institución*. Mexico City: Museo Nacional, 1940.

Flynn, Dennis O., and Arturo Giráldez, eds. *Metals and Monies in an Emerging Global Economy*. Aldershot, UK, and Brookfield, Vt.: Variorum Reprints, 1997.

Flynn, Dennis O., Arturo Giráldez, and James Sobredo, eds. *European Entry into the Pacific: Spain and the Acapulco-Manila Galleons*. Aldershot, UK, and Burlington, Vt.: Ashgate, 2001.

Forbin, Claude. *The Siamese Memoirs of Count Claude de Forbin, 1685–1688* (1731). Chiang Mai, Thailand: Silkworm Books, 1997.

Fortescue, J. W., et al., eds. *Calendar of State Papers, Colonial Series: America and West Indies*. Vols. 7 (1685–1688), 8 (1689–1692), 9 (1693–1696), and 12 (Addenda, 1621–1698). London: His Majesty's Stationery Office, 1901.

Fortificaciones del Caribe: Memorias de la reunión de expertos, 31 de julio, 1 y 2 de agosto de 1996, Cartagena de Indias, Colombia. Santafé de Bogotá: Instituto Colombiano de Cultura, World Heritage, UNESCO, 1997.

Frey, Edward. *The Kris: Mystic Weapon of the Malay World*. New York: Oxford University Press, 2003.

Furbank, P. N., and W. R. Owens. *The Canonisation of Daniel Defoe.* New Haven: Yale University Press, 1988.

Galvin, Peter R. *Patterns of Pillage: A Geography of Caribbean-Based Piracy in Spanish America, 1536–1718.* New York: Peter Lang, 1999.

García Bernal, Manuela Cristina. *Campeche y el comercio atlántico yucateco (1521–1624).* Campeche, Mexico: Universidad Autónoma de Campeche, 2006.

———. *Desarrollo agrario en el Yucatán colonial.* Merida, Mexico: Universidad Autónoma de Yucatán, 2006.

———. *Economía, política y sociedad en el Yucatán colonial.* Merida, Mexico: Universidad Autónoma de Yucatán, 2005.

———. *La sociedad en Yucatán, 1700–1750.* Seville: Escuela de Estudios Hispano-Americanos, 1972.

———. *Población y encomienda bajo los Austrias.* Seville: Escuela de Estudios Hispano-Americanos, 1978.

García Bernal, Manuela Cristina, and Julián Ruiz Rivera. *Cargadores a Indias.* Madrid: MAPFRE, 1992.

Garibay K., Angel María. *Diccionario Porrúa de historia, biografía y geografía de México.* Mexico City: Porrúa, 1995.

Gasser, Jacques. "De la mer des Antilles à l'océan Indien: L'odysée du flibustier Desmarestz (1688–1700)." *Bulletin du Cercle Généalogique de Bourbon* 38, 39, 40, and 41 (1992–1993).

Gerhard, Peter. *Pirates of New Spain, 1575–1742.* Glendale, Calif.: Arthur H. Clarke Company, 1960; reprint, Mineola, N.Y.: Dover, 2003.

Gervaise, Nicolas. *The Natural and Political History of the Kingdom of Siam.* Bangkok: White Lotus, 1999.

Gill, Anton. *The Devil's Mariner: A Life of William Dampier, Pirate and Explorer, 1651–1715.* London: Michael Joseph, 1997.

Glamann, Kristof. *Dutch-Asiatic Trade, 1620–1740.* Copenhagen: Danish Science Press, 1958.

Goñi Gaztambide, José. *Historia de la bula de la cruzada en España.* Vitoria: Editorial del Seminario, 1958.

Goodman, David. *Spanish Naval Power, 1589–1665: Reconstruction and Defeat.* Cambridge: Cambridge University Press, 1997.

Gracián, Baltasar. *El criticón.* Barcelona: Ediciones Orbis, 1982.

Granier, Hubert. *Marins de France au combat, XVIIe siècle.* Brest and Paris: Editions de la Cité, 1989.

Grant, W. L., James Munro, and Sir Almeric W. Fitzroy, eds. *Acts of the Privy Council of England, Colonial Series: Volume 2, 1680–1720.* Hereford: H. M. Stationery Office, 1910.

Grey, Charles. *Pirates of the Eastern Seas: A Lurid Page of History.* London: S. Low, Marston and Company, 1933.

Grotius, Hugo. *Commentary on the Law of Prize and Booty* (1603). Ed. by Martine Julia van Ittersum. Indianapolis: Liberty Fund, 2006.

Guérin, Léon. *Histoire maritime de France*. 6 vols. Paris: Dufour et Mulat, 1851.

Gutiérrez, Ramón. *Las fortificaciones de Iberoamérica*. Madrid: Ediciones el Viso, 2005.

Gutiérrez Coronel, Diego. *Historia genealógica de la Casa de Mendoza*. Cuenca: Instituto Jerónimo Zurita del Consejo Superior de Investigaciones Científicas, 1946.

Gutiérrez Lorenzo, María Pilar. *De la corte de Castilla al virreinato de México: El Conde de Galve (1653–1697)*. Guadalajara, Spain: Diputación Provincial, 1993.

Hairul, Awang Sudjai. *Kamus Lengkap*. Petaling Jaya, Malaysia: Pustaka Zaman, 1977.

Hall, Kenneth R. *Maritime Trade and State Development in Early Southeast Asia*. Honolulu: University of Hawaii Press, 1985.

Hall, Kenneth R., and John K. Whitmore, eds. *Explorations in Early Southeast Asian History: The Origins of Southeast Asian Statecraft*. Ann Arbor: Center for South and Southeast Asian Studies, University of Michigan, 1976.

Hanke, Lewis. *Guía de las fuentes en el Archivo General de Indias para el estudio de la administración virreinal*. Cologne and Vienna: Böhlau, 1977.

Haring, C. H. *The Buccaneers in the West Indies in the XVII Century*. Hamden, Conn.: Archon, 1966.

Hebb, David Delison. *Piracy and the English Government, 1616–1642*. Aldershot, UK: Scholar Press, 1994.

Herbermann, Charles G. et al., eds. *The Catholic Encyclopedia*. New York: Robert Appleton, 1910.

Herrera y Tordesillas, Antonio de. *Historia general de los hechos de castellanos en las islas, y tierra firme, del mar océano*. 3 vols. Madrid: Nicolás Rodríguez Franco, 1725.

Herzog, Tamar. *Defining Nations: Immigrants and Citizens in Early Modern Spain and Spanish America*. New Haven: Yale University Press, 2003.

Hill, A. H. "The Keris and Other Malay Weapons." In *The Keris and Other Malay Weapons*, ed. Malaysian Branch of the Royal Asiatic Society, 1–92. Reprint No. 16. [Kuala Lumpur]: Malaysian Branch of the Royal Asiatic Society, 1998.

Hill, S. Charles. "Episodes of Piracy in the Eastern Seas, 1519–1851." *Indian Antiquary* 48 (1919): 217–219.

———. *Notes on Piracy in Eastern Waters*. Bombay: Indian Antiquary, 1920.

Howell, Thomas Bayly. *A Complete Collection of State Trials*. 33 vols. London: T. C. Hansard, 1811–1826.

Humboldt, Alejandro de. *Ensayo político sobre el reino de la Nueva España*. Mexico City: Porrúa, 1966.

Hutchinson, E. W. *Adventurers in Siam in the Seventeenth Century*. Bangkok: DD Books, with permission of the Royal Asiatic Society, 1985.

Ibn Ahmad, Raja Ali Haji. *The Precious Gift (Tuhfat al-Nafis)*. Ed. and trans. by Virginia Matheson and Barbara Watson Andaya. Kuala Lumpur: Oxford University Press, 1982.

Irizarry, Estelle. *Infortunios de Alonso Ramírez por Carlos de Sigüenza y Góngora y Alonso Ramírez*. San Juan, Puerto Rico: Comisión Puertorriqueña para la Celebración del Quinto Centenario del Descubrimiento de América y Puerto Rico, 1990.

Irwin, Graham. *Nineteenth-Century Borneo: A Study in Diplomatic Rivalry*. Singapore: Donald Moore Books, 1955.

Ittersum, Martine Julia van. "*Mare liberum* in the West Indies? Hugo Grotius and the Case of the *Swimming Lion*, a Dutch Pirate in the Caribbean at the Turn of the Seventeenth Century." *Itinerario (International Journal on the History of European Expansion and Global Interaction)* 31 (2007): 79–84.

Jacq-Hergoualc'h, Michel, ed. *Etude historique et critique du Journal du Voyage de Siam de Claude Céberet*. Paris: L'Harmattan, 1992.

Jasper, J. E., and Mas Pirgadie. *De Inlandsche Kunstnijverheid in Nederlandsch Indië*. 5 vols. The Hague: Mouton, 1912–1930.

Jenkin, A. K. Hamilton. *Cornish Seafarers: The Smuggling, Wrecking, and Fishing Life of Cornwall*. London: Dent, 1932.

Johnson, Captain [Daniel Defoe]. *A General History of the Pyrates* (1724 and 1728). Ed. by Manuel Schonhorn. Mineola, N.Y.: Dover, 1999.

Juárez Moreno, Juan. *Piratas y corsarios en Veracruz y Campeche*. Seville: Escuela de Estudios Hispano-Americanos de Sevilla, 1972.

Judice Biker, Julio Firmino. *Collecção de tratados e concertos de pazes que o Estado da India Portugueza fez com os Reis e Senhores com quem teve relações nas partes da Asia e Africa Oriental desde o principio da conquista até ao fim do século XVIII*. 14 vols. Lisbon: Imprensa Nacional, 1881–1887.

Jumsai, Manich. *History of Anglo-Thai Relations*. Bangkok: Chalermnit, 1970.

Kaempfer, Engelbert. *The History of Japan, together with a Description of the Kingdom of Siam, 1690–92*. Glasgow: James MacLehose and Sons, Publishers to the University, 1906.

Kamen, Henry. *Spain in the Later Seventeenth Century, 1665–1700*. London and New York: Longman, 1980.

Keene, Donald. *The Battles of Coxinga: Chikamatsu's Puppet Play, Its Background and Importance*. Cambridge: Cambridge University Press, 1971.

Kemp, Peter, ed. *The Oxford Companion to Ships and the Sea*. Oxford, New York, and Melbourne: Oxford University Press, 1976.

Kemp, Peter, and Christopher Lloyd. *Brethren of the Coast: Buccaneers of the South Seas*. New York: St. Martin's Press, 1960.

Kerr, Robert. *A General History and Collection of Voyages*. 18 vols. Edinbugh, 1811–1824.

Kinkor, Kenneth J. "Black Men under the Black Flag." In *Bandits at Sea*, ed. by C. R. Pennell, 195–210. New York: New York University Press, 2001.

Klinkert, Hillebrandus Cornelius. *Nieuw Maleisch-Nederlandsch Zakwoordenboek, ten behoeve van hen, die het Maleisch beoefenen.* Leiden: E. J. Brill, 1918.

Ladero Quesada, Miguel Angel. *Fiscalidad y poder real en Castilla (1252–1369).* Madrid: Editorial Complutense, 1993.

Lafaye, Jacques. *Quetzalcóatl and Guadalupe: The Formation of Mexican National Consciousness, 1531–1813.* Chicago: University of Chicago, 1976.

Lagmanovitch, David. "Para una caracterización de *Infortunios de Alonso Ramírez.*" *Sin Nombre* 5 (1974): 7–14.

Lane, Kris E. *Pillaging the Empire: Piracy in the Americas, 1500–1700.* Armonk, N.Y., and London: M. E. Sharpe, 1998.

Lanier, Lucien. *Etude historique sur les relations de la France et du royaume de Siam de 1662 à 1703.* Versailles: Imprimerie de E. Aubert, 1883.

Lantéry, Raimundo. *Un comerciante saboyano en el Cádiz de Carlos II (Las memorias de Raimundo Lantery, 1673–1700).* Ed. by Manuel Bustos Rodríguez. Cadiz: Caja de Ahorros de Cádiz, [1983].

Leal y Leal, Luis. *Diccionario naval inglés-español español-inglés.* Madrid: Ministerio de Marina, Editorial Naval, 1963.

Le Blanc, Marcel, S.J. *The History of Siam, 1688* (1692). Trans. and ed. by Michael Smithies. Chiang Mai, Thailand: Silkworm Books, 2003.

Leonard, Irving. *Don Carlos de Sigüenza y Góngora: A Mexican Savant of the Seventeenth Century.* Berkeley: University of California Press, 1929.

———. *Spanish Approach to Pensacola, 1689–1693.* Albuquerque: Quivira Society, 1939.

Leur, J. C. van. *Indonesian Trade and Society: Essays in Asian Social and Economic History.* The Hague: W. van Hoeve Publishers, 1967.

Lévesque, Rodrigue. *History of Micronesia: A Collection of Source Documents.* 20 vols. Gatineau, Canada: Lévesque Publications, 1992.

Lizana, Bernardo de. *Devocionario de Nuestra Señora de Izamal y conquista espiritual de Yucatán* (1633). Mexico City: Universidad Nacional Autónoma, 1995.

López Cantos, Angel. *Historia de Puerto Rico (1650–1700).* Seville: Escuela de Estudios Hispano-Americanos de Sevilla, 1975.

López de Cogolludo, Juan. *Historia de la provincia de Yucathán.* Madrid: Juan García Infanzón, 1688.

López Lázaro, Fabio. "Labor Disputes, Ethnic Quarrels, and Early Modern Piracy: A Mixed Hispano-Anglo-Dutch Squadron and the Causes of Captain Every's 1694 Mutiny." *International Journal of Maritime History* 22 (2010): 73–111.

———. "La mentira histórica de un pirata caribeño: El trasfondo histórico de *Los infortunios de Alonso Ramírez* (1690)." *Anuario de Estudios Americanos* 64 (2007): 87–104.

———. "Pirates of the Caribbean: Early Modern Spain and Latin America as Part of the Atlantic World." *Bulletin of the Society for Spanish and Portuguese Historical Studies* 33 (2008): 9–22.

Lorente Medina, Antonio. *La prosa de Sigüenza y Góngora y la formación de la conciencia criolla mexicana.* Mexico City: Fondo de Cultura Económica, Universidad Nacional de Educación a Distancia, 1996.

Lothrop, Samuel. *Tulum: An Archaeological Study of the East Coast of Yucatan.* Washington, D.C.: Carnegie Institution of Washington, 1924.

Loubère, Simon de la. *A New Historical Relation of the Kingdom of Siam.* Trans. by David K. Wyatt (1693). Facsimile, Kuala Lumpur, Singapore, London, and New York: Oxford University Press, 1969.

Louis XIV. *Oeuvres de Louis XIV.* Paris: Treuttel and Würtz, 1806.

Lucena Salmoral, Manuel. *Piratas, bucaneros, filibusteros y corsarios en América: Perros, mendigos y otros malditos del mar.* Madrid: MAPFRE, 1992.

Lundy, Derek. *The Way of a Ship: A Square-Rigger Voyage in the Last Days of Sail.* New York: Ecco Press, 2003.

Lussan, Raveneau de. *Raveneau de Lussan, Buccaneer of the Spanish Main and Early French Filibuster of the Pacific: A Translation into English of His Journal of a Voyage into the South Seas in 1684.* Cleveland: Arthur H. Clark, 1930.

Lynch, John. *The Hispanic World in Crisis and Change, 1598–1700.* Oxford and Cambridge: Blackwell, 1992.

Lynum, Edward. *William Hack and the South Sea Buccaneers.* London: Orion, [1948].

MacKay, Ruth. *"Lazy, Improvident People": Myth and Reality in the Writing of Spanish History.* Ithaca: Cornell University Press, 2006.

Maggs Bros. *Catalogue #442.* London: Maggs Bros., 1923.

Malaret, Augusto. *Diccionario de americanismos.* San Juan, Puerto Rico: Imprenta Venezuela, 1931.

Manacy, Albert. *The History of Castillo de San Marcos and Fort Matanzas from Contemporary Narratives and Letters.* Washington, D.C.: United States Department of the Interior, National Park Service, 1955.

Manwayring, Henry. *The Seaman's Dictionary.* London: Printed by G. M. for John Bellamy, 1644; facsimile edition, Menston, UK: Scolar Press, 1972.

Maura Gamazo, Gabriel, ed. *Correspondencia entre dos embajadores: Don Pedro Ronquillo y el Marqués de Cogolludo, 1689–1691.* Madrid: [Duque de Maura], 1951.

———. *Vida y reinado de Carlos II.* Madrid: Espasa-Calpe, 1954.

Mayer González, Alicia. *Dos americanos, dos pensamientos: Carlos de Sigüenza y Góngora y Cotton Mather.* Mexico City: Universidad Nacional Autónoma de México, 1998.

Means, Philip Ainsworth. *The Spanish Main: Focus of Envy, 1492–1700.* New York: Gordian Press, 1965.

Meehan Hermanson, Patricia. "Criterios y procedimientos para la elección de navíos insignia: El caso de *Nuestra Señora del Juncal*, capitana de la flota de la Nueva España de 1630." In *La flota de Nueva España: Vicisitudes y naufragios*, ed. Flor Trejo Rivera, 79–112. Mexico City: Instituto Nacional de Antropología e Historia, 2003.

Meehan Hermanson, Patricia, and Flor Trejo Rivera. "*Nuestra Señora del Juncal*: Her Story and Her Shipwreck." In *Underwater and Maritime Archaeology in Latin America and the Caribbean*, ed. Margaret E. Leshikar-Denton and Pilar Luna Erreguerena, 67–90. Walnut Creek, Calif.: Left Coast Press, 2008.

Molina, Antonio M. *The Philippines through the Centuries*. 2 vols. [Manila?]: UST Cooperative, 1960–1961.

Moncada Maya, José Omar. "En torno a la defensa de la península de Yucatán durante el siglo XVIII." *Biblio 3W: Revista Bibliográfica de Geografía y Ciencias Sociales* 8 (2003) [http://www.ub.es/geocrit/b3w-474.htm, accessed on May 20, 2007].

Montemayor y Córdoba de Cuenca, Juan Francisco de. *Discurso político, histórico, jurídico del derecho y repartimiento de presas y despojos aprehendidos en justa guerra, premios y castigos de los soldados*. Facsimile edition by Oscar Cruz Barney. Veracruz: Consejo Nacional para la Cultura, Instituto Nacional de Antropología e Historia, and Internacional de Contenedores Asociados de Veracruz, S.A., 2001.

Montero y Vidal, José. *Historia de la piratería malayo-mahometana en Mindanao, Joló y Borneo*. 2 vols. Madrid: Imprenta y Fundición de Manuel Tello, 1888.

Montes González, Francisco. "Reflejos de una ambición novohispana: Los retratos de los I condes de Pérez Gálvez por el pintor José María Guerrero (1792)." *Anales del museo de América* 16 (2008): 155–171.

Moreau, Jean-Pierre. *Une histoire des pirates des mers du Sud à Hollywood*. Paris: Editions du Tallandier, 2006.

Moreyra y Paz-Soldán, Manuel, and Guillermo Céspedes del Castillo. *Virreinato peruano: Documentos para su historia*. 3 vols. Lima: Instituto Histórico del Perú, 1954.

Morineau, Michel. *Incroyables gazettes et fabuleux métaux: Les retours des trésors américains d'après les gazettes hollandaises (XVIe–XVIIIe siècles)*. New York and Cambridge: Cambridge University Press; Paris: Maison des Sciences de l'Homme, 1985.

Mota, Francisco. *Piratas en el Caribe*. Ciudad de La Habana: Casas de las Américas, 1984.

Mukherjee, Ramkrishna. *The Rise and Fall of the East India Company*. New York and London: Monthly Review Press, 1974.

Murillo Velarde, Pedro, S.J. *Geographia histórica de las islas Philipinas*. 10 vols. Madrid: Gabriel Ramírez, 1752.

Nadelmann, Ethan. "Global Prohibition Regimes: The Evolution of Norms in International Society." *International Organization* 44 (1990): 479–526.

Navarro García, Luis, and Manuela Cristina García Bernal, eds. *Elites urbanas en Hispanoamérica: De la conquista a la independencia.* Seville: Universidad de Sevilla, 2005.

Nys, Ernest. *Etudes de droit international et de droit politique.* Brussels: A. Castaigne, 1901.

Ordenanzas del buen govierno de la armada del mar océano de 24 de henero de 1633. Barcelona: Francisco Cormellas, 1678; facsimile edition by José Luis Morales. Madrid: Consejo Superior de Investigaciones Científicas, Instituto Histórico de Marina, 1974.

Orléans, Fr. Pierre Joseph d', S.J. *Histoire de M. Constance, premier ministre du Roy de Siam, et de la dernière revolution de cet Estat.* Tours: Philbert Masson, 1690.

Ovington, John. *A Voyage to Suratt, in the Year 1689.* London: Jacob Tonson, 1696.

Parthesius, Robert. *Dutch Ships in Tropical Waters: The Development of the Dutch East India Company (VOC) Shipping Network in Asia, 1595–1660.* Amsterdam: Amsterdam University Press, 2010.

Patch, Robert. *Maya and Spaniard in Yucatan, 1648–1812.* Stanford, Calif.: Stanford University Press, 1993.

Peissel, Michel. *El mundo perdido de los mayas: Exploraciones y aventuras en Quintana Roo.* Barcelona: Editorial Juventud, 1981.

Pelras, Christian. *The Bugis.* Oxford: Blackwell Publishers, 1996.

Peña Izquierdo, Antonio Ramón. *La crisis sucesoria de la monarquía española: El Cardenal Portocarrero y el primer gobierno de Felipe V (1698–1705).* 4 vols. Barcelona: Universidad Autónoma de Barcelona, 2005.

Pepys, Samuel. *The Shorter Pepys.* Ed. by Robert Latham. Berkeley and Los Angeles: University of California Press, 1985.

Pérez Blanco, Lucrecio. *Infortunios de Alonso Ramírez.* Series: Crónicas de América. Madrid: Historia 16, 1988.

Pérez-Mallaína, Pablo E. *Los hombres del océano: Vida cotidiana de los tripulantes de las flotas de Indias, siglo XVI.* Seville: Diputación de Sevilla, 1992.

———. *Spain's Men of the Sea: Daily Life on the Indies Fleet in the Sixteenth Century.* Baltimore and London: Johns Hopkins University Press, 1998.

Perusset, Macarena. *Contrabando y sociedad en el Río de la Plata colonial.* Buenos Aires: Dunket, 2006.

Peter, Jean. *Le Port et l'Arsenal de Toulon sous Louis XIV: La construction navale et les approvisionnements.* Paris: Economica and Institut de Stratégie Comparée, 1995.

Phillips, Carla Rahn. *Six Galleons for the King of Spain: Imperial Defense in the Early Seventeenth Century.* Baltimore: Johns Hopkins University Press, 1992.

Pimentel, Manoel. *Arte de navegar.* Lisbon: Francisco da Silva, 1796.

Poole, Stafford. *Our Lady of Guadalupe: The Origins and Sources of a Mexican National Symbol, 1531–1797.* Tucson: University of Arizona Press, 1995.

Popescu, Oreste. *Studies in the History of Latin American Economic Thought.* New York: Routledge, 1997.

Pötting, Francis Eusebius, Count of. *Diario del Conde de Pötting, embajador del Sacro Imperio en Madrid (1664–1674).* 2 vols. Madrid: Escuela Diplomática, Biblioteca Diplomática Española, 1990.

Poussou, Jean-Pierre. "Journaux et récits de voyage: Le regard de l'historien." In *13e Colloque International du Centre de Recherche sur la Littérature des Voyages: L'Aventure maritime, pirates, corsaires et flibustiers,* Château de La Napoule, May 25–28, 2000 [available as an oral presentation online at the Centre de Recherche sur la Littérature des Voyages: *Encyclopédie sonore* website, http://www.crlv.org /swm/Page_Conference.php?P1=124, accessed on January 4, 2007].

Prakash, Om, ed. *European Commercial Expansion in Early Modern Asia.* Aldershot, UK, and Brookfield, Vt.: Variorum Reprints, 1997.

Preston, Diana, and Michael Preston. *A Pirate of Exquisite Mind—Explorer, Naturalist, and Buccaneer: The Life of William Dampier.* New York: Walker and Company, 2004.

Puertos y fortificaciones en América y Filipinas. Madrid: MOPU, CEHOPU, 1985.

Purcell, Victor. *The Chinese in Southeast Asia.* London, Kuala Lumpur, and Hong Kong: Oxford University Press, 1965.

Quiason, Serafin D. *English "Country Trade" with the Philippines, 1644–1765.* Quezon City: University of the Philippines, 1966.

Quirino, Carlos. *Philippine Cartography (1320–1899).* Amsterdam: N. Israel, 1963.

Real Academia Española. *Diccionario de la lengua castellana.* Madrid: en la imprenta de Francisco del Hierro, 1726–1737; facsimile ed., Madrid: Editorial Gredos, 1969.

Recopilación de leyes de los reynos de Indias. Madrid: Viuda de D. Joaquín Ibarra, 1791.

Records of the Relations between Siam and Foreign Countries in the Seventeenth Century, Copied from Papers Preserved at the India Office. Bangkok: Council of the Vahirañana National Library, 1915.

Rediker, Marcus. *Between the Devil and the Deep Blue Sea: Merchant Seamen, Pirates, and the Anglo-American Maritime World.* Cambridge and New York: Cambridge University Press, 1987.

Reid, Anthony. *Southeast Asia in the Age of Commerce, 1450–1680.* New Haven and London: Yale University Press, 1988.

Rico de Mata, Juan Antonio. *Tratado de galafatería* (1689). Ed. by Cesáreo Fernández Duro. Barcelona: Llagut, 1995.

Riqué Flores, Juan. "'Tupak': Un adoratorio costero en Quintana Roo." In *Homenaje a Julio César Olivé Negrete,* ed. by Beatriz Barba de Piña Chán, 237–247. Mexico City: Universidad Nacional Autónoma de México, Instituto Nacional de Antropología e Historia, 1991.

Risso, Patricia. *Merchants and Faith*. Boulder, Colo.: Westview, 1995.

Ritchie, Robert. *Captain Kidd and the War against the Pirates*. Cambridge, Mass.: Harvard University Press, 1986.

Robles, Antonio de. *Diario de los sucesos notables (1665–1703)*. 3 vols. Ed. by Antonio Castro Leal. Mexico City: Porrúa, 1946.

Rodilla, María José. *Infortunios de Alonso Ramírez*. Mexico City: Alfaguara, 2003.

Rodríguez del Valle, Mariana. *El Castillo de San Felipe del Golfo Dulce: Historia de las fortificaciones de Guatemala en la edad moderna*. Seville: Consejo Superior de Investigaciones Científicas, 1960.

Rojas Sandoval, Carmen. "Nautical Charts and Measurement Systems of the 17th Century." In *Underwater and Maritime Archaeology in Latin America and the Caribbean*, ed. by Margaret E. Leshikar-Denton and Pilar Luna Erreguerena, 91–102. Walnut Creek, Calif.: Left Coast Press, 2008.

Rubio Mañé, Jorge Ignacio. *Introducción al estudio de los virreyes de Nueva España, 1535–1746*. 4 vols. Mexico City: Ediciones Selectas, 1955–1963.

Sáiz Cidoncha, Carlos. *Historia de la piratería*. Madrid: Editorial San Martín, 1985.

Salazar y Castro, Luis de. *Historia genealógica de la Casa de Silva*. 2 vols. Madrid: M. Alvarez y M. de Llanos, 1685.

Sánchez Belén, Juan A. *La política fiscal en Castilla durante el reinado de Carlos II*. Madrid: Siglo XXI, 1996.

Sánchez Bella, Ismael. *La organización financiera de las Indias (siglo XVI)*. Mexico City: Escuela Libre de Derecho, Fondo para la Difusión del Derecho Mexicano, 1990.

Santamaría, F. J. *Diccionario general de americanismos*. Mexico City: Pedro Robredo, 1942.

Schmidt, H. D. "The Idea and Slogan of 'Perfidious Albion.'" *Journal of the History of Ideas* 14 (1953): 604–616.

Scholes, Frances V., and Ralph L. Royes. *The Maya Chontal Indians of Acalan-Tixchel: A Contribution to the History and Ethnography of the Yucatan Peninsula*. Norman: University of Oklahoma Press, 1968.

Seabra, Leonor de. *A embaixada au Sião de Pero Vaz de Siqueira (1684–1686)*. Macao: Universidade de Macau, 2003.

Seed, Patricia. *Ceremonies of Possession in Europe's Conquest of the New World, 1492–1640*. Cambridge: Cambridge University Press, 1995.

Seijas y Lobera, Francisco de. *Gobierno militar y político del reino imperial de la Nueva España (1702)*. Ed. by Emilio Pérez-Mallaína Bueno. Mexico City: Universidad Nacional Autónoma, 1986.

Selden, John. *Of the Dominion, or Ownership, of the Sea*. London: William Du-Gard, 1652.

Shaffer, Lynda Noreen. *Maritime Southeast Asia to 1500*. Armonk, N.Y., and London: M. E. Sharpe, 1996.

Sigüenza y Góngora, Carlos de. *Alboroto y motín de México del 8 de junio de 1692: Relación de Don Carlos de Sigüenza y Góngora en una carta dirigida al almirante Don Andrés de Pez*. Ed. by Irving Leonard. Mexico City: Museo Nacional de Arqueología, Historia y Etnografía, 1932.

———. *Infortunios de Alonso Ramírez*. Buenos Aires: Espasa-Calpe, 1951 [available online in the University of Wisconsin-Madison's Ibero-American Electronic Text Series, http://digicoll.library.wisc.edu/IbrAmerTxt/, accessed on September 17, 2004].

———. *Libra astronómica y philosóphica*. Mexico City: Herederos de la Viuda de Bernardo Calderón, 1690.

———. *Obras históricas*. Ed. by José Rojas Garidueñas. Mexico City: Editorial Porrúa, 1944.

———. *Seis obras: Infortunios de Alonso Ramírez, Trofeo de la justicia española, Alboroto y motín, Mercurio volante, Teatro de virtudes políticas, Libra astronómica y filosófica*. Ed. by William Bryant. Caracas: Ayacucho, 1984.

———. *Trofeo de la justicia española en el castigo de la alevosía francesa que al abrigo de la armada de Barlovento, executaron los lanzeros de la isla de Santo Domingo, en los que de aquella nacion ocupan sus costas. Debido todo à providentes ordenes del ex.mo señor d. Gaspar de Sandoval Cerda Silva y Mendoza, conde de Galve, virrey de la Nueva-España*. Mexico City: Los Herederos de la Viuda de Bernardo Calderon, 1691.

Sioris, George. *Phaulkon, the Greek First Counsellor at the Court of Siam: An Appraisal*. Bangkok: Siam Society, 1998.

Smithies, Michael. "Madame Constance's Jewels." *Journal of the Siam Society* 88 (2000): 111–121.

———. *Mission Made Impossible: The Second French Embassy to Siam, 1687*. Bangkok: Silkworm Books, 2002.

———. *A Resounding Failure: Martin and the French in Siam, 1672–1693*. Chang Mai: Silkworm Books, 1998.

———. *A Siamese Embassy Lost in Africa, 1686: The Odyssey of Ok-Khun Chamnan*. Bangkok: Silkworm Books, 1999.

Smithies, Michael, and Dhiravat na Pombejra. "Instructions Given to the Siamese Envoys Sent to Portugal, 1684." *Journal of the Siam Society* 90 (2002): 125–135.

Spate, O. H. K. *The Spanish Lake*. Minneapolis: University of Minnesota Press, 1979.

Spencer, Thomas. *A True and Faithful Relation of the Proceedings of the Forces of Their Majesties K. William and Q. Mary, in Their Expedition against the French in the Caribby Islands in the West-Indies*. London: Robert Clavel, 1691.

Stanhope, Alexander. *Spain under Charles II: or Extracts from the Correspondence of the Hon. Alexander Stanhope, British Minister at Madrid, 1690–1699*. London: John Murray, 1848.

Stephens, John L. *Incidents of Travel in Yucatan.* New York: Harper and Brothers, 1868.

Storrs, Christopher. *The Resilience of the Spanish Monarchy, 1665–1700.* Oxford: Oxford University Press, 2006.

Stradling, R. A. *Europe and the Decline of Spain: A Study of the Spanish System, 1580–1720.* London: Allen and Unwin, 1981.

Suárez Gil, Luis. *Diccionario técnico marítimo.* Madrid: Alhambra, 1983.

Subrahmanyam, Sanjay. "Holding the World in Balance: The Connected Histories of the Iberian Overseas Empires, 1500–1640." *American Historical Review* 112 (2007): 1359–1385.

Sutton, Jean. *Lords of the East: The East India Company and Its Ships.* London: Conway Press, 1981.

Tachard, Père Guy. *Second voyage du Père Tachard et des jesuites envoyez par le roy au Royaume de Siam.* Middelbourg: Gilles Horthemels, 1689.

Tagliacozzo, Eric. *Secret Trades, Porous Borders: Smuggling and States along a Southeast Asia Frontier, 1865–1915.* New Haven and London: Yale University Press, 2005.

Tcheong-ü-Lâm, and Ian-Kuong-Iâm. *Ou-Mun Kei-Lèok* (ca. 1750). Translated by Luís Gomes as *Monografia de Macau.* Macao: Imprensa Nacional, 1950.

Teixeira, Manuel. *Macau e a sua diocese.* Vol. 14: *As missões portuguesas no Vietnam.* Macao: Imprensa Nacional, 1977.

———. *Os militares em Macau.* Macao: Imprensa Nacional, 1984.

———. *Portugal na Tailândia.* Macao: Imprenta Nacional, 1983.

Terrones González, Enrique. "Algunas evidencias de sacrificio en el asentamiento prehispánico de Chac Mool, Quintana Roo." In *Homenaje a Jaime Litvak*, ed. by Antonio Benavides, Linda Manzanilla, and Lorena Mirambell, 357–378. Mexico City: Instituto Nacional de Antropología e Historia: Instituto de Investigaciones Antropológicas, UNAM, 2004.

———. "Informe de los trabajos de mantenimiento mayor en los asentamientos prehispánicos de Chac Mool y Tupac de julio a diciembre de 1995." Unpublished report. Cancun, Quintana Roo: Centro Instituto Nacional de Antropología e Historia of Quintana Roo, 1996.

Tomás y Valiente, Francisco. *Los validos en la monarquía española del siglo XVII: Estudio institucional.* Madrid: Siglo Veintiuno de España Editores, 1982.

Torres Ramírez, Bibiano. *La Armada de Barlovento.* Seville: Escuela de Estudios Hispano-Americanos, 1981.

Trabulse, Elías. *Los manuscritos perdidos de Sigüenza y Góngora.* Mexico City: Colegio de México, 1988.

The Truest and Largest Account of the Late Earthquake in Jamaica, June the 7th 1692, Written by a Reverend Divine There to His Friend in London, with Some Improvements Thereof by Another Hand. London: Thomas Parkhurst, 1693.

Urdaneta, Ramón. *Marco y retrato de Granmont: Francia y el Caribe en el siglo XVII.* Caracas: Universidad Simón Bolívar, 1997.

Vallés Formosa, Alba. *Infortunios de Alonso Ramírez.* San Juan de Puerto Rico: Editorial Cordillera, 1967.

Veitia Linage, Joseph. *Norte de la contratación de las Indias Occidentales* (1672). Buenos Aires: Comisión Argentina de Fomento Interamericano, 1945.

Vidargas, Francisco. *San Juan de Ulúa y Carlos de Sigüenza y Góngora.* Veracruz: Instituto Veracruzano de Cultura, 1997.

Vilar y Pascual, Luis. *Diccionario histórico, genealógico y heráldico de las familias ilustres de la monarquía española.* Madrid: Librería de Don M. Guijarro, 1859–1866.

Villars, Marie Gigault de Bellefonds, Madame de. *Lettres de Madame de Villars à Madame de Coulanges.* Paris: Plon, 1868.

Vindel, Pedro, ed. *Infortunios de Alonso Ramírez, descríbelos d. Carlos de Sigüenza y Góngora.* Madrid: Viuda de G. Pedraza, 1902.

Viraphol, Sarasin. *Tribute and Profit: Sino-Siamese Trade, 1652–1853.* Cambridge, Mass., and London: Harvard University Press, 1977.

Wafer, Lionel. *A New Voyage and Description of the Isthmus of America* (1699). Ed. by L. E. Elliott Joyce. Oxford: Printed for the Hakluyt Society, 1934.

Wilbur, Marguerite Eyer. *The East India Company and the British Empire in the Far East.* New York: Russell and Russell, 1945.

Wilkins, Harold T. *Captain Kidd and His Skeleton Island.* New York: Liveright Publishing Company, 1937.

Wilkinson, Clennell. *Dampier: Explorer and Buccaneer.* New York: Harper and Brothers, 1929.

Wilkinson, R. J. *A Malay-English Dictionary (Romanised).* 2 vols. London: Macmillan and Company, 1926.

Williams, Glyndwr. *The Great South Sea: English Voyagers and Encounters, 1570–1750.* New Haven: Yale University Press, 1997.

Winstedt, Richard. *An Unabridged Malay-English Dictionary.* Singapore: Kelly and Walsh, 1955.

Wood, W. A. R. *A History of Siam.* Bangkok: Chalermnit, [1924?].

Yun Casalilla, Bartolomé. "From Political and Social Management to Economic Management? Castilian Aristocracy and Economic Development, 1450–1800." In Paul Janssens and Bartolomé Yun Casalilla, eds., *European Aristocracies and Colonial Elites: Patrimonial Management Strategies and Economic Development, 15th–18th Centuries,* 85–98. Aldershot, UK: Ashgate, 2005.

———. *La gestión del poder: Corona y economías aristocráticas en Castilla (siglos XVI–XVIII).* Madrid: Akal, 2002.

Zahedieh, Nuala. "'A Frugal, Prudential and Hopeful Trade': Privateering in Jamaica, 1655–89." *Journal of Imperial and Commonwealth History* 18 (1990): 145–168.

———. "The Merchants of Port Royal, Jamaica, and the Spanish Contraband Trade, 1655–1692." *William and Mary Quarterly* 43 (1986): 570–593.

———. "Trade, Plunder, and Economic Development in Early English Jamaica, 1655–89." *Economic History Review* 39 (1986): 205–222.

Zapatero, Juan Manuel. "Las 'llaves' fortificadas de la América Hispana." *Militaria: Revista de Cultura Militar* 1 (1989): 131–140.

Zubillaga, Felix, and Walter Hanisch. *Guía manual de los documentos históricos de la Compañía de Jesús*. Rome: Institutum Historicum Societatis Iesu, 1971.

Index

Academy of Mexico. *See* Royal Academy of Mexico

Acaponeta, 20

Acapulco, *9 (map)*, 22, 28, 30, 31, 40, 42, 88, 110–111

Achin, 54, 69

Acosta, Francisco de, 35

Aeneas, 103

Africa, 10, 49, 67, 122–123, 190n118; source of slaves for Philippines, 191n132. *See also* Pedro

Aguia Real (ship), 63–65

Aguilar, Diego de, 20

Aguilar, Luis Ramírez de. *See* Ramírez de Aguilar

Agulhas current, 69

alcaldes, 28–29, 73, 75, 146–147; defined, 199n218

Alcántara, 101

Alden, Dauril, 8

Alexander VI, 24

Alguacil alguacilado, El, 16

Alsedo y Herrera, Dionisio de, 25, 158n34

Altobelo Island, *71 (map)*, 134n171

Alvarez Nazario, Manuel, 4

Amazon, 123, 190n116, 193n154. *See also* Brazil; Guinea; Ramírez, Alonso (released by or separated from pirates)

Ambil Island, 112

Amboina, 54

America (Spanish America), 4, *9 (map)*, 10, 33, 46, 68, 70–71, 78, 87, 115, 133; elites, 11–12, 89–90, 141, 194n164; solidarity, 13–14, 82, 85, 149, 193n151; Asian commerce, 22; coastal defense, 22–23, 48, 71–72, 149, 158n29, 196n199; Spanish sovereignty, 24–25; as distinct from Spain (monarchy), 48, 151n1. *See also* Asia (commerce, contraband and piracy); Castile, Castilian language, Castilians; ethnicity; Hispanic World; Indians; *indultos*; merchants; patriotism; race; Ramírez, Alonso (as patriot); Spain (monarchy: diversity and solidarity of subjects); Spaniards

Amor de Dios Royal Hospital. *See* Royal Hospital

Amsterdam, 23, 75

www.ingramcontent.com/pod-product-compliance
Ingram Content Group UK Ltd.
Pitfield, Milton Keynes, MK11 3LW, UK
UKHW031840110225
454967UK00001B/101